PHILOSOPHICAL ISSUES
IN THE
PSYCHOLOGY OF C. G. JUNG

D1712809

PHILOSOPHICAL ISSUES

IN THE

PSYCHOLOGY OF C. G. JUNG

MARILYN NAGY

State University of New York Press

Cover engraving by Mr. Max Boegli
Cover Design by Charles Martin

Published by
State University of New York Press, Albany

© 1991 State University of New York

For information, address the State University of New York Press,
State University Plaza, Albany, NY 12246

Library of Congress Cataloging-in-Publication Data

Nagy, Marilyn.
    Philosophical issues in the psychology of C.G. Jung / Marilyn
Nagy.
        p.   cm.
    Includes bibliographical references.
    ISBN 0-7914-0451-X (alk. paper). — ISBN 0-7914-0452-8 (pbk. :
alk. paper)
    1. Psychoanalysis and philosophy.   2. Jung, C. G. (Carl Gustav),
1875-1961.   I. Title.
BF175.4.P45   1991
150.19'54—dc20   89-78451
                                                                    CIP

10 9 8 7 6 5 4 3 2

Contents

Acknowledgments

I wish to acknowledge permission from *VOICES: The Art and Science of Psychotherapy* to reprint portions of my essay on Paracelsus which appeared in Vol. 21, Nos. 3 & 4, 1985–86.

Claude Welch, Durwood Foster, George Lucas, David Winston, and Margaret Morrison gave most generous assistance during various stages of my thinking and writing on this project.

Pauline Tooker brought order and correct form to the manuscript; I feel fortunate that I could rely on her skill and knowledge.

I am grateful to the Swiss Post, Telephone and Telegraph for permission to use an image from their 1978 Helvetia stamp series, and to Mr. Max Boegli for his drawing and for his original engraving of C. G. Jung, which serves as the cover illustration for the book.

My children, Peter and Cathy, have done most of their growing up during the years when this book was taking shape. Their memories of childhood will always include Mother's book. I hope they will feel that the big events in our family were always shared.

Above all, I offer grateful thanks to my husband, Géza, whose unquestioning, matter-of-course acceptance of equality in all things made it possible for me to continue my work.

Preface

This book stands as a contribution to the history of ideas. But the reason why it came to be written has more to do with social than with purely theoretical ends. It aims to facilitate discussion about Jung at an interdisciplinary level on a more objective basis than has heretofore been possible. Teaching as I have in a professional school which trains psychologists as social scientists, with a doctorate in philosophy from a theological school, and with an analytical technique learned many years ago in Zürich at the feet of Jung's first pupils, I have nearly every day occasion to experience how greatly such communication is needed.

Although Jung made important, even germinal contributions to the psychology of the unconscious processes, to psychotherapeutic technique, to the history and psychology of religion, and to folkloristic studies, he, and the Jungians of our own time as well, are dangerously isolated from the principal currents of thought in these very disciplines. The reason for this has only partly to do with what Jung actually taught. It has even more to do with the ambiguities and contradictions of his style and method and with the fact that he created for his psychology a unique vocabulary, whose nuances are understood only by those who have been initiated through the analytic process. I know at first hand the value of being in a community of initiates. The opposite and more negative value arises however with the difficulties at communication beyond the borders of the inner circle. Others cannot reach in to us, and we cannot reach out. A common language is needed.

By analyzing the internal structure of Jung's theory, following carefully its developmental stages, and then by cultural and historical cross-referencing, it is possible to situate Jung within a specific philosophical tradition. With this identity, avenues of communication may be opened.

In the background of my mind as I write these lines I hear the voices of some of my colleagues, admonishing me softly that knowledge is not just of the mind—that with mind and heart

viii

together, or perhaps with mind and heart against each other, but anyway with both impulses being felt as real, we come nearest to truth. They are of course right, but still I press my point: what *kind* of truth is that?

Work on this project during the last ten years has served more than a professional purpose, although it began as a work-oriented task. Along the way there were many discoveries. Some of them brought me joy, some created sharp dismay. I am after all not a neutral party in the investigation of my own mentor. All of the work however served the process of my own self-discovery.

I discovered Jung for the second time, this time as a figure in the world, whereas my first discovery of him, twenty-nine years ago, was rather as a figure within me. In the light of new understanding I had now to restate my own identity, in relationship both to Jung and to the historical world. The process is by no means finished.

If, beyond its contribution as a scholarly study of Jung's philosophical views, a reader of this book should also be served in this more personal respect, I shall of course be deeply pleased.

Philosophy and psychology are linked by indissoluble bonds which are kept in being by the interrelation of their subject-matters. Psychology takes the psyche for its subject, and philosophy—to put it briefly—takes the world.... Neither discipline can do without the other, and the one invariably furnishes the unspoken—and generally unconscious—assumptions of the other.

—"Basic Postulates of Analytical Psychology"

Introduction

The name of Carl Jung is associated, as that of no other formative figure in twentieth-century psychological thought, with care and respect for a religious perspective in human life. Jung even believed that most of our psychological illnesses are at root religious in nature. He said that "a psychoneurosis must be understood, ultimately, as the suffering of a soul which has not discovered its meaning."[1]

Yet Jung himself barred the path to those who wanted to understand more closely just what he meant by the religious attitude he prescribed for his patients. He insisted over and over again that his psychology had in fact no philosophical significance—that his was a purely psychological theory. As early as 1914 we find him objecting—he must have had former Freudian colleagues in mind—that a psychological view does not amount to a theory of reality as a whole:

> To be suspected of having a *Weltanschauung* is something one could put up with easily enough. There is, however, a greater danger that the public will come to believe that the view of the world worked out by the constructive method is a theoretical and objectively valid view of the world in general. Again and again I have to point out that it is a chronic misunderstanding... not to be able to distinguish between a view of the world that is purely psychological, and a nonpsychological theory that is concerned with the nature of the object itself.[2]

Jung struggled his whole life long to explain to inquirers that he did not intend to do philosophy and that "the psyche is a phenomenal world in itself, which can be reduced neither to the brain nor to metaphysics."[3] Sometimes he exhibited great patience and attempted long and detailed answers to questions, as for example in the correspondence with H. L. Philp and the Reverend David Cox.[4] At other times he could be quick and irritated. "You criticize me as though I were a philosopher," he wrote to Pater Raymond Hostie. "But you know very well that...I have no doctrine and no philosophical system, but have presented new *facts* which you studiously ignore."[5]

As for his personal religious convictions, Jung made such apparently blatantly contradictory statements that even his closest students tend to retire in discouragement with the attempt to follow him. "Everybody is free to believe anything which seems to fit about things of which we know nothing," he wrote to an American correspondent.[6] Yet in a famous and often cited BBC television interview with John Freeman, Jung responded to the question, Do you believe in God? by saying, "I know. I don't need to believe."[7]

For myself, I question that it is possible for any psychology, least of all Jung's, to get along without philosophical assumptions. In one sense, all those who have pursued Jung's connection with religion were entirely appropriate in their concern.[8]

In another sense, however, I think I understand at least some of the reasons why Jung was so adamant in separating a psychological view from philosophy. The first of these reasons has to do with the psychotherapeutic process. What so frequently ails the patient coming into analysis is a conscious point of view that once served well enough, but that now no longer "works"—an attitude that hinders rather than helps the person to live, so that troublesome symptoms of dis-ease have now appeared. The analyst must try to lead the patient away from all conscious "set" answers in order that the inner trouble can be listened to. Inner feelings—powerful emotions of fear, longing, despair, sorrow, love, anger—are the "stuff" from which all creativity and change are wrought. It is a professional task, then, to discredit rationalized systems of thought which serve as a defense against secret or unconscious feelings. Much of what Jung wrote insisting on "real experience" as over against dogmatic systems of thought must be understood *not* as an attack on the system as such, but on *any* rational view which precludes the primacy of inner feeling.

Jung knew philosophy in the systems taught in German universities at the turn of the century; that he did not regard them for the most part as therapeutic for the individual may be understood. He did sympathize with religionists who emphasized the reality of inner feeling. Jung once wrote a letter to Henry Corbin affirming that Schleiermacher "really is one of my spiritual ancestors," and had baptized his Catholic-born grandfather. "The vast, esoteric, and individual spirit of Schleiermacher was a part of the intellectual atmosphere of my father's family...unconsciously he was for me a spiritus rector."[9] On the side of mysticism Jung wrote on Nicolas von der Flüe, on Hildegard of Bingen, and on Jacob Boehme. He repeatedly drew attention to and quoted from the Cabala.[10]

A second reason for Jung's insistence that psychology is a discipline in itself, and not a philosophy, is that at the turn of the century when Jung began his career, the concept of psychology as a discrete field of study was hazy at best. Freud had just published his *Interpretation of Dreams*. Mesmer, Charcot, and Janet had taught hypnotism to medical doctors and the basic facts about conversion hysteria and an unconscious aspect of psychic functioning were beginning to be known.[11] Beyond that there were the laboratories of Wilhelm Wundt and his pupils. A few textbooks of psychology were beginning to appear, mostly speculative in nature. Those of Nicolas von Grot, Theodor Lipps, and Kurd Lasswitz may be mentioned.

In America, William James had published his *Principles of Psychology* in 1890, but James went on to use that text as a base line from which to develop his philosophy. Jung himself, on another occasion, could boast that in 1914 he had attended in London a joint session of the Aristotelian Society, the Mind Association, and the British Psychological Society to discuss the question, "Are individual minds contained in God or not?"[12] It was at another such joint meeting of the three societies in 1919 that Jung delivered his seminal address, "Instinct and the Unconscious," in which he introduced the concept of the archetype after reviewing the philosophical history of the idea of instinct.[13] Psychology was separating itself from philosophy, but was still not *very* separate until the first quarter of the century had gone by. It was important for Jung to be able to point out that a theory of the psychology of the human person is not necessarily a doctrine about reality as a whole.[14]

The situation is reversed today; in the United States at least, philosophy is seldom mentioned as an aspect of psychological concern. There is such a proliferation of different psychologies that we can scarcely keep up with the names of the specialties, let alone know what is happening in them. A recent council on curriculum studies listed "clinical psychology, social psychology, psychophysics, physiological psychology, educational psychology, cognitive psychology, the psychology of perception, of learning, of emotion, of motivation, of personality, and of reasoning."[15] Except for psychophysics, physiological psychology, and clinical psychology, all of them were non-existent or in their infancy sixty years ago.

Psychologies that pursue their course with experimental methods and continue to garner respectable results from their research may well be able to afford to let the problem of philosophical assumptions be relegated to the status of an academic question. It is not so with the clinical psychologies which rely largely on the relationship between therapist and patient for their therapeutic effect. The very fact that two people sit facing each other in a room produces a powerfully suggestive atmosphere. Here the analyst must understand as much as possible what he/she is "teaching" the patient in every interpretation which is offered, both verbal and non-verbal. In some moods Jung of course knew this. He remarked in 1942 that:

> A man's philosophy of life forms the counterpole to the physiologically conditioned psyche, and, as the highest psychic dominent, it ultimately determines the latter's fate.... I can hardly draw a veil over the fact that we psychotherapists ought really to be philosophers or philosophical doctors—or rather that we already are so.[16]

Still, for the most part, Jung wanted to emphasize how different his psychology was from anything going by the name of philosophy. Here we come to the third and most important reason for his often polemic denial. It had to do with the *kinds* of philosophical assumptions which Jung did in fact hold, and which it is the task of this essay to discover.

A distinguished philosopher and theologian, D. C. Macintosh, a number of years ago considered Jung's theory of religion and decided that he was basically a positivist, "entangled in the subjectivism of religious psychologism."[17] I shall try to show that the evidence actually supports a completely different kind of conclusion.

The philosophical views which Jung incorporated into his psychology were conditioned by events and relationships in his own family. In addition, the recent publication of the Zofingia Lectures, talks which Jung gave to his student society in Basel between 1896 and 1899, has enormously increased our knowledge of Jung's own philosophical sources—sources which were suspected or about which Jung had given clues in a few words of later books, but which could not have been positively demonstrated.[18] That situation has changed. Jung's own publications document his entire adult life, and the student lectures have the additional virtue of having been delivered in a philosophical idiom, so that we have direct evidence of the kinds of materials that shaped Jung's mind.

Besides Jung's own concepts and the way in which they came about, we must try to understand the philosophical and intellectual atmosphere of the late nineteenth century—the milieu in which Jung's ideas took shape. Jung has remained so alive for those who continue to read his books, through his pupils who analyze in his spirit, in the Jungian institutes that train analysts and provide a public educational forum for Jung's perspective, that it is perhaps difficult to remember that his psychology was necessarily conditioned by his own time and his own place. The late nineteenth century saw enormous developments in physics, biology, and physiology. Turn-of-the-century philosophy was a response both to the new science and to the only recently deceased nature philosophies. German-speaking Europe was at the very center of the intellectual ferment of the age, and Jung's theory may be seen as a kind of position-taking on the issues.

A feeling of inner hesitancy comes over me at this point. Jung is much more than an object of scholarship for all those who have found renewal in their own lives through the vehicle of his thera-peutic method—for people who can now understand their own dreams and who have found a symbolic language in which to express deep inner feelings. One ought perhaps to leave it at that. Yet knowl-edge is a very good thing, even when it forces change, or possibly on account of the fact that it brings about change. I must finally believe that increased objectivity about who Jung was and what he believed will lead into the future, and to the goals still hidden there by our own unconsciousness.

A note for the reader: The form of this book has been shaped by its interdisciplinary aims. I hope to make Jung's thought more intel-ligible to fellow students of the history of ideas, to historians of philosophy and religion, and to people who work in the field of psychology of religion. To colleagues in Analytical Psychology I hope to bring stimulation to think in new ways about the coherence between theory, personal belief, and methodology in clinical practice.

Because it is interdisciplinary, a dialectical approach to the organ-ization of the essay has been used. In each of the three parts, the material dealing with Jung's own work has first been set out, along developmental lines. Then I have attempted to situate Jung's view in the historical and philosophical context in which it belongs. Lastly, I have returned to Jung, with the larger context now freshly in mind, for a detailed discussion of some points which exemplify the philo-sophical attitude being presented. Part I of the essay has to do with Jung's epistemology, Part II deals with his ontology, and Part III with teleological questions. This traditional philosophical format is a con-venient "universal language" in the history of ideas, and it is well able to contain the major features of Jung's thought, which were scarcely influenced by twentieth-century philosophical developments.

Among scholars in any field, generalizations about matters which everyone may be expected to know serve as a kind of short-hand notation; they speed the course of an argument and facilitate discourse. At an interdisciplinary level just the opposite is the case. An unsupported general statement may prevent the inquirer from understanding the terminology and assumptions of a discipline not one's own. More than that, the authoritative use of summary state-ments may be psychologically damaging to cross-disciplinary inquiry between specialists in different fields. We can define our own "turf" and send "outsiders" into defensive withdrawal when we neglect to explain what we mean and how our field has arrived at a point of general understanding. In this book I have tried therefore not to make assumptions about the reader's prior understanding, but have in each case imagined a reader with a specialty outside Jung, or outside the history of philosophy. The source material has been laid out, at least briefly, so that the background of doctrine can be seen. I must beg the indulgence of the reader who experiences impatience with material already familiar in his/her own field.

Notes to Introduction

1. C. G. Jung, "Psychotherapists or the Clergy" (1932), in *The Collected Works of C. G. Jung*, translated from the German by R. F. C. Hull, Bollingen Series XX, and published by Pantheon Books and Princeton University Press (hereafter abbreviated as CW), vol. 11, para. 497. See also "The Aims of Psychotherapy" (1929), CW 16, para. 83: "About a third of my cases are not suffering from any clinically definable neurosis, but from the senselessness and aimlessness of their lives." Para. 99: "People blind themselves to their own religious promptings because of a childish passion for rational enlightenment."

2. Jung, "On Psychological Understanding" (1914), CW 3, para. 422.

3. Jung, *Mysterium Coniunctionis* (1955), CW 14, para. 667.

4. Jung's answers may be found in vol. 18 of the CW: "Jung and Religious Belief," para. 1583–1690.

5. *C. G. Jung Letters*, 2 vols. (1906–50 and 1951–61), translated from the German by R. F. C. Hull, selected and edited by Gerhard Adler in collaboration with Aniela Jaffé, Bollingen Series XCV (Princeton: Princeton University Press, 1973), hereafter cited as *Letters*; the letter quoted is from vol. 2, April 25, 1955. See also *Mysterium Coniunctionis*, CW 14, para. 781: "In every attempt to gain an adequate understanding of the numinous experience use must be made of certain parallel religious or metaphysical ideas which have not only been associated with it from ancient times but are constantly used to formulate and elucidate it. The consequence, however, is that any attempt at scientific explanation gets into the grotesque situation of being accused in its turn of offering a metaphysical explanation. It is true that this objection will be raised only by one who imagines himself to be in possession of metaphysical truths."

6. Jung, *Letters*, 2, Jan. 26, 1953.

7. "Face to Face," broadcast Oct. 22, 1959, in *C. G. Jung Speaking: Interviews and Encounters*, ed. William McGuire and R. F. C. Hull, Bollingen Series XCVII (Princeton: Princeton University Press, 1977), p. 428.

8. James W. Heisig's bibliography, "Jung and Theology: A Bibliographical Essay," *Spring* (1973), pp. 204–55, covers the period through 1973. Heisig's

own *Imago Dei: A Study of C. G. Jung's Psychology of Religion* (Lewisburg: Bucknell University Press, 1979) catalogs a specific image throughout Jung's work and attempts to understand Jung's use of the term.

9. Jung, *Letters*, 2, May 4, 1953.

10. See also Jung, "Brother Klaus," in CW 11.

11. Henri F. Ellenberger, *The Discovery of the Unconscious* (New York: Basic Books, 1970).

12. Jung, "Basic Postulates of Analytical Psychology" (1931), CW 8.

13. Jung, "Instinct and the Unconscious," CW 8.

14. Jung, "On Psychological Understanding," CW 3, para. 422.

15. *Psychology and the Philosophy of Mind in the Philosophy Curriculum* (San Francisco: Council for Philosophical Studies, San Francisco State University, 1983), p. 9.

16. Jung, "Psychotherapy and a Philosophy of Life," CW 16, para. 180–81; see also para. 185; "Psychotherapy Today," CW 16, para. 218.

17. Douglas Clyde MacIntosh, *The Problem of Religious Knowledge* (New York: Harper & Brothers, 1940), pp. 68–73.

18. C. G. Jung, *The Zofingia Lectures. The Collected Works of C. G. Jung. Supplementary Volume A*, ed. William McGuire, trans. Jan van Heurck, with an Introduction by Marie-Louise von Franz, Bollingen Series XX (Princeton: Princeton University Press, 1983).

PART I

To Know Only the Soul: Jung's Epistemology

1

Childhood and Youth: Taking Up the Problem of the Father

Jung's own account of how he arrived at the epistemological views which were to characterize his psychology is set down in two early chapters of his autobiographical memoirs, *Memories, Dreams, Reflections.* He grew up in the last quarter of the nineteenth century as a country parson's son in small parishes along the Rhine near Basel. Writing as a very old man, Jung's memory was flooded with the images of his early childhood. His experience of that world was of Sunday sermons in which his father spoke of the "good" God, "praising God's love for man and exhorting man to love God in return." Yet, he remembered, no one spoke of the unrest in his parents' marriage, and the fact that they now slept in separate bedrooms. At lunch on Thursdays in the home of his uncle, pastor of St. Alban's in Basel, there was sophisticated talk about various points of religion. But Jung dared not bring up the subject of the powerful dreams which had troubled him since earliest childhood, or the worrying episode of the dead man washed up by a flood on the Rhine. On the day of his first communion he wore a new black suit and a new black felt hat, and all the members of the congregation were suitably solemn and correct. "My father, too," wrote Jung, "seemed to be chiefly concerned with going through it all according to rule, and it was part of this rule that the appropriate words were read or spoken with emphasis...[but] I saw no sadness and no joy....I knew that God could do stupendous things to me, things of fire and unearthly light; but this ceremony contained no trace of God—not for me, at any rate."

Jung suffered as a child from the Pharasaic, stultified "religion by the rules" that German-speaking Protestantism had become in those years. But it was his father whom he saw as the chief victim of a professionalized religious tradition which he could not connect to meaningful, living experience. His "dear and generous father" became ever more moody and irritable. Jung tried to talk with him about problems of faith but these talks were always failures. Jung came to understand years later that "my poor father did not dare to think, because he was consumed by doubts." He counseled his son on no account to opt for a religious profession, but if on the other hand he studied medicine he "should in Heaven's name not become a materialist." At last the abdominal symptoms of which his father had hypochondriacally complained for years became clearly worse and he died early in 1896, during Jung's first year of medical studies at the University of Basel.[1]

How much the story of his father's fate actually became connected in the mind of the young student Jung with his own vocational choice we can of course never know. In the last years of his life Jung in any case chose to devote nearly eighty-five pages of his memories to the theme of his childhood religious dilemmas, to his philosophical readings as a young student, and to their connection with his experience of his father. He was able to write only four of the twelve chapters of the book from his own hand, the rest being written from interviews and previous material by Aniela Jaffé. But of those four chapters, two were devoted to his father and to religion. In an earlier letter he had written to Pastor Walter Bernet that "it was the tragedy of my youth to see my father cracking up before my eyes on the problem of his faith and dying an early death."[2] I believe that Jung quite literally took on as his own the unsolved problem of inner belief of his father and made the *reality of the psyche* the motive of his life.[3]

Jung's autobiographical memoirs are very late. Their referential accuracy with regard to some details cannot be guaranteed, but they are important just because they serve as Jung's own retrospective view of the significant features of his early history. The publication of the Zofingia Lectures has however provided a direct bridge from those late memories of childhood to Jung's actual theoretical formulations as a young man. We can now follow the entire course of Jung's development, from the youth who sought answers in the libraries of his father and his father's friends, to the student who lectured on philosophy to his comrades, to the physician who invented a terminology of his own to express what he understood of human experience. What the Zofingia Lectures reveal is a thoroughgoing consistency of philosophical attitude. Jung's earliest convictions were also his last ones.

The first of these student lectures ("The Border Zones of Exact Science," 1896) is a passionate exhortation against the claims of mechanistic science to exhaust the limits of reality and a plea in favor of a vitalistic view. Life, thought Jung, cannot possibly spring from dead matter; "the first cell must have come about through contact with pre-existent life."[4] Chapters 4 and 5 of Part III of this essay have to do with the relationship between Jung and vitalism. This lecture is considered in the context of the discussion in those chapters (see esp. p. 251), and will be passed over with this brief mention for the time being.

In the second lecture ("Some Thoughts on Psychology," 1897), Jung continues his arguments for a non-mechanistic world view, plunging directly into the grand philosophical questions of the origin of life and the origin of consciousness. The focus of his attack is the so-called empiricism of modern science, most especially that of the physiologist Du Bois-Reymond.

Four famous German physiologists, Carl Ludwig, Hermann von Helmholtz, Emil Du Bois-Reymond, and Ernst Brücke (the so-called Berlin group because of alliances of friendship formed during their student days at mid-century), together with the French Claude Bernard, practically created the modern science of physiology. As physiological reductionists they held to a strict Darwinian hypothesis and struggled to establish a non-vitalistic interpretation of organic nature in the university system.[5]

In a famous and often cited speech to the forty-fifth assembly of German Naturalists and Physicians in Leipzig in 1872, Du Bois-Reymond had attempted to set the limits of knowledge, and he distinguished between the things that we do not now know (ignoramus) and things that we will never be able to know (ignorabimus). What we *can* know is everything which has to do with matter in movement; we must only assume that matter does exist and that a perceiving mind also exists. What we *cannot* know is what matter is in itself and what mind is in itself:

> Despite all the discoveries of science, man has made no more significant progress in understanding the derivation of psychic processes from their material conditions than he has made in understanding force and matter.[6]

This speech gained a tremendous currency within the intellectual class in Europe. Over two thousand people were present at its first reading and a quarter century later it was still being mentioned. Both those in favor of religion and those against religion found it objectionable. Theologians might object to the premise that we can know only about matter. But confirmed materialistic monists like

Ernst Haeckel objected too. Haeckel, who thought he knew that mind is ultimately only a form of matter, reproached Du Bois-Reymond for leaving a door open to a "defence by all representatives of the mythological view of the world... [who] extolled it as a refutation of 'monistic dogma.'" Du Bois' view was antiquated. "For my part," wrote Haeckel, "the fact of consciousness and the relation of consciousness to the brain are to us not less, but neither are they more puzzling than the fact of gravitation, than the connection between matter and energy."[7]

For Jung, Du Bois-Reymond was one of the "esteemed scientists" who had closed the door to knowledge of the spirit. His entire lecture is a refutation of the type of authority and the evidence of Du Bois and his ilk. In the opening paragraph he sets forth his challenge:

> No doubt people will call it an act of mad adventurism to abandon the safe path laid out for us by esteemed science and accredited philosophy, to make our own independent raids into the realm of the unfathomable, chase the shadows of the night and knock on doors which Du Bois-Reymond had locked forever with his little key that says "Ignorabimus." People will accuse us of fancifulness and superstition.... Those who will do this are the same people who fill every Sunday of their lives chockful of edifying words, deeds, and thoughts, but on weekdays parade around with a sign that says, "We will never know."... Despite all this, and despite the danger of arousing the keenest displeasure, I have chosen to speak on this theme before all others.[8]

The speech reveals with all possible clarity exactly what Jung was aiming at; the object of his attack is scientific positivism of the end of the nineteenth century, together with the pious anti-intellectualism of the Sunday morning church-goer. "They will claim that ours is a fruitless and a hopeless enterprise, a self-tormenting brooding on the absurd," says Jung. He apparently intends to offer something with which to combat both scientific and religious doubt.

The further importance of these lines is that they show us Jung at a psychologically crucial period of his development—a year after his father's death, in the heroic mode of the young man seeking his future, beginning to experience his strength and laying down the ground-motives of his future life's achievement. It is a period of what recent psychological terminology would call "grandiose narcissism."[9] The connection of the motives here declared to the problematic of Jung's father, as Jung himself saw it, is unmistakable.

What Jung proposes in his lecture is that psychology itself has its own kind of empiricism—that there are factual data with which the skeptical authority of the sciences can be positively counter-manded, and which support the first principle of *rational* psychology, namely the proposition that "the soul is an intelligence independent of space and time."[10] The evidence which Jung adduces is that of spiritualism (he mentions the famous names of Carl du Prel, Johann Karl Friedrich Zöllner and Sir William Crookes), of hypnotism, and of telepathic phenomena. It is possible in fact, thinks Jung, to prove the existence of spiritual or psychic phenomena which are indepen-dent of the space-time contingencies of material phenomena. As allies in his cause he cites David Strauss's book on Justinus Kerner and the Seeress of Prevorst, Arthur Schopenhauer, and Immanuel Kant.

Kant's essay, *Dreams of a Spirit Seer* (1766), may well be taken as the motto for this period in Jung's life.[11] He quotes from it seven times in the course of his lecture. *Dreams of a Spirit Seer* is itself an interesting document of a transitional period in Kant's own life, written at a time when Kant was beginning to move away from rational views of the possibility of metaphysics in the direction of a more critical assessment. The essay records both intense interest and intense skepticism concerning the idea of a psyche independent of space and time.

The occasion of the book is well known. In a letter to Fräulein Charlotte von Knoblauch, Kant reports receiving a letter from a friend who had personally verified the amazing telepathic experi-ence of Emmanuel Swedenborg in Gothenburg. Just arrived from England in 1759, Swedenborg had been invited for dinner in the home of friends. He soon became pale and alarmed, went outside, came back and announced to the party that a great fire had broken out in Stockholm. Over the next hours he told the assemblage just how the fire was progressing, whose houses were destroyed. Then at eight o'clock he said with great relief that the fire was extin-guished, just three doors from his own house. Two days later, with the arrival of couriers from Stockholm, the entire report was con-firmed in every detail.[12] Kant was gripped by this report. He went to the trouble and expense of obtaining Swedenborg's eight-volume *Arcana Coelestia* (London, 1749–56), studied it carefully, and wrote to the great Swedenborg. He awaited the reply with anticipation, but received none. Swedenborg was at that time at the pinnacle of his career, rich and world-famous. Kant was an exceedingly poor docent at a provincial university. *Dreams of a Spirit Seer* is the work which resulted from Kant's encounter with Swedenborg. It intersperses eager consideration of a pre-subsisting immaterial world of spiritual beings entirely independent of material substances "and capable of animating the dead matter of the material world"[13] with bitterest irony, so that one is never quite sure which side of the issue Kant endorses:

> How could I blame a reader who instead of regarding the spirit seers as half citizens of another world, merely considers them without further ado as candidates for the nearest lunatic asylum?

And again:

> The soul must be regarded, even in this life, as linked to two different realms simultaneously.... As soon as the union with the body ceases, the soul continues to remain in communion with the spiritual world.... It becomes more and more difficult for me to express myself in the language of careful reasoning. But then why shouldn't I be permitted to write in an academic style which is far more decisive and which allows the author and the reader to dispense with the painful task of thinking, a task which in the long run can only lead to frustration (and disappointment)?[14]

The *Spirit Seer* is still a rather marvelous book to read. In it one can see Kant involved in what today might be termed a profound exercise in self-analysis, struggling to emerge from rational philosophy and deeply caught in the reality of his own experience: "I confess that I, too, am inclined to affirm the existence of immaterial beings in the universe and to include my soul in the class of such beings."[15] Yet Kant understands that it is not reason, as such, which provides the basis for that belief, but "the specific bent of the human mind" which tends to decide the case in a manner which is "prejudiced beforehand":

> The scale of reason is not quite as impartial as we might think: the lever carrying the inscription "Future Hopes" has mechanical advantage; it always succeeds in outweighing, even with the smallest weights on its side, the speculations of far greater weight placed in the opposite tray.[16]

The historian of philosophy may discern in the *Spirit Seer* the seeds of Kant's mature critical philosophy which would reach fruition only fifteen years later. In the *Critique of Pure Reason* the role of reason in the human mind would receive a thoroughgoing re-evaluation. Yet Kant's roots were in Leibniz's doctrine of the supremacy of rational reason. In this small polemical essay Kant feels those roots as still very powerful.[17]

Jung, however, as a young man of twenty-two, completely passed over the evidence of doubt and struggle in the *Spirit Seer*. He quotes only the passages which seem to be evidential in favor of spirits, and in favor of an immaterial soul.[18] His mood is missionary. What Jung got from Kant at this stage of his life was surely a) Kant's increasing interest in an empirical standpoint and b) Kant's willingness at least to consider that inner, psychic experience might be a part of reality. The ringing tones of Jung's heroic conclusion reflect these motifs:

> We must combat crass sensualism with the weapons of certain transcendental truths. But whence are we to derive these truths? From religion? What use is all the idealism in the world? *Deeds* are needed to wake up religion, miracles are needed, and men endowed with miraculous powers. Prophets, men sent by God! Religions are created by men who have demonstrated with deeds the reality of mystery and the "extrasensory realm."[19]

From the light of this early student lecture the whole of Jung's future theory of knowledge and, actually, the basis of his unique psychological point of view, becomes clear. As he matured Jung soon came away from the idea that hypnotism, telepathy, or spiritualism might match the kind of science that Ludwig and Du Bois-Reymond were doing in the physiology he so much despised. What remained for him however was the emphasis on *experience*. We may summarize those elements of Jung's epistemology which have already become visible. 1) The primary orientation of Jung's career will have to do with experience of a religious nature. What this means can probably best be indicated by referring to the original, etymological sense of the term, which means to bind back (into one's ethic or inner faith). On a personal level the motivation of that career is connected back to Jung's childhood and to his relationship with his father. 2) No rational or formulaic expression, that is, no dogmatic formula, will suffice to achieve the goal of a religious point of view. 3) Real knowledge is based on real experience, and that means experience in which the individual is moved by numinously felt inner feelings which convince him/her of the reality of the mental/psychic/spiritual sphere.

One question remains unanswered in the above summary. What is the *reason* for Jung's religious point of view? To say that it stems from the crisis of faith which Jung observed in his pastor-father, and from the fact that he could then never fully assume his place in the world as a man among men is to say no less than the truth which the evidence supports. But this is a reduction to material causes which cannot, I believe, adequately explain the mountain of impassioned creative work which Jung produced over the next sixty years.

A year following his lecture on psychology, in the third of his lectures to the Zofingia Society, Jung did make a statement about the broader, underlying basis for his emphasis on knowledge as personal experience. This statement is extremely important, for Jung's work was in later years subjected to the ministrations of philosophers, theologians, and psychologists of various breeds who thought they saw in Jung everything from a positivist to a man caught in obscurantist mystical twaddle:

It is the gratification of two *a priori* requirements—the categorical imperative and the category of causality—that, under certain circumstances, makes a person happy and gives him a feeling of contentment which no external factor can confer. The frail and transitory nature of all the external factors in human life is so apparent that there is no need to discuss it. A man can survive all his friends and relatives, bury what he loves most and lead a lonely existence as a stranger in an alien time; but he cannot survive himself and the inner factors of his life, for they are his very self, and thus are inalienable. . . . Do philosophy and pure science really represent an intellectual luxury in the transcendental sense, and can metaphysical reality be attributed to the as yet ideal goal of gratifying the need to think in causal terms? Radical subjectivists, i.e. those who regard the world as illusion, and multiplicity as a show of flittering nothingness, deny any objectivity of purpose. That is, they do not acknowledge the existence of any teleology external to man, and instead claim that we ourselves have projected onto the world, out of our own heads, the idea of the purposefulness of nature. At least the epigones of Kant have this much in common with the materialists. . . . It means despair to any healthy person of heart and sensibility. The only true basis for philosophy is what we experience of ourselves and, through ourselves, of the world around us.[20]

Jung inquires in this lecture whether a philosophical standpoint, which is to say an attitude based on the factors of mental life, has not become superfluous in the modern world of scientific and exteriorized facts. His answer is no, for the *objective needs* of the human person cannot be satisfied in this way. It is important to examine this passage, for it contains the first intimations of Jung's later doctrine of the *self*. The passage also reveals the final use to which Jung will in future years direct his doctrine of knowledge through experience; through acknowledgment and acceptance of the realities of personal experience we come at last to true self-knowledge and to the transcendent center of the personality, to the self. Jung's doctrine is not hedonistic, and not pragmatic.[21] It is inspired by Kant's conviction that through our experience of innate moral knowledge we come as close as is humanly possible to knowledge of reality in itself.[22]

While in his *Critique of Pure Reason* Kant had reduced the role of reason to a merely *regulative* function, aiding the judging mind by providing transcendental principles that enable us to unify the knowledge gained by the understanding, in his moral essays that same reason finds its authority—its proper *constitutive* function—as determiner of the moral law and guide to action in the world. In this role as moral arbiter reason is independent of the interlocking relationships between knower and thing known which necessarily determine our knowledge of phenomena. The will is free.[23]

The will must indeed be free if we are even to speak of the possibility of moral action, or to think of ourselves (of human beings) as intrinsically valuable. Being free means having choices: to go to war or not to go to war, given a certain level of provocation. To buy this piece of goods or not to buy it, given that there are a number of ways in which the money can be used. Of course, the individual's sense of being a free agent does not rest on any metaphysical certainty, either a posteriori, by way of experience, or as a result of purely logical analysis. There are no guarantees, certainties coming from outside ourselves, which would ensure our status as free. If there were, we would by that very certainty be robbed of the dignity and the reality of our freedom.[24] But we do experience ourselves as free.

The fact is, in each instance where a moral decision must be made and a course of action taken, we do know what it is that we *ought* to do. There is something in us (pure practical reason) which knows, a priori—before the fact of outer experience—what action would express the value of the human person. The formal law expressing this value is that one should "act only according to that maxim by which you can at the same time will that it should become a universal law" (*Foundations*, p. 39; Akademie Edition 421). The experience of this inner moral knowledge, of the "categorical imperative," as Kant called it, over against such other facts of our experience as are determined by interactions with the environment — desire, jealousy, anger, hunger, disgust, impulses of all kinds — means that we are not entirely of a piece with the world in which we live. There must be something in us, namely the moral faculty, which is different in kind from the material world.[25]

Of course we cannot always act in accordance with our moral knowledge. We are so closely bound to ourselves as phenomenal beings in a merely phenomenal world that we scarcely approximate the truth we actually know. But if we can conceive of the truth we must also be able to achieve it, if not in this life then in an eternal realm. The human being must be thought of as immortal. And if there is a non-material, moral first principle in us, there must also be a *summum bonum*, a Highest Good, if we are to make sense of our experience. Kant did not however intend a metaphysical argument for God. He disdained all knowledge not based on experience and he had shown in the first *Critique* that there is no knowledge of what is beyond our experience. We do not even need to consciously believe in God or immortality. But in the moment when we act in accordance with the inner moral imperative we implicitly acknowledge a belief in the ultimate reality of that moral principle. The only theology was therefore moral theology, for Kant. It was based on the individual's experience of an inner center of consciousness and will which is not identical with, or bound to, outer experience.[26] The phrases of Kant's moral convictions ring through Jung's student lectures. They will be heard throughout his entire career in the form of Jung's emphasis on the authority of individual experience, and they find their final formulation in his doctrine of the self.[27]

With this background on the Kantian context in mind, as well as a forward glimpse of the way in which Kant would appear in Jung's later theory, we may now return to the crucially important passage from Jung's student lecture on "Speculative Inquiry." We are looking not only at the central source reference of Jung's doctrine of the self, but at an epistemological claim for *experience* which has not been well understood by students of Jung. Much confusion has arisen in the attempt (as we shall see in later texts) to understand Jung's description of himself as an empiricist and at the same time his insistence on the ultimate reality of psychic life. We are helped by the realization that Jung adopted a stance which was deeply influenced by his reading of Kant. In his ethical treatises Kant proposed a concept of experience as a non-empirical, a priori organizing factor. The experience of moral knowledge was for Kant the central fact of life.

Jung later on adapted late nineteenth-century versions of Kant's first *Critique* to the doctrine of moral experience expressed in the ethical works, thus conflating what Kant had most carefully differentiated, namely moral and phenomenal knowledge. But in Kant's ethical writings we see Jung's own most basic philosophical orientation.

After saying that it is after all the validation of the categorical imperative (the conviction of inner freedom and the capacity to make moral choices) and the category of causality that make life seem worthwhile Jung goes on to deny the subjectivist epistemology of some Kantian followers who claim that such ideas are mere human illusion, even that the empirical world itself is so far unknown that we see it only as a projection of internal states of mind.[28] Inductive science *together* with religious convictions stand or fall on the question of the reliability of "what we experience."[29] This experience is not primarily the experience of objects in the empirical world. It is an experience of internal states.

Secondly, the kind of happiness which results from adherence to a priori factors in life is for Kant, as for Jung, not of the "hypothetical" kind which says, If I do thus and so I will obtain that pleasure or that advantage. It is rather of a kind which results as an accident of moral action. Certainly it is a fact, said Kant, that fulfillment of duty "instills a feeling of pleasure or satisfaction."[30] One cannot really conceive how this is possible. All we know is that what we do "is valid for us not because it interests us...but that it interests us because it is valid for us." The happiness that results from the experience of the inner moral law has more to do with the realization that the human being is of immense value. In his famous conclusion to the second *Critique* Kant spoke of this:

> Two things fill the mind with ever new and increasing awe and admiration the more frequently and continuously reflection is occupied with them; the starry heaven above me and the moral law within me....The first...expands the connection in which I find myself into the incalculable vastness of worlds upon worlds, of systems within systems over endless ages....The second starts from my invisible self, from my personality, and depicts me as in a world possessing true infinitude....[It] raises my value infinitely, as an *intelligence*,

through my personality...[and] is not restricted to the conditions and limits of this life, but radiates into the infinite.[31]

True happiness, then, for both Kant and Jung, is connected with "the inalienable inner factors of a man's life which are his very self" (word order transformed). It has to do with self-knowledge and with the capacity to feel that the human person has permanent, even universal value. Jung once remarked many years later that "man is worth the pains he takes with himself, for he has something in his soul that can grow."[32] As a very young man Jung was already convinced that we must take our longings for the final value of the human person entirely seriously.

I propose that the evidence reveals, and will continue to show in the texts of his later years, that Jung's emphasis on the primacy of inner experience grows from a philosophical root that values moral feeling. His first hero of the mind was surely Kant. Kant was soon replaced by Schopenhauer and by Eduard von Hartmann, and then, as Jung matured, by any of a myriad of scholars and philosophers, mystics and alchemical physicians who offered support for his point of view.

Of course these student lectures are not in themselves the stuff of Jung's later fame nor the cause for his thousands of devoted followers. The lectures are the eager reflections of a young medical student, seeking to understand his own heart and his own purpose in life. The thoughts they contain were later forgotten for a number of years during which Jung became a professional psychiatrist and earned a reputation with his work on hysteria, on schizophrenia, on the unconscious complexes revealed in association experiments, and as a close associate and protégé of Sigmund Freud. But about the time that Freud's and Jung's confidence in each other began to fade, the ideas of the early lectures began to re-emerge as the structural elements of Jung's own psychology. One way of 'reading' Jung's psychology is to see it as an eminently practical instruction manual with directions on how to get there from here—"there" being a state of mind in which one lives with hope and a conviction that one's own life process is of ultimate value, and "here" being a state of mind in which skepticism prevails, along with a sense that one's own life is neither meant nor needed. It is on account of the quality of Jung's work as a manual of instruction that he gained his followers.

2

From Experience as Value to Experience as Knowledge

In 1911–12 Jung took a series of fantasies and dreams belonging to a young American woman (Miss Miller) which had recently been published by her physician, Theodore Fluornoy, and poured into his explication of their meaning the whole of what he had been learning in the last several years about myths, about the symbolism contained in unconscious material, and about the psychology of the human being. *The Psychology of the Unconscious: A Study of the Trans-formations and Symbolisms of the Libido* was Jung's first major book. It was written at the brink of Jung's break with Freud and it shows just what Jung had learned from his mentor as well as where his own views were beginning to diverge. *The Psychology of the Unconscious* (in the 1952 revised edition: *Symbols of Transformation*) is also the only one of Jung's books which underwent a drastic revision. We can therefore examine with some precision the changes in Jung's thought between 1912 and 1952. In the present discussion I am quoting from the original edition,[1] which is no longer easily available except in larger research libraries. Later on I shall quote from the revised edition.

In Chapter 5, "The Symbolism of the Mother and of Rebirth," Jung has been discussing a particular group of symbolic images which have to do with being swallowed by the big fish, traveling a long sea journey toward the east, and emerging then out of the fish in the eastern land in a new-born form. On the one hand, such symbolic tales are clearly regressive, concealing an incestuous wish to get inside the mother again. On the other hand, as tales of rebirth, they may provide a pathway over which sexual libido can be unconsciously sublimated: "Man should not merely renounce and repress and thereby remain firmly fixed in the incestuous bond...he should redeem those dynamic forces which lie bound up in incest, in order to fulfill himself."

Christianity, for example, thinks Jung, gained its success in great part because it was psychologically necessary to escape the brutality of antique culture, marked by such "incredible contrast between slavery and the freedom of the citizens and masters" that people had "entirely lost the consciousness of the common bond of mankind." Sexuality was easily available and so women also were terribly depreciated. Christianity provided an idealized image of the family which served to re-cathect libido and allow for spiritual and cultural progress. But Christianity at the same time keeps man infantile—bound as a child in love for the parents. "Man can remain a child for all time and satisfy his incest wish all unawares."

What to do? Should we give up all religious belief we abandon ourselves to the licentiousness of primitive times and the anxiety of life with no transcendent ruling principle. But a positive creed "keeps us infantile and, therefore, ethically inferior."

> The world is not a garden of God, of the Father, but a place of terrors. Not only is heaven no father and earth no mother and the people not brothers and sisters, but they represent hostile, destroying powers, to which we are abandoned the more surely, the more childishly and thoughtlessly we have entrusted ourselves to the so-called Fatherly hand of God. One should never forget the harsh speech of the first Napoleon, that the good God is always on the side of the heaviest artillery.

Now follows the passage for whose sake this discussion has been undertaken. The religious myth, says Jung, is one of the most important of human institutions because it reassures man and protects him from the monsters of the universe. "The symbol, considered from the standpoint of actual truth, is misleading, indeed, but it is *psychologically* true, because it was and is the bridge to all the greatest achievements of humanity."

Jung appends a long footnote to these lines in which he explains that what he has in mind is a "relentless fulfillment of the standpoint of the theory of cognition, established by Kant." We are ethically obliged to seek moral autonomy and not play around with "infantile images of the world."[2]

We ought to do good for its own sake, he says, continuing on in the main text, and not because we have to have a metaphysical belief in order to do so. *This would be the course of moral autonomy, of perfect freedom.* The solution to the dilemma, Jung believed in 1911, was that "belief should be replaced by understanding; then we would keep the beauty of the symbol, but still remain free from the depressing results of submission to belief. This would be the psychoanalytic cure for belief and disbelief."

Most of this remarkable passage was excised from the revised version of *Symbols of Transformation*, no doubt because it offers a merely rational solution to the epistemological dilemma—our conflict between the reality we see in the world around us and the reality we feel within. Jung is still very much the young, sophisticated professional, trained by Freud. In spite of that we can observe: 1) Jung's emphasis on the necessity of a *psychological* or inner truth as over against the material or outer truth. In these years Freud had denied that. 2) Jung's dependence on the fact of an inner moral imperative to support the idea of an "inner truth." Jung is very doubtful, and deeply conflicted. The psychological reality is "merely a functional phenomenon," he says in the footnote. But if things were reversed, if in a way Jung says he does not expect will happen, the psychological truth were suddenly no longer an epiphenomenon and became a "physical entity" then the psychological reality would have an *even greater worth* as a mark of the real, "because of its directness." To anticipate, we may look to the coming theory of archetypes to replace the Kantian categorical imperative as guarantor of the reality of the inner world.

In his Foreword to the revised edition of *Symbols of Transformation* Jung remarks that "hardly had I finished the manuscript [of the original version] when it struck me what it means to live with a myth, and what it means to live without one."[3]

In 1913 Jung delivered to the Fourth Psychoanalytic Congress in Munich a lecture on typology which was to be a preliminary sketch of his second major book (*Psychological Types*, 1921). Many scholars have believed that *Types* was motivated in great part by Jung's attempt to work through for himself an understanding of the differences with Freud. That is surely the case with the 1913 "Contributions to Psychological Types." Jung had just read William James' lectures on *Pragmatism*,[4] and James' description of the tough- and tender-minded types provided Jung with an enormous "aha" reaction; it led to his delineation of extraversion and introversion—two naturally occurring attitudinal types which account for much of the failure of people to understand one another. In a later essay, "The Psychology of the Unconscious Processes," Jung openly labels Freud an extravert.[5] In this early lecture, we will not err in supposing that Jung had Freud in mind when he described the typology of the tough-minded man, borrowing from James' description of two different philosophical temperaments:

The tough-minded man is "sensationalistic," giving more value to the senses than to reflection. He is "materialistic and pessimistic," for he knows only too well the uncertainty and hopeless chaos of things. He is "irreligious," being incapable of asserting the realities of his inner world against the pressure of external facts; a fatalist, because resigned; a pluralist, incapable of all synthesis; and finally a sceptic, as a last and inevitable consequence of all the rest.[6]

Jung has clearly taken sides on the issue of whether "inner" or "outer" knowledge is to be preferred. Since the publication of his student lectures we know that Jung's recriminatory attitude toward the tough-minded scientific stance did not originate with the break from Freud. But it was at this time decisively reaffirmed. In his later work on typology Jung tried to describe the extraverted approach to life as in polar but balanced relationship to the introverted attitude. It is nonetheless a fact that neither extraverted analysts nor extraverted patients have ever felt very much at home in Jungian circles. What is particularly important is that in 1913, Jung recognized that the differences between Freud and himself were primarily differences in *religious* attitude. Jung would later describe the difference between the extravert and the introvert as a difference in object relatedness. The extravert perceives primarily an external object; the introvert perceives primarily an internal object. This has been the epistemological division line since Plato.

By 1914, in "On Psychological Understanding," Jung was already proposing a remedy for the overly objective attitude which leads to resignation and skepticism about life. Freud's analytic method reduced the content of dreams as well as the symptomatic behavior of neurotic process to its causal elements, thus freeing his patients from projective defenses. It promoted a reality oriented attitude. Jung now suggested, instead, what he call a "constructive" or "prospective" method of analysis. The prospective method begins analysis by asking the question of purpose. What does this behavior intend? Why did the dreamer need this dream? What story is the dream wanting to tell? What is the potential of this person and how is the psyche attempting to reach this goal?[7]

Jung realized very well that from the objective point of view his "constructive understanding" might seem to be mere "infantile fantasy." But, he pointed out, if we for example try to understand *Faust* from a causal prospective we entirely miss its living meaning as a work of art. "That meaning only lives when we experience it in and through ourselves." The subjectivity of the prospective method means creativity and redemption for the human person. "As Nietzsche says, 'Creation—that is the great redemption from suffering; that is ease of living.'"[8]

During these years when his theory was taking shape Jung was undergoing a deep personal crisis. The break with Freud had cost him most of his relationships with professional colleagues, and professional activities came almost to a standstill. His own conscious point of view was endangered. Although he carried on his analytic practice, served his regular term in the Swiss Army, and continued in family life, at an inner level he was dangerously depressed. Jung decided to subject his psychological theory to the experiment with his own life, and for several years every spare moment was devoted to the probing exploration of inner fantasy and dreams. He began to keep a journal, the famous Red Book. As a private diary it has never been published, although late in his life Jung entrusted it to his secretary and collaborator Aniela Jaffé with permission to quote from it at her discretion. In 1971, in a lecture at the Eranos Conference in Ascona, she read several passages from the opening chapters. A poem entitled "The Rediscovery of the Soul" reveals Jung in an intimate dialogue with himself, on the brink of giving over the authority for his life entirely to the inner voice:

I have returned, I am once again there—
I am with you—after long years of long wandering
I have come again to you.
Should I tell you everything I have seen, experienced, drunk into myself?...
    I thought and spoke much about the soul; I knew many learned words about the soul; I judged it and made a scientific object of it.
    I did not consider that the soul cannot be the object of my judgment and knowledge. Much more are my judgment and knowledge the object of my soul....
    The spirit of the depths sees the soul as an independent, living being, and therewith contradicts the spirit of the times, for whom the soul is something dependent on the person, which lets itself be ordered and judged, that is, a thing whose range we can grasp.[9]

From this time on, the "soul" or the "unconscious psyche" became, for Jung, the positive source of knowledge. In his writing it is hypostasized as though it were a nonmaterial being connected to but actually distinct from the conscious ego. In several 1931 essays which were later collected into the much loved little book *Modern Man in Search of a Soul* Jung emphasized that his psychology is based on a theory that what we know comes directly from within:

> Today we have a psychology founded on experience, and not upon articles of faith or the postulates of any philosophical system.[10]

> It would be so much simpler if only we could deny the existence of the psyche. But here we are with our immediate experiences of something that *is*—something that has taken root in the midst of our measurable, ponderable, three dimensional reality. . . . We can easily understand why higher and even divine knowledge was formerly attributed to the soul.[11]

> Do we ever understand what we think? We only understand that kind of thinking which is a mere equation. . . . But besides that there is a thinking in primordial images, in symbols which are older than the historical man, which are inborn in him from the earliest times, and, eternally living, outlasting all generations, still make up the groundwork of the human psyche. It is only possible to live the fullest life when we are in harmony with these symbols; wisdom is a return to them. It is a question neither of belief nor of knowledge, but of the agreement of our thinking with the primordial images of the unconscious, no matter what our conscious mind may cogitate.[12]

3

Inner Experience as True Knowledge: The Apologetics of Subjectivism

Jung continued to speak of the moral or psychological *value* of an attitude which takes inner experience as objective. (From the point of view of anyone with a healing vocation there is scarcely any difference between a moral and psychological stance.)[1] "A life directed to an aim is in general better, richer, and healthier than an aimless one." "What we want is a practical psychology which yields approvable results...justified by the outcome for the patient." But more and more, his appeal for the inner life was based not on the ethical value of recognizing an alternative to the objective, scientific view, nor on the prophylactic value for the patient, but on an *epistemological assumption* that the *only* certainty we have is our knowledge of the inner world. We are in fact imprisoned in the symbolic realm of the psyche.

By the time the revised edition of *Symbols of Transformation* came out in 1952 there was no longer any trace of the rational understanding and rational valuation of the religious myth which Jung had recommended in 1912. Instead, he states, conscious life is governed and shaped by the numinous impact of the inner symbolic images. In place of the excised passage quoted on pages 24 f. we now read:

> Psychological truth by no means excludes metaphysical truth, though psychology, as a science, has to hold aloof from all metaphysical assertions. Its subject is the psyche and its contents. Both are realities, because they *work*. Though we do not possess a physics of the soul, and are not even able to observe it and judge it from some Archimedean point "outside" ourselves, and can therefore know nothing objective about it since all knowledge of the psyche is itself psychic, in spite of all this the soul is the only experient of life and existence. It is, in fact, the only immediate experience

we can have and the *sine qua non* of the subjective reality of the world.[2]

What does this passage contain? 1) Jung begins with the statement that while there may be metaphysical realities beyond the possibility of our knowing them, psychology, being a *science* cannot claim to know anything about that. 2) Indeed, he goes on, psychology cannot even know for certain anything about its own subject matter, the psyche, since there is no way in which I myself or anyone else who is not "me" can objectively observe what I am thinking and feeling. 3) More than that, the objectivity of our experience of external reality must also be called into question since everything we perceive is filtered through the contaminants of the psyche—the limitations of our perceptive faculties and the bias of our affective states.[3]

Therefore, Jung concludes (though these are not his own words), we might just as well trust our inner feelings and our inner experience since that is all there is to know. If we do not trust it, what religious faith in life we do have will be infantile and dependent on someone else's authority. If we do trust it, we have a chance that our lives may be governed by the kind of " 'legitimate' faith . . . [which] must always rest on experience."

Many followers of Jung to this day defend Jung's theories with this subjectivistic argument. I did so myself, until I began to be troubled by the observation that many people obviously "knew" other things, and that I could not in any practical sense actually live my life as though there were no objective outer reality.

Before going on to examine in detail the background of the subjectivist epistemology which Jung embraced, it is worthwhile to look at the philosophical content of his statement. Knowledge of God is expressly rejected. But real knowledge of the physical world is also rejected. Thus we are returned to the world of the mind, or, as Jung preferred to say—the world of the psyche or soul. This formulation allowed him to accept mental contents as valid while denying rationalized or dogmatic expressions of those contents. But what comprises the non-rational arena of the mind? What is it that is to be validated? The inmost longings of the human person, now as in every age, are to be able to believe that the course of life is toward a good end, that one's life is developing toward its ultimate potential and fulfillment, that love is finally to be gained, and justice achieved, if not in this life then surely in some kind of continuation of existence beyond the barrier of death. To believe in these dictates of the soul rather than in the physical evidence of the perceivable world has been the purport of every metaphysical idealist since Plato. We are thus in Jung's argument returned through the back door to a metaphysical position without, apparently, having to carry the onus which belief in realities "beyond physics" brings with it in the modern world.

There are many good reasons for being a follower of Jung's psychological views. Among them are his insights into the projective phenomena of transference relationships. Still more, his symbolic approach to the meaning of dreams is a most fruitful factor of my professional and my personal life. Still again, his writings are replete with a deep "wisdom of life" from which I have personally profited. However, Jung's subjectivist argument for the validity of psychic contents has brought, to my mind, only unhappy results.

It has earned Jung isolation from both the scientific community on the one hand and from the philosophical and theological community on the other hand. It is likely that isolation from the scientific community would have occurred in any case, for we lack even today an appropriate philosophical or biological context for the kinds of contents Jung studied.[4] But the subjectivist argument, if taken in earnest, makes nonsense of scientific endeavor. This is unnecessary.

Among philosophers and theologians, if I may speak now from years of personal experience in another discipline, the subjectivist argument has felt like an unjustified slam at metaphysicians from one of their own ilk who won't admit it. Students have frequently been charmed by Jung; their professors often deeply irritated. In defense of Jung, I can only remark that while he was so well read that his entire psychology may be understood as a kind of philosophy, he was nevertheless a passionate philosophical amateur. He may well not always have understood the implications of what he said. But it must also be said that he didn't much try. If he could arouse an emotional reaction in an overly rationalistic patient by showing his own feelings he would surely not prevent himself from responding. Emotion can be transforming; it stirs the depths. It is *genuine experience*, for Jung, and always to be preferred over an organized intellectual presentation which is two or three steps away from the real thing. In at least one instance Jung admitted being deliberately ambiguous because he thought this way of speaking is more true to the yes and no of the flow of human experience than a straight rational exposition.[5]

Among Jungians, in the professional societies and in the communities surrounding the various training institutes, the subjectivist argument has often had the devastating effect of squelching critical thinking and creating a kind of confessionalist atmosphere. Jung himself, as we have seen, had solved critical life problems arising from the break with Freud by a sacrifice of the intellect, a "return to the soul" and to the life of the inner feelings which had been the theme of his earliest reflections as a young man. There is no doubt in my mind concerning the efficacy of this procedure; this is the essence of a psychological attitude. What has sometimes happened in Jungian groups however is something like what churches in a confessional tradition have long observed among themselves. The faith experience becomes a doctrinal position which excludes or discriminates against open inquiry and hard thinking. Fringe groups and sects of various kinds may get attached to the Jungian centers, for Jungians accept experience which is not hard science. It is not easy to take a stance toward the theoretical formulation with which borderline types of experience are expressed, for in a subjectivist framework, all real experience is valid. Some Jungians would say it's better not to try to discriminate—better to err on the side of acceptance of all views. In any case, they add, we cannot know what is real truth; we can know only what we individually experience.[6] Yet a neglect of comparative research and the work of careful thinkers in related fields will eventually cost Jung's followers the very trust which their emphasis on the experience of the individual seeks to earn.

Jung did not always in his later years use the three-step subjectivist argument. In his writings on psychology of religion and in his answers to queries about whether he really believed in God, since he wrote so much about the need for a religious attitude, Jung usually replied quite reductively that "it is a thoroughly outmoded standpoint, and has been so since the time of Immanuel Kant, to think that it lies within the power of man to assert a metaphysical truth."[7] One example of this type of response is the dispute with Martin Buber. Buber had published an article in which he accused Jung of being a gnostic. Jung was shocked and offended and published a rejoinder defending and explaining his own position. Buber replied again. Buber's book, *Eclipse of God* (1952) contains his two essays. Jung's reply is reprinted in the *Collected Works*.[8] A number of letters written between 1952 and 1960 also discuss his position. If we do not have the means of knowing God, we do nevertheless have the possibility of observing what the psyche says about God. This does not make us gnostics, said Jung; it makes us empiricists.[9] Buber did not know what psychiatric observation was all about, wrote Jung. In order to convince himself of the devastating *reality* of people's ideas of God, he ought to "take a reflective tour through a lunatic asylum."[10] What psychology can prove is that people actually believe in God, but "not that [those beliefs] are true or untrue in the philosophical or religious sense." Jews, Christians, and devotees of Islam, Buddhism, and Hinduism all believe in God but each has a God concept peculiar to himself:[11]

> I am sorry to say that everything men assert about God is twaddle, for no man can know God. Knowing means seeing a thing in such a way that all can know it, and for me it means absolutely nothing if I profess a knowledge which I alone possess.[12]

Kant's proof against the possibility of transmundane knowledge was brought forth again and again in order to show that our ideas of God have a psychological origin. But this *psychic* or *psychological* origin of metaphysical ideas had also another status with Jung. From a reductionist explanation of religious beliefs the psyche became the source of all knowledge whatsoever, and even, speculatively, the ground of reality. I am going to number the progressive stages of Jung's subjectivist argument in the following paragraphs, so that their content is conceptually clear. These stages do not follow a developmental time-line. Jung seems to have used the various parts of it to suit the apologetics of his theory throughout his career. The more extreme forms of the argument do tend to show up in the later works, perhaps as Jung found more courage to say in public everything he was thinking himself!

1) One way of understanding the subjectivist view is to see it as the *innate disposition of introverted people*. In his 1921 *Psychological Types* Jung made a typological analysis of the introverted attitude which characterizes idealists in general. Because the internal idea is the strongest factor for the introvert, as an invisible inner dominant, it gains ascendancy over all external facts and communicates a sense of its own autonomy and freedom to the subject, who, in conse-quence...feels independent and free in relation to the object.[13] Plato, with his doctrine of forms and Kant with his threefold postulate of God, freedom, and immortality would be typical examples from philosophy of how the introverted attitude may be expressed in philosophical doctrine. Darwin might be an example of the normal extraverted thinking type. (It is interesting that Jung apparently makes this judgment on account of Darwin's relation to the world of objects as a scientific personality, and not on account of his personal habits and manner.)

Yet even in *Types* Jung did not stop with a relativizing description of the object-oriented versus the subject-oriented attitudes. In Chapter 8, which focuses directly on philosophy and typology, Jung goes on to declare that it is simply not true, as empirical science would have it, that the idea is an epiphenomenal abstraction from concrete experience. The mind is not a *tabula rasa*; it comes already equipped with certain categories of thinking which supply us with all the potential for experience which we will ever have:

> What Kant demonstrated in respect of logical thinking is true of the whole range of the psyche....The...inherited and preformed functional disposition...gives the stuff of experience a specific configuration, so that we may think of them, as Plato did, as *images*, as schemata, or as inherited functional possibilities which...exclude other possibilities or at any rate limit them to a very great extent.[14]

Not only do we inherit a tendency to experience the world as (subject) introverted or (object) extraverted personalities, but *all* knowledge is governed by a priori existing potential images, which become activated in the act of perception. It sounds as though, for Jung, the categories or the archtypes do not so much enable us to know the world as they mask or filter our perceptive capabilities.

2) If we must live in a state of uncertainty about the transcendent inner objects of knowledge so must *we also remain uncertain about outer objects*:

> We must always bear in mind that despite the most beautiful agreement between the facts and our ideas, explanatory principles are only points of view, that is, manifestations of the psychological attitude and of the *a priori* conditions under which all thinking takes place.[15]

> In contrast to any other scientific theory, the object of psychological explanation is consubstantial with the subject: one psychological process has to explain another.[16]

3) Because we have no Archimedean point outside the psyche from which to guarantee either inner *or* outer perception, the contents of the unconscious, *the objects of inner feeling, have just as much right to be called "real" as our outer observation*: "The fact that we are totally unable to imagine a form of existence without space and time by no means proves that such an existence is in itself impossible."[17]

4) Inner and outer objects are both uncertain. *What we can be sure*

is real is psychic experience. The psyche is the key to all consciousness and to all knowledge:

> Without the psyche you can neither know *nor* believe. There-
> fore everything about which we speak at all lies in the psy-
> chic realm; even the atom is in this sense a psychic model.[18]

> I can say of nothing that it is "only psychic," for everything
> in my immediate experience is psychic in the first place.[19]

> *Esse in intellectus* lacks tangible reality, *esse in re* lacks mind.
> Idea and thing come together, however, in the human psyche,
> which holds the balance between them...What indeed is
> reality if it is not a reality in ourselves, an *esse in anima*?[20]

The reader may remember back to the second of Jung's student lectures, where he proposed to overcome the hybris of scientific knowledge and the skepticism which lay behind religious platitudes with empirical proofs of spirits — telepathy, hypnotism, and spiritualism. In maturity Jung found a new empiricism with which to achieve these goals. The *reality of the psyche* became the banner of his psychology. I would really like to say that it became the banner of his faith, for his position amounts to little less than that.

5) In a few passages of his later writings, Jung speculated that if all our knowledge is psychic, if consciousness arises out of an unknown, unconscious matrix, *it may be that this unknown psychic matrix is the primary substance of all reality.* In a 1955 interview with the Australian analyst Rix Weaver, she asked him on impulse, What is the difference between me and that table? "Jung leaned forward and tapped the table with his middle finger and said, 'We are of the same substance as that table. Our discrimination, the 'I' awareness is the difference.'"[21] In *Psychology and Alchemy* Jung remarked that "nothing that exists could be discerned were there no discerning psyche. Only by virtue of psychic existence do we have any 'being' at all...all consciousness rests on a sort of unknown *prima materia*.[22] In his late and most important theoretical essay, "On the Nature of the Psyche," Jung declared that "the psyche is the greatest of all cosmic wonders and the *sine qua non* of the world as an object."[23] Is this a kind of idealist monism, or is it Pyrrhonic skepticism, or is it merely a more extreme formulation of how limited our perceptive capacity really is? Jung would have jumped in the air at such labels. It is enough to observe that in his most far-reaching meditations, we are breathing in an atmosphere in which the things of the mind are all in all.

In the preceding three chapters we have followed the development of Jung's epistemological views from their origin in personal family issues, through his response in university years to scientific and philosophical problems of the turn of the century, to his development of subjectivist psychological premises which should offer the possibility of preserving and affirming important human values. The three chapters which follow now seek to widen the historical basis of Jung's theory of knowledge and to prove the direct lineage of Jung's theory in late nineteenth-century thought.

4

Epistemology as a Value Term:
Plato's Theory of Recollection
as a Solution to the Problem of Justice

Jung's assertion that all our substantial knowledge stems from the authority of inner experience is far from being the phenomenological record of an empirically oriented psychology. I have given evidence in the three preceding chapters that the subjectivist epistemology developed by Jung found its original inspiration in Kant's second *Critique*, and that Jung, like Kant, was motivated by religious and ethical considerations. Jung eventually adopted arguments supporting his doctrine of inner experience which had to do not with Kant's moral writings but with a particular strain of neo-Kantian epistemology prominent at the end of the nineteenth century. We shall examine those arguments, as well as their source in Kant's first *Critique*, in Chapters 5 and 6. This chapter however continues on with the theme of the ethical grounds of both Kant's and Jung's position. What sort of philosophy characterizes views like those which have been described?

Jung substituted "inner experience" for Kant's concept of a priori reason. Both men meant that there is something *inside the individual* which knows what to do and how to act. Knowledge which is of crucial importance for the human individual is won at the moment when we acknowledge a priori inner experience, experience which is not dictated by the perceptual and sensual power of the outer object. For Kant this was the experience of the categorical imperative. For Jung it was the experience of the self.[1]

In the second edition of the *Critique of Pure Reason* Kant stated that he had "found it necessary to deny *knowledge* in order to make room for *faith*" (Bxxx). Kant's philosophy aimed not only at establishing a proper basis for scientific work, but also and more importantly at establishing the possibility of a moral universe.[2] Jung's theory seems also to have been motivated by the desire to satisfy objective moral demands. (See pp. 18 f. and 24 f. above.)

We need the *reasons inside the mind* and not outside in the external object, if we are to believe in the value of the human individual and have hope for justice. There is always a moral reason for epistemological idealism.

A case can be made that at the core of Western idealism as it originated in Plato the solution to a moral problematic was being sought.[3] One of the best proofs of that case lies in a critical passage of Plato's dialogue called the *Meno*. The *Meno* marks the end of the first group of dialogues in which Plato has Socrates endlessly and fruitlessly ask the question: Is there such a thing as virtue, or truth? Can we know it? In the *Meno* Plato finds an answer to this question, at least a theoretical answer. This answer, while satisfying moral demands, was to initiate the split between mind and body which has characterized Western philosophical thinking ever since. If I suggest a moral (or some might say, a psychological) background to the epistemological dilemma, it is not in order to reduce the metaphysical question to a moral-psychological one. I mean instead to show how intertwined they are; we cannot ask either side of it without meaning and saying a great deal about the other side of it. To the point of this essay: Jung's appreciation of subjective internal experience gives *prima facie* evidence of the kinds of moral values he intended to affirm.

In the *Meno*, Socrates is involved in a heated discussion with Meno, a rich young Thessalian aristocrat, about whether virtue can be taught. Socrates says he doesn't even know what virtue is. Meno throws up his hands and says, but how can you possibly look for something when you don't even know what it is (80d)? Previous dialogues have essentially stopped at this point, with eristic Sophist declarations that it is impossible to even get a start on such a vague idea, and Socrates insisting that it's nevertheless better to go on looking for an answer (e.g. 86b). But now, at 81b, something completely new in the dialogues happens. Socrates replies that he thinks in fact that he has a better answer to the question of how virtue is to be sought, "from men and women who understand the truths of religion." Socrates explains what he means, in a passage which is the key to all of Plato's philosophy henceforth:

> Meno: What did they say?
> Socrates: Something true, I thought, and fine.
> Meno: What was it, and who were they?

Socrates: Those who tell it are priests and priestesses of the sort who make it their business to be able to account for the functions which they perform. Pindar speaks of it too. ...What they say is this.... They say that the soul of man is immortal: at one time it comes to an end—that which is called death—and at another is born again, but is never finally exterminated. On these grounds a man must live all his days as righteously as possible.... The soul, since it is immortal and has been born many times, and has seen all things both here and in the other world, has learned everything that is. So we need not be surprised if it can recall the knowledge of virtue or anything else which, as we see, it once possessed. All nature is akin, and the soul has learned everything, so that when a man has recalled a single piece of knowledge—*learned* it, in ordinary language—there is no reason why he should not find out all the rest, if he keeps a stout heart and does not grow weary of the search; for seeking and learning are in fact nothing but recollection.[4]

Plato proposes a new theory of knowledge which should have a more authoritative base than the Sophistic dilemmas which have until now halted the progress of epistemological discussion. The final referent is the inborn capacity of the mind to know. We know, says Plato, because we remember what we already know, and have known since before our birth when the discarnate soul in other incarnations was able to learn everything that is. The soul/psyche is separate from its bodily incarnations.

In order to understand the import of that statement we need to follow the doctrine of immortality back some hundreds of years into a period of Greek history when there was no such thing as immortality for human beings. Early Greeks believed that the gods were immortal, but that men were not. Crucial moral problems were left unsolved.

a. Immortality and Justice in Homeric Society

Greek religion is an amalgam of religious beliefs belonging to an original Mediterranean stock of people persisting through a succession of invasions beginning about 2000 B.C., and the last Dorian invaders of about 1100 B.C., who brought with them a "Nordic" father religion, the aristocratic attitudes of a conquering race, together with the capacity for clear reasoning thought which we think of as the 'light of Hellas'. Whatever religious attitudes the more ancient Greeks had is lost to us, but the Homeric society of the *Iliad* and *Odyssey* from which our first records derive is dominated by a practical, this-worldly rationality.

We may remember the passage in the *Iliad* where the gods have taken sides with their favorite warriors and begun to fight each other in earnest (21. 385). Poseidon wants to draw Apollo into the battle, but he answers:

> Lord of the earthquake, you would not call it wisdom in me
> to fight with such as you, for the sake of miserable mortals,
> who are like the leaves; today the flame of life burns bright
> in them, and they eat the fruits of the ground, and tomor-
> row they are withered, and die away. No, let us even now
> take our rest from fighting, and let them do battle by
> themselves.[5]

Man is mortal, and destined in any case to disappear, so it is not worthwhile for the gods to concern themselves with him overly much. Although the gods could have quite a lot to do with the passionate events of men's lives, they were of no benefit to man as regards his death, for death had no meaning.

To be sure, certain great heroes, relatives or favorites of the gods, were said to have been conveyed to the "Elysian Plain at the ends of the earth...where life is easiest for men" (Hom. *Od*. 4. 561).

> There they have their dwelling place
> and hearts free of sorrow
> in the islands of the blessed
> by the deep-swirling stream of the ocean,
> prospering heroes, on whom in every year
> three times over
> the fruitful grainland bestows its sweet yield.[6]

But these heroes had always lived a long time ago, in a former age, and their felicitous fate is related to the life of those now living only insofar as it draws out feelings of longing for a thing men cannot hope to enjoy. And even here there was no real sense of immortality—that is, of an indestructible "essence" or essential core of the personality which would live on after death. For the heroes of Elysium had not died at all—they had been literally transported in their living, bodily form to the far green isles.

It is true that the Homeric Greeks did have a belief in a certain continuity after death. But it was a destiny to be awaited with utter horror. The souls of the dead led a wraith-like, powerless existence in Hades, deprived of all joy, and of all capacity for effective action. When Odysseus goes to Hades in order to demand advice from Teiresias he meets the shade of his mother, but when he tries to embrace her she escapes his arms like a shadow or a dream (*Od.* 11. 475). The spirit of the dead Patroclus hovers all night around the sleeping Achilles, begging for proper burial so that he need trouble the living no more. But when Archilles reaches out his hand, Patroclus flies shrieking from him—a petty ghost (Hom. *Il.* 23.59). Although Achilles himself becomes a prince in the land of the Dead, he tells Odysseus, "I would rather be on earth as the hired servant of another, in the house of a landless man with little to live on, than be king over all the dead." (Hom. *Od.* 11. 490). The early Greek word for soul was *eidolon*, and it meant simply "image." The soul, and with it, existence after death, is a shadowy image of life. This is the crucial point—*real* life is the life of the body. The soul is an unreal reflection of life.

Such a realistic world view was without hope, especially in the sense that there could be no recompense for bad fortune or injustice. But it had the admirable virtue of focusing man's attention on the living of life. We may guess that the miracle of ancient Greece— a culture which developed in the space of some five hundred years from a primitive tribal state to a level of civilization whose architecture, poetry, mathematics, and philosophy ever since cause wondrous admiration—this miracle may be due to the fresh and steady eye of the Greek who knew that *now* is the moment for his life to find its meaning. The great classicist, Herbert Weir Smyth, expressed the matter in these lines:

> The early Hellene gains his buoyancy of spirit, his serenity, nay even...his very impulse to heroic endeavor, not only from his realization of the inevitableness of sorrow and of the cruelty of death, which awakens in him no thought of relief from suffering, but also, and perhaps in no small measure, from his cheerless view of the destination of his soul when once it has left its fleshy tenement.[7]

Tribal Homeric society had enormous energy and impetus for growth, as well as an astonishing presence of mind about the psychology of human behavior. Left completely unsolved, however, were *moral problems* that affected the life of the individual. We may be deceived by the very familiarity of the *Iliad* and the *Odyssey* into thinking that the men and women of the poetic sagas felt very much as we do about such questions as virtue and justice—how a man ought to be in relationship to his fellows. Our keen sense of affinity with those long-ago heroes lies however mainly in the psychological realism with which their angers and ambitions, their loves and their mourning, their sense of honor and shame are drawn: We easily overlook the fact that Agamemnon kills the sons of Antimachos although they beg him for mercy, cutting off their heads and arms and sending them rolling like logs down the battlefield (Il. 11.146 f.). Hector strips the body of Patroclus and intends to draw the body behind his chariot until the head falls off and the Trojan dogs devour it (Il. 17.125 ff.). Nobody thinks there is anything wrong with this.

Wars are fought over women as property and prizes. To take vengeance on one's enemy by raping and enslaving his wife is a usual procedure (Il. 9.591 ff.; Il. 22.63ff.; Od. 8.523 ff.; Il. 1.113; Il. 2.354 ff.). Piracy is a respectable profession (Od. 3.71; Il. 9.406). To steal another's property and get away with it makes one not only admired but virtuous (Od. 19.395 ff.). Indeed, what it means to be a virtuous man—to have arete—is that one comes of aristocratic lineage, owns land, flocks, house, and slaves, and has the wealth and strength to defend them. There is no such thing as a poor but virtuous man. Conversely, there is no way that a man who success-fully protects his household can lose his virtue, no matter how unself-controlled or how unjust he is.[8] There is little sense of indi-vidual rights, and what is more important, no power of recourse if the individual has been wronged.

The problem of justice and the meaning of virtue became a lead-ing theme of Greek life in the fifth century. The life of Socrates and the dialogues of Plato would be devoted to it. But already in Hesiod we find signs of longing, coupled with doubting hope that a better solution to the problem of justice might be found:

The eye of Zeus sees everything. His mind
understands all.
He is watching us right now, if he wishes to,
nor does he fail
to see what kind of justice this community keeps
inside it.
Now, otherwise I would not myself
be righteous among men
nor have my son be so; for it is a hard thing
for a man

to be righteous, if the unrighteous man
is to have the greater right.
But I believe that Zeus of the counsels
will not let it end thus.

(*Works and Days*, 269–70)

Zeus is there, but only "if he wishes to be." Because of the possibility that the god above might be watching over, the poet is himself righteous and teaches his son to be likewise. But there is as yet no real conviction. Elsewhere Hesiod turns pessimistic again and is sure that

There will be no favor for the man
who keeps his oath, for the righteous
and the good man, rather men shall give
their praise to violence
and the doer of evil. Right will be in the arm.

(*Works and Days*, 190)

The form of the ethical question today scarcely differs from the ancient debate over *nomos* vs. *physis*. This was the problem underlying Plato's epistemological discussion in the *Meno*. Is virtue simply the conventional custom of the society in which we happen to live and ought we to adapt ourselves to it and be satisfied? Or is there some ultimate standard—something that we could label "Virtue" and "Justice"? If so, how can we know it? And even more: How will the good man be rewarded? Who gives the wicked man recompense?

b. The Orphic Vision

The priests and priestesses of whom Plato speaks in the *Meno*, whose business concerned the immortality of the soul, and whose doctrine helped Plato develop an idealist solution to the problem of knowledge, appeared quite suddenly in the body of Greek literature at the end of the sixth or the beginning of the fifth century B.C. In a fragment from the hand of Pindar there is a remarkable statement which contradicts the Homeric view of the soul as a shadowy reflection of the true life in the body:

The body of all men is subject to all-powerful death,
but alive there yet remains an image of the living man;
for that alone is from the gods.
It sleeps when the limbs are active, but to them that
sleep in many a dream it reveals an award of joy or sorrow.

(Fr., 131)

The Greek word for soul in this passage is still *eidolon*, but the soul image is no longer seen as a witless wraith drifting about in the realm of Hades. Instead, it is completely alive, indeed, the only truly living part of the person, for the soul comes from the gods and is divine and cannot die, whereas the body suffers the fate of everything corporeal and will pass away.

Moreover, while the body is active and awake the soul sleeps, but when man sleeps, the soul awakens and in a man's dreams indicates to him the truth about his life and whether he is headed for a good or a bad end. These doctrines, of the body as a prison house of the soul and of a last judgment, are Orphic teaching, which seems to have appeared in the Greek world, especially in south Italy and in Athens, about the middle of the sixth century, or perhaps somewhat earlier.

There were other religious sects in Greece which taught something about immortality, notably the Eleusinian and Dionysian mysteries, and the Pythagorean colonies of Magna Graecia. But only the Orphics combined their theory of the immortal soul with a decisive doctrine of retributive justice which promised an answer to the questions of men like Hesiod, who doubted that a good man can win out in life.

The Orphics held initiations which were supposed to purify a man from the sinful part of his nature and guarantee him a happy fate in the land where Persephone was queen, provided that he continued to lead a righteous life. It is the Orphics, and no one else, who brought the concept of heaven and hell to the Western world. There is nothing similar to their formulation of these states either in the Eleusinian initiation or in the Dionysian mysteries. Plato's *Republic*, at 363d, has a satiric account from Adeimantus of how the righteous and the wicked are to be judged according to Orphic tenets. But Plato's more serious thoughts about what awaits the soul after death are to be found in his impassioned account of judgment and purgatory in the *Gorgias* (523 ff.), in his magnificent myth of Er in the tenth book of the *Republic*, and in the story which Socrates tells in order to comfort his followers, gathered with him in prison on the day of his death (*Phaedo.* 109 ff.). In each case, there is to be a dividing of the path between the good and the wicked, between men who have followed the life of the mind, and those who have been attached to the body. Socrates says:

> If at its release the soul is pure and carries with it no contamination of the body, because it has never willingly asso-

ciated with it in life...then it departs to that place which is, like itself, invisible, divine, immortal, and wise, where, on its arrival, happiness awaits it, and release from uncertainty and folly, from fears and uncontrolled desires, and all other human evils, and where, as they say of the initiates in the Mysteries, it really spends the rest of time with God. Shall we adopt this view, Cebes, or some other?

This one, by all means, said Cebes.[9]

c. Inner Knowledge and Transcendent Order

It was therefore the new doctrine of immortality—the notion of an "image of the living man," the soul, which might survive the "all powerful death" of the body and if it is just "spend the rest of time with God"—which inspired Plato's theory of knowledge as anamnesis in the Meno. Plato depended for validation of his theory on a religious doctrine which he accepted as given: an essential differentiation between body and mind. What is real and true is known by the mind.[10]

Learning does not depend on conclusions which may be drawn as a result of interaction with an external object. It is a process of recollection of internal truths. The theory of recollection rests on a non-empirical base and on an absolute standard always present in the mind which serves as reference point for phenomenal experience. Plato's theory of recollection led directly to his doctrine of forms and to the idea of the good. There is probably no clearer statement in all the dialogues of what the doctrine of forms is about than this passage at Meno 81b where Plato reveals its connections with a separable soul and a stable, non-material source of knowledge.[11]

At the same time, the theory of recollection satisfied Plato because it is based on a doctrine of immortality which in its turn satisfies the moral problem of retributive justice. Otherwise Plato would surely not have chosen the solution he did. This is the main point. "On these grounds," he says in the Meno passage we have been studying, "a man must live all his days as righteously as possible."

I have been maintaining that Jung's theory of knowledge as inner experience, Kant's theory of the categorical imperative, and Plato's theory of anamnesis are essentially similar examples of epistemological idealism. They give authority to the reasons in the mind *in order to* guarantee a moral world order and/or they grant authority to the things of the mind *because of* the moral order which is thought to exist.

Jung would have been shocked to hear that he belonged to any kind of category in which world order is to be believed in. He made a great to-do about his belief in the existence of evil, both in the polemical little book, *Answer to Job,* and in his discussions of the doctrine of the *privatio boni* in Part I of *Aion* as well as in his correspondence with Father Victor White.[12] Much excitement has been created around Jung's denial of "an only good God," and a morality which seeks perfection rather than a wholeness of psychological attitude, including both "dark" and "light" qualities. In the years after World War II Jung meditated about the ominous potential of human beings to destroy the world entirely. As an analyst he never shied away from honest acknowledgment of the dark motives in the soul.

These explicit facts lie flagrantly in the path of our search to understand Jung's philosophical views, but they are in many respects false leads. I make so bold as to say that the issues which have arisen around Jung and Evil are not so interesting as they appear to be on the surface. The problem of the *privatio boni* rests on an insufficient understanding on Jung's part of the Aristotelian doctrine of substance and its accidents, as well as on Jung's apparent determination not to be labelled a "religionist." In *Answer to Job* Jung is angry at God in a way no unbeliever ever could be. Most modern ethical theory considers the complexity of the human situation and recognizes that perfection is rather the heart's dream than a human possibility; also that love of self is part of love of humankind. (It must be admitted however that a religious *persona* of moral perfection often still sadly masks the human condition.) If Jung saw deeply into human darkness he also posited a transcendent directive center of the psyche in the self.

What this essay attempts to examine is not so much Jung's explicit statements about what he believed about metaphysical questions as the much broader, internal structure of his theory. I have identified Jung as belonging to the epistemological tradition whose most prominent members were Kant and Plato. I have now to turn to the closer historical background of the subjectivist argument with which Jung defended his doctrine of knowledge as inner experience.

We have observed in this chapter how epistemological idealism arose in Western culture as a solution to moral and religious problems in ancient Greece. Plato posited an ultimate standard for truth and justice when he declared that we know because we can recollect, step by step, back to ultimate standards (the forms). By and large, Plato's solution—that truth is in the rational mind, or else in an ultimately rational being, God, who has created in the human mind an approximation of divine rationality—held through until the beginning of the modern era. Then new problems arose which demanded a reconsideration of the question: how and what do we know? Moral and religious questions of course remained, and with them the need for guarantees that we live in an ordered universe under the aegis of a rational God. But, from about the middle of the seventeenth century, scientific questions were also becoming more and more important. How can we understand cause and effect relationships in observable objects? What is the relationship between sense experience and rational thought? What is real—the world of observable objects or the mind which thinks them? Opposing considerations put scientists and religionists increasingly at war with each other, but until the twentieth century philosophers attempted to build systems which would answer both scientific and religious questions. Chapter 5, to follow, reviews the historical development of philosophical discussion of these issues up through Immanuel Kant's "Copernican revolution," which reversed the focus of authority on matters of knowledge from God to man. Chapter 6 follows the course of Kantian disputes, including the version of Kant taught by Schopenhauer, until the end of the nineteenth century, when Jung chose among competing versions of Kant's philosophy a position which expressed his own philosophical views.

5

Theories of Perception and Knowledge: From Descartes to Kant

According to Plato, we are so far removed from knowledge of true reality in our ordinary lives as to be like chained prisoners in a deep cave, with only the reflected light from an anterior fire to guide our perception of the flitting shadows crossing the visual field (*Rep.* 514b).[1] We imagine that these shadows are real things, but they are four times removed from the light of the sun as the true life and source of the visible world. Plato's truth was in the transcendent forms, known by reason and not by sense perception.

The empiricist of ancient times, on the other hand, was Epicurus. For him, it is *only* the senses which are to trusted, and we can never go wrong in our apprehension of objects if we accept our sense impressions immediately as true.[2] Where we err is when we start to think about things and add in our own opinions. Not only are the objects of our perception material, but the perceptual image traveling from the surface of the object to our eyes is a "material effluence"—a sheet of matter one atom thick which comes to meet us from the object. The soul of the perceiver is itself a kind of fine matter. So on the principle of like being able to know like it is easy for the material soul to perceive the material object. But we must not, said Epicurus, confuse the clarity of our judgments by thinking in too complicated a way abut what we know.[3] Reason can get in the way of knowledge.

Both Plato and Epicurus were trying to deal with the disparity between what we know by way of bodily sense perception and what we know by way of the reasoning and imagining experience of the mind, Plato by declaring that there *is* no knowledge of objects of sense, and Epicurus by declaring that there is no knowledge *except* for sense perception. Plato's epistemology expressed a deeply religious belief in transcendent and permanent values. The goal of Epicurus in applying a materialistic standard was to free people from

49

fear of the fate of the gods. If gods have no power over men, and immortality and a last judgment are also not to be reckoned with, then we may live with inner peace. Even death is not to be feared, "for while we exist death is not present, and when death is present we no longer exist."[4] The Epicurean religion spread widely throughout the Hellenistic period because it offered to an uncertain and changing society the solace of a universe contained in a modest framework of known quantities.

In the moment when we proclaim a "higher meaning" to human life, a God with real power in the universe, or moral values which transcend self-interest, we also have to assert the *primacy* of inner knowledge, be it "reason" or "inner feeling" *over* the knowledge produced by sense perceptions. We must explain how and to what extent we know the world of sense and how and what we know of the inner world. And we must try to connect the two realms. The metaphysical idealist must explain how the external world is an epiphenomenon of mind and the empiricist must show how mental phenomena spring from a non-mental physical base. It has always been the peculiar problem of the empiricist to show how general categories of understanding are reached by inference from the object, and the never quite solved problem of the idealist to demonstrate how apprehension of the particular object can be deduced from purely a priori inner knowledge.

So long as the Western world remained secure in the rational theology of scholasticism only one set of standards—that of reason—was applied to the quest for knowledge.[5] But with the advent of science in the early seventeenth century the claims of the empiricists grew much stronger.[6] It became the special task of philosophy to judge the status of scientific knowledge and to ask whether or not we can have objective knowledge of the world. Throughout the seventeenth and early eighteenth centuries philosophers were involved in intense discussion, without, however, being able to arrive at a causal theory of knowledge and reference which might secure the path between sense perception and rational reflection. Not until 1781, in the *Critique of Pure Reason*, would Immanuel Kant find that way. Kant's solution upended the heretofore accepted criteria for knowledge, presumably for all time to come.

René Descartes (1596–1650) succeeded, after doubting everything that he could not be absolutely sure of, in establishing that at least he could not doubt his own existence since someone must actually exist who was thinking these thoughts (the *Cogito ergo sum*). But in order to reach to the world of outer objects Descartes resorted to a form of the ontological argument for God. If Descartes existed, then a more perfect mental being than he must surely also exist outside him and this more perfect being (God) would not deceive him about the existence of external objects. The argument is still scholastic in form.[7]

It was left to John Locke (1632–1704) to establish the epistemological bases for an empirical view. All our ideas, he said, derive from experience, either through sense perception of outer objects or by way of reflection on those objects. Our general notions are the mere *nomina* which the customs of verbal language bestow upon us. Yet perception itself is a veridical reflection of sensation. How, then, do we know that our perceptions record real objects? How can we be assured without an independent authority that our ideas have anything to do with what is outside the mind itself?

Bishop George Berkeley (1685–1753) thought that Locke's arguments must lead to complete skepticism—to skepticism about the objective world and about the existence of God as well. So he turned the material substance world of Locke outside-in and made mind the substance of the universe. He did this not in order to desecrate common sense observations of the perceptual world but in order to guarantee a believable universe. Berkeley's study of the process of perception was of primary importance to Hume, Kant, and Schopenhauer. Although, as we shall see, Jung attributed his epistemological views to Kant, Schopenhauer's view of the world of objects as emanating from the primal Will was also a powerful influence on his thinking.

Berkeley doubted that our possession of ideas of space, time, motion, and substance in any way proves their existence in the world.[8] He doubted that insentient objects have any causative power either to interact among themselves or to cause perceptual images of themselves in the percipient's mind. Vital life and causative power are rather in the mind, and we must give back to the mind what we have abstracted from it and projected onto what we think is matter.

On the ancient theory that only like can know like, Berkeley decided that what we perceive with our minds must be all that exists; otherwise nothing that we perceive is true. If the existence of material substances cannot be guaranteed then the material world must be eliminated.

It is only in the mind that trees are in the park, or books in a closet, or a table in the room, for "when we do our utmost to conceive the existence of external bodies, we are all the while only contemplating our own ideas.[9]

Does this mean that the table no longer exists when we leave the room and no longer see it or think about it? No, for in fact our sense impressions are even livelier and have more stability than the fantasies of our imagination. All it means is that those external objects are held under the steady gaze of some other mind or spirit (God) which by means of this act in fact produces them. The world is entirely real, only it is not material.

> The ideas imprinted on the senses by the Author of Nature are called *real things*; and those excited in the imagination, being less regular, vivid and constant, are more properly termed *ideas* or *images of things* which they copy and represent. But then our sensations, be they never so vivid and distinct, are nevertheless ideas, that is, they exist in the mind, or are perceived by it, as truly as the ideas of its own framing.[10]

Both the objects of our immediate perception and the continuing existence of the objective world beyond our seeing of it are the manifestation of the "Eternal Invisible Mind which produces and sustains all things" (94). Like Schopenhauer after him, Berkeley solved the epistemological dilemma of dissimilar kinds by declaring that there is after all only one kind; the material world is a phenomenal manifestation of non-material reality.[11] Indirectly, through Schopenhauer, Jung's own speculations about an ultimately non-material universe took inspiration from Berkeley.[12]

David Hume (1711–1776) accepted the arguments of Locke and Berkeley that what we know depends on personal experience, but saw that when Berkeley's theological proposition that mental experience equals spiritual experience is removed we are left in a completely skeptical dilemma. If knowledge is experience then there is no validating criterion which assures me that what I seem to perceive and what I personally experience is objective reality. We cannot even know that natural events occur in a necessary causal chain. We can only observe a succession of events in regular order. The imputation of relations is what the percipient imposes on this order. We think we know, but seeming and believing is all it amounts to.

A position exactly opposed to that of Hume was occupied by Gottfried Wilhelm Leibniz (1646–1716) and by his pupils, prime among them Christian von Wolff. Leibniz, like Hume, was deeply interested in problems of causation and in scientific method in general. But he considered that the cause and effect order which we see exhibited in mechanics is the corollary effect of an order which is ultimately rational in nature and which comprises the existing universe. In Leibniz's scheme, mechanical cause and effect operate in a not quite real phenomenal world. Logic and final cause operate at the level of true being. At both levels order is preserved, each order reflecting or validating the order seen in the other. The phenomenal level of reality is actually however subsumed within the larger reality of non-material, rational being.[13]

For Leibniz, God is the true substance of the world, and he operates the world, which consists of individual monadic units, according to the laws of logic. The monadic world gives rise to the phenomenal world, an artifact operating according to contingent mechanical laws. We may trust in the lawfulness of our observations of nature because God could never create any but the best possible of worlds, insofar as logic allows. Our perspective is limited, and different in kind from the totality of God's understanding, but it is not directly false.

Leibniz was educated in both scholastic and Neoplatonic philosophy, was deeply influenced by mystical traditions (Robert Fludd, Rosicrucianism, Jakob Boehme, Paracelsus). He was also a superb mathematician and a practiced emissary of government. He discovered the differential and integral calculus, was committed to the mechanical methodology of Descartes, served as diplomat for the throne at Hanover and exerted himself ecumenically on behalf of Protestant and Catholic reunification. Leibniz stood just between the old and the new, in science and in the cultural themes of his era. The customary interpretation of Leibniz's philosophy shows it as an application or model of his mathematics, and as supremely rational in intent. Newer work however suggests that Leibniz encompassed the conflicting themes of his intellectual experience in a kind of Neoplatonic myth. It was, to be sure, a myth which placed the principle of reason at the pinnacle of the interpretive scheme.[14]

According to Leibniz, God is the one fully actualized, simple substance, containing in his own being the potential for everything which is created, "by continual fulgurations from the divinity" (*Monadology* 47).[15] Through his creative activity, God fills the world with living elements—the monads. Monads, both soul-monads which have reason and memory and which therefore are a shadowy form of God himself, and other types of monadic elements such as plants and fish and rocks, fill the entire universe in a plenum of created being, down to the most infinitesimal portions of what we view as the material world (*Monadology* 60–69).[16] Monads are themselves non-material, but they are attached to bodies, for which they function as an entelechy (*Monadology* 62–63), that is, as an active and directive center for the activity of the body which they inhabit (*Monadology* 17,18). The activity of monads is governed not by external motion or by causes which impinge on the monad itself, but by internal motivations which express the character or the nature of the monad, just as, in a larger sense, God expresses his own nature in and throughout the universe created by him. That motivation may be expressed as desire, or appetition, or as final cause (*Monadology* 79).[17]

Although the monad is alive and is an indestructible unit and thus mirrors the indestructible universe and participates in some degree in the nature of God, its perspective and therefore its possibility of true knowledge is limited to whatever degree of perfection it may possess, and is indeed qualitatively different from the knowledge possessed and exercised by God (*Monadology* 48, 77). One may imagine a city as metaphor for the universe. The individual monads live in the city and they may obtain perspectives of the city from a number of positions, depending on how they are placed in it. Each perspective is limited and none yields an image of the whole town (*Monadology* 57). If God, or perhaps an angel of God, were however to view the city from the top of a tower situated in the center of town a perfect understanding could be obtained.[18] One could see the town as it *really* is—not from the point of view of perspective as we know it, from whence we arrive at clear ideas of magnitude, figure, and motion—but from the point of view of the logic of the entire plan.

Different methods must therefore be applied to different tasks. The material bodies which completely fill the palpable universe and are in continual mechanical, jostling contact with each other are not nothing, but they are not quite real either. They comprise the *phenomenal* world, and here the mechanical method of Descartes must be applied to achieve understanding.[19] What we thereby realize is not however knowledge; it is awareness of the causal relationships between bodies. True knowledge has to do with understanding the activity of the monads which operate so-to-say from within the bodies they inhabit, and with God, who alone possesses perfect knowledge. From without, bodies behave according to mechanical laws. From within, their monads behave in perfect harmony with outer mechanical reactions, but actually according to divine laws which express their essential nature. Robert Butts says:

> The preferred methodology for studying bodies is the mechanical method. The problem is this: Bodies are not real, only spirits are. . . . Perception is the real state of things, not mechanical action. From the aspect of eternity, purpose replaces efficient cause, reason replaces cause.[20]

True knowledge has to do with metaphysics, with approaching more closely the viewpoint of the angel on the tower, with fitting things together in a logical whole. True knowledge does away with the phenomenal world of time and space, for from the divine perspective there are no such things as contingent facts. There are only necessary truths. In the later language of Kant, we ought according to Leibniz to reduce synthetic statements to analytical statements in order to obtain knowledge.[21]

From the point of view of sense perception we remain, according to Leibniz, as citizens on the streets of the village, envisioning our world in a series of partial vistas limited by considerations of time and space. Only by using another faculty—reason—are we able to envision reality as a whole. The reasoning faculty of human beings is also limited, but we must trust, thought Leibniz—and here he was in accord with ancient and scholastic tradition—that the divine nature in which we share, as rational beings, is wholly rational. The truest knowledge of reality is therefore obtained from the tower. Spatial and linear perspective on the streets below is to be sure flattened out, but we obtain in its place a clear view of the design of the town as a whole, when we "see" it from the point of view of logic. Understanding the "design as a whole" means seeing with the vision of the rational mind, and participating thus with God in true knowing.

The reader who is familiar with Jung's own work two hundred years later will recognize in the Leibnizian theory of knowledge not, to be sure, his belief in the superior perspective of the *rational* monad, but yet a definite connection to Jung's belief that a mental, or psychic perspective takes precedence over sensory data of time and space. It may fairly be said that the direct line of descent to Jung's own theory begins early in the eighteenth century with Berkeley and with Leibniz, passing then through Kant to Schopenhauer and von Hartmann and to turn-of-the-century academic quarrels about whether Kant had intended to affirm or deny the reliability of our knowledge of phenomena.

While Immanuel Kant (1724–1804) began his career with, and indeed for a time followed the precepts of the Leibnizian school, he was finally unable to buy on faith or to accept by reason of the authority of long tradition the idea that reason alone leads to knowledge of reality. Reason in itself, he concluded, leads us neither to knowledge of God nor to knowledge of the objects of our world, although it must play a crucial role in the *way* we fashion our understanding of things. Ever since Plato had enthroned reason in the place of the divine in order to ensure a moral universe (see

Chapter 4, above), Western thought ascribed to a transcendent God both perfect reason and perfect knowledge. It will not do, said Kant. We cannot give over to an externalized authority, even to the idea of God, the responsibility for our own understanding. Whatever there is that is to be known, is known by *us*.[22] We must transpose our model of knowledge as something existing outside ourselves (a theocentric model) to a view of the human being as percipient knower (an anthropocentric model).[23]

Even more, we must abandon the Leibnizian conviction that if only we could attain the angel's perspective from the tower our understanding of reality as a whole would be more perfect. There are no grounds for expecting that a different or more complete perspective would yield a reality other than what we now know.

But if the authority of reason, and even more, the authority of God as author and commander of reason, is dismantled, are we not delivered over to the Human dilemma? Who or what is to guarantee that our perceptions make any sense? Do we perhaps live in a solipsistic world of our own imaginings? That idea doesn't seem to make even ordinary sense of our everyday lives, but eighteenth-century philosophers before Kant were unable to propose a theory of knowledge which could answer these kinds of objections.

It was exactly at this point of Hume's skeptical impasse that Kant was startled into reconsideration of the Leibnizian/Wolffian postulates in which his own philosophical thinking had first been nurtured. "I openly confess," he later wrote, that "my recollection of David Hume was the very thing which many years ago first interrupted my dogmatic slumber and gave my investigations in the field of speculative philosophy a quite new direction."

> The question was not whether the concept of cause was right, useful, and even indispensable for our knowledge of nature, for this Hume had never doubted; but whether that concept could be taught by reason *a priori*, and consequently whether it possessed an inner truth independent of all experience. . . . If we start from a well-founded, but undeveloped thought which another has bequeathed to us, we may well hope by continued reflection to advance farther than the acute man to whom we owe the first spark of light.[24]

By way of answering Hume and transforming the authoritative bases of Leibnizian epistemology, Kant proposed in his *Critique of Pure Reason* a close analysis of what comprises the experience of a thinking mind in the human individual. The reader unfamiliar with Kant's analysis may perhaps keep in mind the passage just cited as a guide to the paragraphs which follow. What is being sought is an authoritative standard, a point from which to measure, a beginning place where one can stand on sure ground. Experience is so various and appearances so deceiving that the impressions which come to us from without (a posteriori experiences) do not seem to promise any certainty of knowledge. Is there perhaps such a reliable standard within us (a priori, before the fact of experience), which guarantees the truth of our thought and experience?

Kant said, there is no guarantee of absolute truth, not even any sensible speaking of such a thing, but we do have the possibility of objective knowledge. We must only observe that the process by which we come to any understanding involves not only experiences which impact us from outside ourselves, but also certain innate patterns or categories in our minds which impose on the data of our experience a conceptual framework. When we apply concepts to the data of experience we are able to form judgments. We say that we know.[25]

> Intuitions and concepts constitute, therefore, the elements of all our knowledge, so that neither concepts without an intuition in some way corresponding to them, nor intuitions without concepts, can yield knowledge. (A50/B74)

"There can be no doubt," begins Kant, "that all our knowledge begins with experience" (B1). But in order that the raw data of the *sensible intuition* (Kant's term describing the reception in a mind of a sense impression) can become the conscious possession of the knowing person a series of processing steps are necessary. We may imagine the situation in the language of computer operations, and divide the mind into two interacting sections. In the data input section we have the data input itself, that is, the not yet conceptualized matter of our experience (the manifold of intuitions), and we have the formatting codes. These formatting codes are a kind of pre-processing feature of computer operations which will eventually allow the computer to process the data. For Kant, the formatting codes are the forms of space and time; they are the a priori forms of pure intuition.

Space and time are of the stuff of the machine—they do not belong outside it. It is pointless to ask whether space and time have independent existence outside the perceiving individual. "Space is not a form inhering in things in themselves as their intrinsic property" (B45). It is the form in which the objects of outer sense are necessarily and always perceived by the subject perceiver.

Just as we are unable to perceive the objects of outer sense except in spatial relationships, so are we also constrained by the fact

that the human mind thinks in just this way to conceive of ourselves, as well as the conceptual objects of our experience, in a
temporal framework. Time is the form of inner sense (A33/B50). For
Kant, time does not have the status of absolute reality. It is simply
the pre-condition in virtue of which all perception takes place,
exhibiting "the relation of representations in our inner state." We can
very well experience time without the appearance of objects, but we
cannot experience the appearance of objects except in time (A31/B46,
A34/B51). All appearances of objects of the senses "necessarily stand
·in time relations." They appear to our minds in succession. Our
experience of motion and cause depends on our still prior experience of self and others in time. In itself, time is nothing; it is not a
"thing." It is clearly not attached to the objects perceived by outer
sense, since it is experienced prior to the experience of objects.

Both time and space are thus the a priori forms of our experience; they do not exist in their own right. However, if we turn this
statement around, and observe that time and space are nevertheless
the necessary and universal conditions of whatever knowledge
human beings may be said to possess, we may begin to build a basis
for the objectivity of knowledge (B74). There are certain principles
upon which we can rely. (These principles are furnished by the
categories of the understanding.) They are not contingent on the
particularity of the sensed object nor on the peculiarity of the
knower. Everyone thinks in the same way. We may speak of the
empirical reality of these principles because they are valid "in
respect of all objects which allow of ever being given to our senses"
(A35/B52).

Henry Allison has coined the term *epistemic condition* to describe
the focus of Kant's theory of knowledge.[26] The term is a positive one,
in the sense that it indicates the human person as the subject of
activity: we cannot separate the known from the conditions under
which it can be known. In Kant's theory, the Leibnizian order of
relation, in which the experience of objects in time depends on a
prior existing logical order of relation, is turned upside down:

> For Kant, ... it is only in terms of the prior and independent
> representation of space that we can represent to ourselves
> this order or situation of things. It is, therefore, not space,
> but the things in space that are eliminable, not, to be sure,
> in experience, but in thought. The same applies, *mutatis
> mutandis*, to time.[27]

Copernicus observed that the data of astronomical observation would not fit, so long as one supposed the sun and the planets revolve around the earth as a fixed object. So he remade astronomy on a plan of the earth revolving around the sun. Kant, too, rewrote the plan of his field. He made logic serve sense data and set human experience (the forms of intuition) over the objects of knowledge. Contrary to earlier views, he rejected the idea that material objects form impressions on our minds. Instead, the objects of experience become determinate only through intuition and the understanding. These points will be further considered in a moment, when the meaning of Kant's idealism and his empiricism, and the disputes over his achievement which raged throughout the nineteenth century, are discussed.

Returning now to the analogy of the mind in the language of computer operations, we come to the second main stage of the process. When the data is assembled the program in the computer begins to run. It asks questions and gives directions: "If this...then this....If not this, then move to the next possibility." Now the logic, the intellectual, a priori factoring processes in the human mind come to the fore. These are Kant's *categories*—his pure concepts of the understanding. Unlike the program of the modern computer, which is interchangeable with any number of other software plans which can be made to function in a single hardware environment, we must however imagine a computer with one basic control program. This program contains the general concepts which comprise our understanding. Consciousness consists of *genera*. We are given the raw data or matter of experience, but unless we have a word to describe it—a concept—we do not know it.

The list of a priori concepts, or categories, which Kant himself proposed has long been regarded as the least successful aspect of his theory. Kant did not unfortunately provide any argument to support the claim for his list. The terms he supplied are not really general terms for the objects of experience, but categories which define what happens in the activity of judging—in making an assertion about—an inner or outer sense impression. The categories are forms of judgment, acts of differentiating thought in which the mind asks questions of quantity, quality, relation, and mode about intuited objects.

The objects which are actually treated in the act of judgment— while the control program is running—are the *schematized objects*. The schemata attempt to solve the problem of unlike kinds. (See my commentary on p. 50 above). How does the mind connect the sensible intuitions with logical forms?[28] The distance is too great, as the situation as defined until now stands. Kant states the problem thus:

In all subsumptions of an object under a concept the representation of the object must be *homogeneous* with the concept; in other words, the concept must contain something
which is represented in the object that is to be subsumed
under it. But pure concepts of the understanding being quite
heterogeneous from empirical intuitions, and indeed from
all sensible intuitions, can never be met with in any intuition. (A137/38/B176–77).

Kant proposed a most interesting solution for this dilemma. It is
not the intuition itself which the mind judges in terms of the categories. It is the image of the intuited object, created in accordance
with certain rules, that is, certain schema, by the imagination.[29] All
of this activity is on the input side of the computer. All of it is a
priori. What we are dealing with in the act of thinking about, or
obtaining knowledge about an object is thus not the object itself but
an image of that object created by and limited by the potentials of
our imagination. It is by now a very short step over to the program
proper of the computer—to the pure concepts of understanding.
Here we meet however not with the concepts themselves, which are
logical constructs completely unconnected with the intuited object,
but with *their* schema. The schema of the concepts do not, like the
sensible schema, create images. They provide a kind of universal
grammar by means of which the whole process of cognition gains
significance and meaning.[30] Taken together, the transcendental schemata "subordinate appearances to universal rules of synthesis and
...fit them for thoroughgoing connection in one experience" (A14/
B185). The problem of heterogeneity has nearly been overcome, for
we see that what we know is largely defined and limited by internal
mental processes. These processes are nevertheless objective; they
operate according to rules and they are the same for all human
beings.

Now the final stage of the computer's processing activity takes
place. The *output* appears on the screen or the printer. What is the
result?

1. The process has been shown to take place in the computer
and to define the computer in terms of its activity. In the case of the
computer this is perfectly obvious. This is what the computer does:
it computes. In the case of the human mind it is perhaps not so
obvious, and certainly not so in the eighteenth century. This is what
the mind does: it thinks, in such and such a manner. In fact, this is
what it means to be a self-conscious human being in the environment in which human beings live—to receive intuited impressions

from within or without ourselves and to understand them by means of a priori forms, schemata, and concepts which already operate in the mind. Kant said, "Only in so far, therefore as I can unite a manifold of given representations in *one consciousness*, is it possible for me to represent to myself the *identity of the consciousness in these representations*" (B133). There is a reciprocal and necessary relationship between knower and object being known. I am aware of myself because I know objects, including myself. Objects are knowable because I can know them.

2. Kant considered that he had shown that we do have very substantial knowledge. We are not in fact caught between Humean skepticism and Leibnizian rationalism. While it is true that with regard to objects appearing to us from without ourselves we may know them only within our own parameters, a synthetic and regularly repeatable process goes on inside us. In the case of mathematics we have an example of this synthetic process occurring without there being any outer object, that is, before the fact of experience. Objects of pure intuition, mathematical objects, serve as stimulus for mental activity which results in new knowledge. We have *synthetic a priori knowledge*. Because this in indubitably so, Kant's entire analysis gains validation.

3. The object of knowledge has been defined epistemically, that is, in terms of the conditions by means of which it can be known. These conditions are centered in processes which take place within the knower, that is, the human person, not outside the knower in the object, nor outside the knower in some authoritative Knower (God) who can however not be known by the human person. The epistemological focus of the question, as Kant set it, should not be interpreted as the question of the existence or non-existence of objects. This latter is an ontological question, one which naturally springs to mind when we consider that objects are, for us, appearances. But it is not Kant's issue. The epistemological focus should also be distinguished from the psychological conditions—cultural background, personal complexes rooted in individual family history, the unique configuration of each personality—which give shape to what we know. Still further, epistemological are to be differentiated from physiological conditions of knowledge, for example, the way in which auditory and optical signals are wired in the brain. (See the section on Helmholtz in Chapter 6, following, for an example of confusion of this sort.) Kant's problem had to do with the nature of the mind, not of body.

Nevertheless, the wretched problem of the object—the thing-in-itself—could not be made to disappear. In part, Kant's transcendental distinction between the object as it appears to us and the object as it may be in its own right forces the ontological question. Must we assume that the impression which affects our sensibility stems from an actually existing object or might it be the case that there is no external referent? If it is conceivable that empirically existing objects have characteristics not knowable by us because these qualities spring the frame of the human conditions of knowability, may there not be *logically* conceivable entities (God or rational unembodied souls) which also exist, though we may not know them nor indeed experience any sensory intuition of their existence? This is, in briefest form, the question of the noumena which necessarily arises when we consider that our knowledge is phenomenal. In the second edition of the first *Critique* Kant carefully rephrased his explication so as mostly to avoid what had seemed in the first edition like a positive doctrine of the noumena. But problematical passages remain.[31]

Modern Kantian scholars consider that it is methodologically consistent with the transcendental analysis to think of things in themselves, indeed that is the very point, that we *do* think of them, while we at the same time recognize the necessary limit of our knowledge. As for the noumenon (the only-intellectually-existing object), Kant considered at least in the second edition of the *Critique* that the conception of such non-sensible entities functions in a negative way as a boundary or limit on sensibility.[32]

More than any other single factor, it was the difficulties attendant on understanding Kant's doctrine of the *Ding an sich* and the noumena that led to enormous divergences of opinion in nineteenth-century philosophical discussion. Depending on how one understood Kant's analysis, he was supporting the new sciences. Or he was justifying belief in God. Or he had anticipated the new physiology, which was discovering how we process information in the brain. The next chapter offers a closer view of these varying interpretations and concludes by exactly matching one version of Kant with Jung's own epistemological assumptions.

6

Nineteenth-Century Kantianism

For a long generation after the death of Kant in 1804, his authority on the problem of knowing disappeared, at least in German-speaking countries, in the flood tide of Hegel, Schelling, and *Naturphilosophie*. But with the approach of the mid-century a new philosophical spirit began to be felt. Great metaphysical systems seemed less in accord with a world of burgeoning scientific discovery. Hard facts and the process by which we know them became the focus of both scientific and philosophical thinking. The term *theory of knowledge* was used for the first time.[1] Major philosophers no longer believed that they could understand the whole of reality. Quite enough would be achieved if we could understand what it is that we human beings know. Physiologists were learning more about the perceptive apparatus of the mind. Philosophers became more involved in logic as a path to knowledge.[2] Metaphysics continued, of course, to be the underlying concern, but in place of the grand schemes, all was focused down on technical epistemological exposition. The name of Kant was heard again.

The nineteenth-century Kantian revival was marked by two major departures from Kant's own work. 1) Many modern students of Kant argue that the first *Critique* should be understood only in the light of the second *Critique*. Kant's ethical concerns provide a guide for understanding the epistemological intentions of the first *Critique*. But the nineteenth century Kantian revival was concerned almost alone with the first *Critique*. The reference point offered by the ethical works was therefore lost. Because important sections of the *Critique* were drastically revised in its second edition, and because Kant's style and conceptual formulations notoriously explored every level of complexity at the cost of clarity, there was plenty of room for argument about what Kant said, and what Kant meant. 2) The epistemological question had an urgency in the nineteenth century that we will scarcely encounter in the late twentieth century, when the scientific world view has so completely won over our everyday thinking that we are apt to think of the *problem* of knowledge only in terms of physiological apparatuses for perception and cognition, or technical innovations which increase our cognitive capacity. Nineteenth-century discussions were fraught with metaphysical significance, both for scientists and for philosophers. To be suspicious of what we can know by means of sense perception meant for the idealists leaving room for the a priori knowledge of the mind, that is, for transcendent truths. To be suspicious of any knowledge which goes beyond the objects of sense perception meant for the positivists that "felt" inner truths or logical constructions about them were pure nonsense—chatter about the irreal.[3] To be suspicious about the veracity of sense perception meant for the scientist however something quite different from what it meant for the idealist. It opened the way for the techniques of the new scientific professions. The invocation of Kant's authority did not necessarily carry the same set of meanings in the nineteenth century then, as it had in Kant's own time. We must expect to find each of the disputants arguing for a different version of what Kant said.

What Kant urged is the objective character but not the apodictic certainty of our knowledge of phenomena. In the following pages we will follow the tangled path by means of which Kant came to be regarded, by influential figures in science and in philosophy, as the hero of a subjectivist view—a view scarcely to be differentiated from that of Berkeley. At the end of the trail we shall find epistemological views that can be matched with Jung's own views, as delineated in the first three chapters of this book. This is a circumstantial proof of the historical sources of Jung's psychology.

For a second proof, namely the influence on Jung of Schopenhauer's philosophy, we have more than circumstantial evidence. Jung refers to Schopenhauer more than seventy times throughout the *Collected Works*. In the *Zofingia Lectures* which are published as a supplement to the *Collected Works*, there are twenty-three references to Schopenhauer and in the *Letters* seventeen citations. This is not to mention the *Seminar Notes*, whose publication is in process and which are not yet indexed as a whole. The chapter therefore concludes with a brief summary of Schopenhauer's theory of knowledge, and particularly of the changes rung by Schopenhauer on Kant.

a. Hermann von Helmholtz and the Skeptical Heritage

Although it was Otto Liebmann, professor of philosophy at Jena, whose motto "Back to Kant"[4] served to express the aspirations of the time, it was a scientist, not a philosopher, who perhaps did most to fuel the new movement. Hermann Ludwig von Helmholtz was born and educated in Potsdam where his father was gymnasial professor of classics and philology. Helmholtz wanted to study physics but his father persuaded him that the only way he could earn a living was as a physician. He obtained a scholarship to study medicine in Berlin, on the condition that he afterwards should serve ten years as an army physician, but he was released from that obligation when at the age of twenty-six he published his essay "On the Conservation of Energy," which set the tasks for philosophy and for physics for the next fifty years.[5] From that time on he served as professor of physiology and professor of physics at Königsberg, Bonn, Heidelberg, and Berlin. Helmholtz became the great polymath of nineteenth-century German science. He influenced an entire generation of German academicians—philosophers, physicians, anatomists, physiologists, physicists. Together with three other famous German physiologists who had become friends as students in Berlin—Emil Du Bois-Reymond (University of Berlin), Ernst Brücke (University of Vienna), and Carl Ludwig (University of Zürich and Leipzig)—he pushed to get rid of the confessional vitalist assumptions for professorships in science at German universities. In this he was absolutely courageous, and his enormous scientific reputation gave him the freedom to speak openly. Science, he insisted, must never begin with metaphysical presuppositions:

> Our knowledge never reaches the status of unconditional truth; it reaches only a degree of probability so high as to be practically equal to certainty. The metaphysicians may amuse themselves at this; we shall take their mocking to heart, however, only when they are in a position to do better, or even as well as can be done by the inductive method.[6]

Just nine years after the publication of his essay on thermodynamics, Helmholtz published the first volume of his *Handbuch der Physiologischen Optik* (Leipzig, 1856–66), which became and remains the principal work in the field. In 1863 came his *Die Lehre von dem Tonempfindung* (translated by A. J. Ellis as *On the Sensations of Tone as a Physiological Basis for the Theory of Music* [New York: Longmans, Green & Co., 1885). This book did for the physiology of hearing what the former work had done for an understanding of vision. It was on this basic work in the physiology of perception that Helmholtz built his philosophical theory of knowledge. He had grown up in a philosophical atmosphere; his father had been a personal friend of Fichte's son. Helmholtz was always aware that his scientific work had profound philosophical implications.

Johannes Müller, Helmholtz's own teacher, had already in his *theory of specific nerve energy* settled the question whether what we perceive is what is really there, in the outer object. With our eyes we perceive the image of the sun. With our skin, however, we perceive only its warmth. Likewise, added Helmholtz, we can próduce a sensation of light by pressing on the eyeball, by passing a weak current of electricity through it, or administering a narcotic drug.[7] What we perceive "does not depend...upon the kind of external impression whereby the sensation is excited, but is determined alone and exclusively by the sensory nerve upon which the impression impinges. Excitation of the optic nerve produces only light sensations.[8]

It is clear, however, that if we do not perceive what is really there, our perceptions do nevertheless depend on external stimuli. How do we interpret these external stimuli? Do our perceptions, although not identical with, correspond in a kind of preexisting harmonic manner with the objects of external perception? This would be a *nativistic theory of perception*. To hold to it requires an assumption of faith that can never be demonstrated, any more than one can refute an extreme idealist who insists and holds on to a conviction that life is just a dream.[9] There is no objective standpoint from which one can reach the dreamer.

The other possible viewpoint, that which Helmholtz advocated, takes a more skeptical view of what we perceive of external stimuli. What we perceive are mere *signs* or *symbols* of external objects (not images), not necessarily resembling them at all. What we perceive is conditioned by the capacities of our physiological sense-perceptive organs. Nevertheless, this perception is not just subjectivistic, for a similar stimulus always provokes a similar sign or symbol as response. And not only we, but all other humans, apparently have the same kinds of symbolic responses to stimuli. So there is a universality or lawlikeness to our response to patterns, even if they do not indicate to us the true nature of the external object.

Even if we do not know that it will lead us to truth, we have to assume an inductive hypothesis. We have to assume that the practical knowledge which enables us to get along in the world is the result of *inferences of causal process* which we have been making all along, albeit unconsciously, since our birth.[10] We cannot know anything just on our own in a moment's observation, for we depend for the *genera* of our knowledge on past experience. "The new sense impression entering in present perception forms the minor premiss."

The major premise to which it is fitted is the past experience of earlier observations. *We can also compare our observations with those of others, and we can repeat our experiences (our experiments) in order to test the lawlikeness of our results.* In these studies Helmholtz effectively laid down the rules of modern scientific procedure. The more frequently our experiments are repeated without variation the more certain we can be that we are observing not just a subjectivistic state of mind but whatever we are enabled to know of the causal lawlikeness of nature.

Nevertheless, we should keep constantly in mind that lawlikenss is the condition of our comprehension of objects. The lawlike operation of what we think of as causality is a regulative principle. It does not guarantee that the world actually operates on that principle.[11] Helmholtz understood the implications of his theory:

> It is apparent that our present inquiry requires us to consider the far-reaching opposition between these two systems of philosophy: one of which [the nativistic theory] assumes that the laws of mental operations are in pre-existing harmony with those of the outer world, and the other [empirical skepticism] which attempts to explain all correspondence between mind and matter as the result of experience.[12]

What we have to pre-suppose, but cannot prove, thought Helmholtz, is the law of causality. In place of Kant's doctrine of a priori synthetic knowledge, that is knowledge independent of experience, Helmholtz hypothesized a causal law which is present in the mind *on account of* past experience. But, as Moritz Schlick noted, Helmholtz adopted in fact not Kant's viewpoint, but that of David Hume.[13] Helmholtz thought he was being true to Kant.

While Kant referred to the categories by means of which *mind* apprehends the *body* of nature, Helmholtz referred to the *physiological* limitations which condition our apprehension of nature. We must rely on science and on scientific experimentation for whatever verification of sense experience we can obtain.[14] Helmholtz's Kantianism was in fact a kind of psychologistic, skeptical positivism.[15] The worst of it was that although the error was detected by some scholars, for example by Hermann Cohen and Paul Natorp of the University of Marburg, Helmholtz's version went on being believed in among other groups. It fed into a stream of skeptical assumptions about human knowledge which nourished both scientific and religious inclinations of the late nineteenth century and gradually became a commonplace academic expression.

b. Lange and the Phenomenal Idealists

The political reform journalist and philosopher Friedrich Albert Lange (1828–75) was the one figure most largely responsible for spreading Helmholtz's view of Kant. His influence was greatest in just that area of northwest Switzerland where Jung lived and went to school. Though German by birth, Lange grew up mostly in Zürich. Between 1855 and 1857, Lange was in Bonn, studying natural science and attending the lectures of Helmholtz in physiology (Helmholtz's *Physiological Optics* was published in 1856). Afterwards Lange taught in the Gymnasium at Duisburg, at the same time editing the town newspaper. But the politics of his journalism forced him to resign his professorship and he moved to Switzerland, where he at first served as editor of the *Winterthurer Landbote* and then in 1870 was appointed professor of philosophy at the University of Zürich. Politics (this time, Swiss sympathies for the French in the Franco-Prussian War) led once again to Lange's resignation and return to Germany, but his prominence in Swiss affairs between Zürich and Basel in the generation where Jung's own gymnasial teachers will have been students must not be overlooked.

Lange's enormously influential *History of Materialism (Geschichte des Materialismus und Kritik seiner Bedeutung in der Gegenwart)* was first published in 1866. Lange used Kantian arguments to demolish the claims of nineteenth-century materialists to absolute knowledge, thus recommending himself to religionists and others who wanted freer scope for the ideas of the mind. But he went further in also endorsing an entirely skeptical view of our cognitive capacities:

> We can no longer dismiss with the predicate "Irrefutable but absurd" even the hypothesis that the whole system...into which we bring our sense-perceptions—in a word, our whole experience—is conditioned by an intellectual organisation which compels us to feel as we do feel, to think as we do think....[16]

Lange took the Kantian Copernican revolution entirely literally:

> Our notions do not regulate themselves according to things but things according to our notions. It follows immediately from this that the objects of experience altogether are only *our* objects; that the whole objective world is, in a word, not absolute objectivity, but only objectivity for men....[17]

Lange thus followed directly in the path laid down by Helmholtz, but as a turn-of-the-century commentator pointed out, he created in the name of Kant a quite new philosophy of Neo-Kantianism.[18] This Neo-Kantian movement took various forms of empiricism and positivism. Lange's physiological view of the categories and his rejection of all metaphysics, which is to say his rejection of positive a priori and a posteriori knowledge, put him in the positivist camp. Unwittingly however he gave greatest support to the idealists.

By 1911 Thomas Case could refer in his long survey of "Metaphysics" to a school of "phenomenal idealists" who followed Kant's analysis of the way in which mind shapes our perception and limits our knowledge of the outer world, but who ended up agreeing with Hume that "as we begin by perceiving nothing but mental phenomena of sense, so all we know at last from these data is also phenomena of sense, actual or possible."[19] Unfortunately, as Case went on to say, no one had noticed the difficulty of the term *phenomenon*, which means a mere mental appearance to the idealist but signifies a positive fact for the scientist; the position of the phenomenal idealists was thus far from clear.

In his essay on "Epistemology" in *Hastings Encyclopedia of Religion and Ethics* (Edinburgh, 1912) James Iverach was sure that Kant has "constructed the world of objects...on the plan of the world of knowledge" thus reaching a solution which "had regard only to the conditions of intelligibility and not to the actual world of human experience. So his intelligible world remained a phenomenal world, purely hypothetical. . . ."[20]

In Germany, the great experimental psychologist Wilhelm Wundt deemed it necessary to devote his 1875 Inaugural Lecture at the University of Leipzig to the relationship between science and philosophy. There was too much serious misreading of Kant. We may recognize that certain a priori elements are effective agents of our knowledge of nature, he said. But we should not confuse the concept of causality with the grounds of knowledge. We should think of the outer object as the direct cause of our perception. The concept of cause is after all always related to an event. What must be inborn in us is to be sure the drive to seek for a reason for the appearance, and this drive has its roots in the logical nature of our thinking process. But it is experience which produces the appearance of the peculiar form of cause and effect relationships, while the nature of our cognitive spirit demands that this connection be universal and necessary.[21] The point for us is that Wundt needed to argue for the real existence of the object and for causality as more than a mere epiphenomenon of mind.[22]

c. Haeckel and Adickes: A Pitched Battle

The escalating tone of charge and counter-charge over the question: what kinds of objects are capable of being known? finally resulted in a real confrontation between a famous scientist and an equally well-respected philosopher.

The zoologist Ernst Haeckel (1834–1919) of the University at Jena had given over most of his career to furthering the evolutionary views of Charles Darwin in German-speaking lands. Haeckel went much further than Darwin in insisting, explicitly and with missionary fervor, on the implications for religious belief of the theory of natural selection. In his later years he even advocated a religion of his own, materialistic monism, and published a charter of its articles of belief: *Der Monistenbund: Thesen zur Organisation des Monismus* (1905). The Bund drew such important figures as Wilhelm Ostwald, the Nobel prize-winning chemist, and for some years the movement seemed likely to attract members from as far away as North and South America. Haeckel's book, *The Riddle of the Universe* (1899), became an instant worldwide best seller which did much to popularize and clarify the struggles between religious and scientific world views.

For Haeckel, the theory of natural selection meant that organic beings can be reduced back to ever simpler and less differentiated organisms and finally to inorganic matter. Mind itself, and certainly the differentiated organs of sensation, are reducible to the epidermal cells of the organism. If the physiological structure of the human being limits apperception of things-in-themselves, we are nevertheless justified in accepting as true those presentations which we do receive. "Our only real and valuable knowledge is a knowledge of nature itself, and consists of presentations which correspond to external things.... We *know* that these facts are not imaginary, but real."[23] Haeckel accepted Helmholtz's physiological interpretation of the Kantian categories but rejected the skepticism attendant on it. As for the possibility of a priori synthetic knowledge, Haeckel would have none of it. Article 1 of the thirty theses of his theoretical monism insists that all knowledge is won a posteriori by human reason reflecting on experience. Article 4 states again even more specifically:

> Just as indefensible and contrary to experience is the contention of metaphysics (Kant) that a portion of the most important kind of knowledge is won a priori, independent of any experience, through the conclusions of reason alone. In fact,

so-called a priori knowledge springs entirely from associations of ideas that originally were acquired a posteriori out
of the chain of experience.[24]

This open attack on what seemed to him to be the heart of the
Kantian enterprise and the essence of a non-materialistic world view
was enough that Erich Adickes, professor of philosophy at Kiel and
a most prominent Kantian scholar, determined to "bring out his
heaviest weapons...in order to sweep Materialism completely
away."[25] In fact, wrote Adickes, new discoveries about how our perception is limited by the physiology of the sense organs have forced
every scientific point of view to make concessions to idealism. It
must recognize the existence of the psychic, even if science itself
does not dare to formulate a theory about it.

Philosophical idealism says that the whole physical world is only
in my consciousness; it is only my idea. The whole world of our
experience is built up out of sensations and exists only within our
consciousness. There is thus nothing in it which is not dependent
on us.

More: spatial order and therewith the whole of space as well as
our sensation of it is nothing more than the symbol of something
which is in itself unknown. Between the green which appears to my
eyes and the property of the thing in itself there is no greater similarity than that between my thoughts and the speech tones through
which I express them. Kant insisted on that, thought Adickes:

> The existence of the psychic is the stumbling block on which
> every materialist falls, let him turn and twist how he will.
> Nothings helps the fact that our sensations and the condi-
> tions of our consciousness...are the only thing which is
> directly given to us. The idol of the materialist is a real fetish
> which he has made himself: Matter, from which conscious-
> ness should spring, exists only within consciousness. It
> [matter] cannot be a thing-in-itself, for all its properties con-
> sist in the contents of sensation and their combinations. It is
> not our spirit which comes out of matter: matter is depen-
> dent on spirit; spirit creates matter, not matter spirit.[26]

Adickes adopted the Helmholtz-Lange skeptical interpretation entirely,
but without the experimental procedures by which Helmholtz
hoped to be able to obtain phenomenal knowledge. A comparison
with texts mentioned earlier in this essay (p. 27 and 34 ff.) will show
that Adickes' formulation of the character of human knowledge is

exactly similar to that of Jung. If matter exists only within our consciousness, then all objects of the psyche have equal right to be called "real." For Jung, as for Adickes, and for the phenomenal idealists in general, a skeptical, subjectivist interpretation of Kant's epistemology serves as a defense against reduction to matter.

d. Arthur Schopenhauer

Although Schopenhauer's monumental book, *The World as Will and Representation*, was published in 1819, Schopenhauer's work did not begin to be widely read until after the mid-century. In his 1925 Seminar in Analytical Psychology Jung specifically acknowledged the formative influence of Schopenhauer on his psychology.[27] It was most particularly what Jung took to be Schopenhauer's teleological views in his second book, *The Will in Nature*, that interested Jung in that referenced note, but Schopenhauer's influence is visible at every level of Jung's thought. At this point we must review Schopenhauer's theory of knowledge, and particularly his views on Kant.

The opening lines of Schopenhauer's major work declare his epistemological assumption: "The world is my representation." What is primary is the subject; what is object is only in phenomenal or secondary relationship to the perceiving subject; a creation of the willing subject:

> No truth is more certain, more independent of all others, and less in need of proof than this, namely that everything that exists for knowledge, and hence the whole of this world, is only object in relation to the subject, perception of the perceiver.[28]

Schopenhauer insisted on the negative side of Kant's critique of our knowledge of the external world, as over against the attempts of Fichte, Hegel, and Schelling to find reasons why we nevertheless know. He heroized Kant's achievement in showing that we have no direct knowledge of phenomena.

The limits which prevent us from absolute knowledge lie not in the qualitative differences between myself as subject and the world as external object, but they lie instead *within* me in the separation between will and its organ, the intellect. The limits placed on perception are the *physiological* limits of the brain and the physical organism. "Man...does not know a sun and an earth, but only an eye that sees a sun, a hand that feels earth...." There was therefore for Schopenhauer no way to bridge the gap between the inner and the outer world—no melding of external a posteriori event with internal a priori knowledge. What we have is our experience, but this is not knowledge. Schopenhauer adopted the view of the English empiricists on this score. A recent commentator remarked: "A point which Schopenhauer, like Berkeley, repeatedly makes, and which the realist persistently misunderstands, is that experience is what it is and not another thing. The realist has somehow got it into his head that experience is being denied when, on the contrary, it is being insisted upon. Experience is experience; it is not something else."[29]

Schopenhauer intensely regretted the second edition of Kant's first *Critique*, which he labelled a "mutilated, spoilt, and, to a certain extent ungenuine text," for it completely obscured what Schopenhauer felt was Kant's great merit, his distinction in the first edition of the phenomenon from the thing-in-itself. There *is* no object without a subject, thought Schopenhauer. "When later I read Kant's principal work in the first edition, which had already become scarce, I saw, to my great joy, . . . that he . . . with just as much emphasis as do Berkeley and I, declares the external world lying before us in space and time to be mere representation of the subject that knows it."[30]

If we should totally give up on the hope of knowing the world as it is, there is nevertheless a "way from within" which penetrates to the "real inner nature of things . . . a subterranean passage, a secret alliance." Far more immediate than any mediated knowledge of "things" is the act of self-consciousness by which we know ourselves as will. There is no explanation beyond this. This *is* the thing-in-itself—the basis of all life and all appearance of reality:

> In the case of every emergence of an act of will from the obscure depths of our inner being into the knowing consciousness, there occurs a direct transition into the phenomenon of the thing-in-itself that lies outside time.[31]

In this passage we glimpse not only Jung's doctrine that knowledge is intrasubjective, but also his later theory of the self as transcendent subject of the ego.

A summary of the ground which has been covered in this chapter is in order. I have attempted to show that the epistemological subjectivism which characterized Jung's psychology in its mature form was not invented by him as a purely empirical conclusion from premises set by clinical experience. The theoretical materials for Jung's position were available to him in late nineteenth-century intellectual life and they carried polemical and political significance in the battle between science and religion. These are the issues which created the intellectual ferment of those years in which Jung was a gymnasial and university student. His lectures to fellow students of the Zofingerverein richly document his familiarity with most of the principal figures of the debate.

Helmholtz's error in understanding the nature of the limitations which Kant had set on the human capacity for knowledge set the stage for skepticism and subjectivism to be used as a political tool both by scientists and by religionists. One of Helmholtz's most influential pupils was the journalist/philosopher F. A. Lange, who studied briefly with Helmholtz and then wrote a book representing Kant as a complete skeptic. Although a materialist like Haeckel accepted the Kantian categories as physiological (as did Helmholtz), he denied that we therefore know nothing. Mind is finally only matter; what we do know is matter and *that* is real. Against such materialism there arose a group of phenomenal idealists, typified by the great Kantian scholar Adickes, who claimed that we have *only* what the mind knows: "Spirit creates matter, not matter spirit."[32] Faced with such sweeping certainty on opposing fronts, an orthodox Kantian like Wilhelm Wundt felt himself almost unheard.

In Schopenhauer Jung found another subjectivist interpreter of Kant, one who hypostasized a psychic quality, the Will, as ultimate Noumeon. The world of objects and the intellect itself possessed for Schopenhauer no more reality than the experience through which they are perceived. In general, for nineteenth-century idealists, establishing a skeptical view of human knowledge meant winning the battle against a science which reduced reality to matter, or at the very least achieving a kind of balancing of the scales, so that both science and human values could claim equal worth.

7

Two Epistemological Discussions by Jung

a. Esse in Anima *as a Solution to the Mind-Body Dilemma*

On two occasions Jung undertook somewhat more extended epistemological discussions, without however announcing them as such. After surveying Jung's view of knowledge through the perspective of his personal life tasks and in the context of his psychological treatises, and then comparing them with the context of late nineteenth-century philosophical idealism and epistemological skepticism, I want to return briefly to Jung's own work.

The first of these longer passages appeared in 1921, in the opening chapter of *Psychological Types*. Jung was attempting to establish the fact of two naturally occurring attitudinal variations in human character—introversion and extraversion—and to show how those two attitudes, as major functions of consciousness, have marked the course of Western philosophy since ancient times. He begins with the example of Tertullian, who was a typical introverted thinking type—a superb theologian and apologist, and creator of Church Latin. His religious development as a Christian eventually led him however, according to Jung, to a *sacrificium intellectus*, a sacrifice of his major function as a thinking type in favor of the irrational inner reality of his faith. Origen, on the other hand, thought Jung, must have been an extraverted thinking type. Origen is reported to have been much loved by his students; his intellectual gifts were more in the direction of objective facts than Tertullian's. As a philosopher and scholar, Origen neatly assimilated current Gnostic and Neoplatonic views. Like Tertullian, he sacrificed the one thing which might have endangered the development of his Christian faith; Tertullian sacrificed the reasoning intellect, while Origen gave up his sensual tie to the world. Origen was bound to the world as object; Tertullian was bound to the rational mind.

We may see the type problem carried on, thought Jung, in ancient theological disputes, the Ebionites representing with their purely human Christ the extraverted, objective view, and the Docetists with an only apparently human Christ the introverted view in which the inner idea predominates over the external object. The Palagians, again, held the extraverted view with their emphasis on human value, as over against Augustine's more introverted insistence on the Church and divine grace. In the centuries which followed, as the church became the dominant force in Western civilization, the extraverted, object-oriented Abbot Radbertus insisted that in the holy communion there is an actual physical transubstantiation of the wine and water into the body and blood of Christ. The more symbolic, introverted doctrine of John Scotus Erigena, that the communion is simply a commemoration of the last supper, was condemned in an age in which religious experience must be concretized in order to be understood.

A similar typological conflict characterizes the philosophical dispute between nominalism and realism. Plato's doctrine of universals was scoffed at by the Cynics and the Megarians, who "denied the substantiality of generic concepts."[1] The issue of what is most real—the objects of sense and the predications we make about them, or the higher concepts by means of which we order the realm of our own being—continues to puzzle us, and presumably it always will, said Jung.

> The question at issue is the typical opposition between the abstract standpoint, where the decisive value lies with the mental process itself, and the personal thinking and feeling which, consciously or unconsciously, underlie orientation by the objects of sense.[2]

In the scholastic period the nominalist position was carried by Johannes Roscellinus, and the realist view by Anselm of Canterbury, who devised the ontological argument for God. Jung quotes Fichte's formulation of it: "The existence of an Absolute in our consciousness proves the real existence of this Absolute."[3] The argument is so logically deficient that one wonders how a mind like Anselm's could advance it. Its real power, Jung believed, lies not in logic but in the fact that it represents for a certain group of people (introverts) the highest value. "The idea represented for them a higher reality or value for life than the reality of individual things." The ontological argument is a statement of value, not a proof. It is in fact a disguised form of an even more ancient argument for God—the *consensus gentium*.[4]

Jung then outlines Kant's demolition of the ontological argument in the first *Critique* in order to reinforce his assertion that what reason requires may be very far from objective reality; the proof is no proof. There is no clearer demonstration, Jung believed, of the division between *esse in intellectu* and *esse in re*.[5]

Now Jung's discussion comes to a climax. There is no logical path, Jung continues, by way of which the distance between the either-or of the ancient nominalist-realist quarrel may be traversed. "But between *intellectus* and *res* there is still *anima*, and this *esse in anima* makes the whole ontological argument superfluous." Kant himself, says Jung, used the *esse in anima* on a grand scale in his *Critique of Practical Reason* where he introduces God as an a priori postulate of respect for moral law, as a value concept inherent in the human person. *Esse in anima* is a psychological fact. Whatever we call God signifies the highest good and the supreme value.

After the early nineteenth century had more than done justice to realism and the "scientism" of the latter half of the century pushed toward nominalism we now, said Jung, have a "mediatory science" in psychology, which "is capable of uniting the idea and the thing without doing violence to either."[6] The problem is real—not just an academic philosophical issue. It is "the daily repeated problem of [man's] relation to himself and to the world":

> For its solution a third, mediating standpoint is needed. *Esse in intellectu* lacks tangible reality, *esse in re* lacks mind. Idea and thing come together, however in the human psyche, which holds the balance between them. What would the idea amount to if the psyche did not provide its living value? What would the thing be worth if the psyche withheld from it the determining form of the sense-impression? *What indeed is reality if it is not a reality in ourselves, an esse in anima?* [my italics] Living reality is the product neither of the actual, objective behavior of things nor of the formulated idea exclusively, but rather of the combination of both in the living psychological process, through *esse in anima*.[7]

Jung then goes on to complete the chapter by explaining what he means by the psychic process which constitutes the *esse in anima*. It is primarily a creative process in which the conscious point of view is in continual dialogue with the unconscious psychic matrix out of which it springs. "The psyche creates reality every day" through an activity which we can only call "fantasy." We must beware of becoming too identified with conscious intellectual viewpoints of all kinds, for they stifle living reality. Religious dogmas are as suspect as the sciences; both exclude feeling and fantasy. Psychology, too, must not become too much of a science, for science is always "an affair of the intellect," and must not be allowed to overstep its proper boundaries and interfere with the practical living of life.[8]

Just as Tertullian and Origen sacrificed their most developed, superior functions for an even higher religious value, so must a psychological epistemology (my term, not Jung's) always be ready to sacrifice its conscious standpoint for something even greater:

> The intellect remains imprisoned in itself just so long as it does not willingly sacrifice its supremacy by recognizing the value of other aims. It shrinks from the step which takes it out of itself and which denies its universal validity, since from the standpoint of the intellect everything else is *nothing but fantasy*. But what great thing ever came into existence that was not first fantasy?[9]

In order to follow the argument which underlies the discussion in this chapter, it is necessary to follow Jung's thought transitions in causal sequence. The central but unannounced theme has to do with validating the ideas of the mind or the soul as over against the more reasonable-seeming nominalist or empirical views which, however, lack deeper values. How shall we justify an "inner" view of reality? The chapter begins with a typological distinction between extraversion and introversion but the discussion quickly slides over to philosophy, so that in the end a psychological view equals an introverted view, and an introverted view means the espousal of subjective values as over against a valueless nominalist or empirical standpoint.

In the ancient world Tertullian sacrificed his intellect and Origen his manhood. These were their "outer" values and they were sacrificed for a more important "inner" value—the Christian faith. Pelagianism, too, fell in favor of the more vital, introverted Augustinian view. The theory of transubstantiation (an extraverted view) succeeded over against Scotus Erigena's commemoration theory only because the medieval period was primitive and concretistic, that is, wedded to an external view of things. Theories which defend universals or inner values continue to have a hard time succeeding in the world. Anselm's ontological argument is valuable not because of its rationalist logical form, which is worthless, as Kant showed, but because it represents a belief in God, or in highest values. Kant himself demolished rationalist arguments while elevating value criteria, especially in his second *Critique*. (1) *Esse in anima* means to affirm inner values as over against either nominalist or purely rationalist views. (2) *Esse in anima* also means that reality itself equals the inner value of the subject. What is valuable is what is real.[10]

All of Jung's psychology may in fact be reduced to this formula. Jung follows Kant, but disavows the conclusions of the first *Critique* which support a view that knowledge begins with the outer object.[11] Jung's view coincides with Kant's view in the second *Critique*, which makes the fact of moral values tantamount to knowledge of God. It is more especially, however, in line with Schopenhauer's skeptical epistemology which has reality created by the inner Will, and with nineteenth-century religious idealism which insisted that we know only what is within.

b. The Lumen Naturae *of Paracelsus as the Paradigm of True Knowledge*

One of the great heroes of Jung's later years was an irascible and passionate physician and alchemist who was always being hounded out of town by his professional colleagues, but sought out and loved by his patients. Theophrastus Bombast von Hohenheim, who called himself Paracelsus, grew up in the Swiss town of Einsiedeln, which had already in the sixteenth century been famous for hundreds of years as a pilgrimage center. Its Benedictine monastery housed the Black Madonna. Paracelsus combined in his person two very typically Swiss characteristics—an attitude of inner piety and a fierce independence of thinking. He took for his motto: *Alterius non sit, qui suus esse potest*: "Let him not be another's who can be his own." Jung liked to cite that motto, for there was much about the rebellious wandering physician which seemed like the history of his own life. He had given up a sure career as Freud's anointed successor in order to follow deep inner intuitions which led he knew not where, but which seemed to him to be a more adequate expression of truth than the psychoanalytic theories which had been so firmly established by Freud.

Paracelsus, too, seemed early in life to have set himself on the good way to riches and fame. He made a spectacular cure of a prominent citizen of Basel and partly as a result of that cure was named official town physician. But he behaved in such an unconscionable manner that he soon had to flee the city to save his life. He despised the old town customs, lectured at the university in German instead of Latin, boasted of his achievements, insisted on practicing surgery as well as medicine (surgery was lowly barber's or field surgeon's work in those days). After leaving Basel he spent the rest of his life in the cities of Austria, Germany, and Switzerland, sometimes even farther afield, never more than a year in one place, for he neither would nor could he keep from innovative and dissension-provoking behavior. He made chemical analyses of the waters of famous spas, did urinalysis, insisted on antisepsis of wounds, and prescribed laudanum (probably opium) for pain. Worst of all, however, was what he wrote in his many books about the causes and cure of illness, for he violently disagreed with the theories that had been taught for hundreds of years in medical faculties in the universities.

It was Paracelsus' theories of illness—its diagnosis and its cure —that were of primary interest to Jung. A lecture on Paracelsus delivered in 1929 was followed in 1935 and 1936 by two Eranos lectures which formed the core of his major book, *Psychology and Alchemy*.[12] "Paracelsus as Physician" was published in 1941, and the long monograph, "Paracelsus as a Spiritual Phenomenon" appeared the following year.[13] Alchemy became the consuming interest of Jung's last twenty-five years. His writings in the field takes up three fat volumes of the *Collected Works*, and part of a fourth volume if we include the 1946 monograph, "Psychology of the Transference," which interprets projective transference phenomena through a series of alchemical drawings.[14]

The core of the matter has to do with a theory of knowledge which is at the same time a theory of the individual's relationship to the world. It was thus of much more than academic interest to Jung as a psychologist, concerning, as it does, a theory of psychic functioning. The term which Paracelsus used for his theory was the *lumen naturae*. Jung devoted the first part of his 1942 Paracelsus monograph to this theme: "The Two Sources of Knowledge: The Light of Nature and the Light of Revelation." Other aspects of the theory, including a more exact exposition of Paracelsus' philosophical theory, were given by Walter Pagel in his 1958 *Paracelsus: An Introduction to Philosophical Medicine in the Era of the Renaissance*.[15]

Although Paracelsus remained a faithful son of the Church his whole life, he rebelled from the authoritative medical traditions of both Church and university. These traditions sprang originally from experimental Aristotelian sources, but they had been passed down as the one true and revealed doctrine, and left no room for the advancement of knowledge. There were two aspects of these doctrines which Paracelsus could not accept. The first was their diagnosis of human ills as a disorder in the *material elements* of the body, of its earth, its air, its fire, and its water. Paracelsus agreed well enough that the body was composed of chemical elements. But material elements were not the true substance of the body, he said.[16] Something else—the inner principle of organization, or the Archeus —is more truly the body than its chemical constituents. We can neither diagnose illness nor cure it by adjusting material elements. The second problem for Paracelsus was the doctrine of revealed knowledge. We cannot accept things on faith, he said, just because someone else has told us that it is so.[17] We must look instead to Nature and to the truth which God has put there for us to read. "Pagoyum" was a favorite neologism, made up of *paganum* and the Hebrew word *goyim*. It meant that the truth is revealed not by authority or dogmatic faith but in nature herself, which is by contrast pagan. We can find out the truth for ourselves.[18]

The path to this knowledge is through direct personal experience. That meant getting away from rationalized theories and being with real people in the world, listening to a story of a strange cure told at a wayside inn, observing not only the pathology but also the life circumstances of an ill woman. You must read nature's book with your feet (you must go and see), he said.[19]

More than that, thought Paracelsus, we must adopt the attitude of the naturalist, believing that Nature does indeed reveal the signs of God. We must not be skeptical, not "drown in work, abandoning research, saying that it is beyond our understanding and thus failing to kindle the torch which will enlighten us."[20] Even in the face of our ignorance we must be obedient servants of this task. "As the light of Nature is like the crumbs from the table of the Lord, for all the heathen to grasp, and has departed from Judah, so it behoves us not to give in, but to pick up the crumbs as long as they fall."

It seems impossible to know, and to expect to know, without guideposts for our search. But personal experience meant for Paracelsus something more, or different from what we today would think of as an empiricist position. What is of primary importance, he thought, is that we experience and understand how nature operates *in ourselves*. There is an *ens seminis*, a spiritual essence or a spiritual principle (an *Archeus*) which gives form and substance to each one of the objects of nature and determines the course of its existence. That same spirit pervades the whole of the universe, so that each individual thing has its own proper qualities, but also shares in the cosmic spirit which informs the universe *as object*. Since human beings are the last and highest of God's creation (and here Paracelsus is a faithful medieval Christian observing a doctrine of the hierarchy of being) they have within their own natures something of the spirit of every part of nature. It means: as it is with me, so is it in the universe. Obversely, as it is in nature as a whole, so is it within my own soul. Further: there is an element inside me (the naturalist or the physician) which corresponds to the illness of this woman, or the properties of that planet.

The method by which we obtain this knowledge and come to the light of nature has to do with coming into contact with a deeper level of our own natures which is connected to the larger processes of nature. For example, we know that scammonea purges, but this does not help us to understand the process itself. Just as there is a kind of science in a pear which teaches it how to be a pear and not an apple, so we should try to listen through to the process of the scammonea. "When you overhear ('ablauschen') from the scammonea the knowledge which it possesses, it will be in you just as it is in the scammonea and you have acquired the experience as well as the knowledge.[21] We find that place in ourselves which is in sympathetic correspondence with the principle of the external object, and we know it because we know ourselves. There is thus a much more direct, internal path to knowledge than the objectivized processes of the rational mind.[22]

From the philosophical point of view, Paracelsus' theory of the *lumen naturae* is easily identifiable as a type of identity theory associated with the doctrine of the microcosm and the macrocosm. Most scholars suppose that Paracelsus may have learned it from Agrippa von Nettesheim, during a presumed period of medical studies in Turin around 1517–18. Late forms of Neoplatonism flourished in Italy during this time. Marsilio Ficino's translation of Plato into Latin and his Platonic Academy in Florence did much to revive Platonic theories. The form in which Paracelsus adopted these ideas was however heavily stoicized. Stoic monistic physics admitted two principles for one substance. All is corporeality, but there is an active principle within it which is reason and form, and a passive principle (matter, or better, prime matter) which receives the formal imprint of the active principle and thus assumes its visible shape. Paracelsus had objected to a diagnosis of material causes for illness. What is more basic is the *Archeus* or the *ens seminis*. It is through our shared connection with the overarching world principle that we know ourselves and each other, thought Paracelsus. Although assimilated by Neoplatonism, this is in origin the purely Stoic doctrine of sympathy.

From Jung's psychological standpoint, the *lumen naturae* is nothing more nor less than the *unconscious psyche,* and the Paracelsian path to knowledge is through what we would today call the *"projective field."* The light through which we are connected to each other is not like the great sun who vanquishes the darkness completely. It is rather, thought Jung, the light of the darkness itself, a "divine spark buried in the darkness... which illuminates its own darkness, and this light the darkness comprehends."[23] We participate in the illuminating activity of the unconscious psyche through imagination and fantasy, but above all through the magic of projection. Who among us has not discovered important aspects of our own character through first discovering feelings of joy or anger and fascination with an outer object? We project our own psychic background onto the persons and things in our world, and the more unknown the object, the more effectively does the projective experience envelop our image of reality. Jung's interest in alchemy lay in that fact. "The real root of alchemy," he wrote, "is to be sought less in philosophical doctrines than in the projections experienced by individual investigators. I mean by this that while working on his chemical experiments the operator had certain experiences which appeared to him as the particular behaviour of the chemical process."[24]

It is in the application of the *lumen naturae,* or the doctrine of sympathy, to the projections operating within the analysis, in the relationship between the analyst and the analysand, that Jung's psychological understanding reached its most profound level. We are here in the realm of the facts of inner feeling. What is to be discovered in the analytic relationship goes as deep as the connection between parent and child, between lover and beloved. Scarcely anything has been written in the non-specialized literature about the details of this process, and it is probably not possible to do so, since every human relationship contains much that is unique to the individuals involved as well as much that is "generally human" and applies to all relationships. The task of analysis is to discover the experienced facts of crucial familial relationships which condition, or predispose the individual to a certain view of reality. To a very great extent the emotional set of the mind determines how we see life. In this sense our view of reality may be said to be projective. Becoming more conscious of these emotional factors frees the individual to let other possible perspectives on the nature of reality enter their claims. Hopefully, the analyzed person is less influenced by unconscious attitudinal determinants than the unanalyzed person.

The doctrine of sympathy, and its Paracelsian version, the *lumen naturae*, may therefore continue to have a validity that can be understood today when it is applied to the realm of human relationships. We are healed, made whole, when we feel ourselves held in the projective web of relationships. Our emotional investment in ideas also enhances the degree to which they are experienced as "real" by us. Belief structures built up on the basis of emotional relationships need to be trusted if we are to function in human society. Human beings are social beings. It was his father's tragic estrangement through loss of faith from the beliefs which he nevertheless had to defend that first led Jung toward his lifelong therapeutic search for a believable reality.

On the other hand, belief structures have also to be distrusted. We must from time to time emerge from our projective containment in persons and ideas, because projection keeps us unconscious, makes us overly vulnerable and finally inhibits our own maturational process. At a philosophical level we may observe this dialectical process over a long historical period, as new philosophical ideas engage us, express for a while the best possible synthesis, and then gradually succumb to increasing consciousness about problems which had not in the first flush of enthusiasm been observed.

It is my conviction that Jung's own powerful leading idea had to do with the engagement of inner sympathy which binds and enlivens the heart. Here lay his ultimate moral values. At some point however the development of his psychology as theory, and I mean specifically the themes which are discussed in this book (Jung's subjectivistic epistemology, his theory of the archetype, and his theory of individuation), tied up the system.[25] The dialectical movement which characterizes personal development could no longer occur. This is to a certain extent the fate of every theory. Becoming more conscious about the way in which Jung's own theory began to conform to a typical pattern is the purpose of this book. A period of wandering, if we do not give up but remain, as Paracelsus counsels, "obedient servants of the task," may bring still new understanding of nature's operations.

Notes to Part I

Chapter 1

1. C. G. Jung, *Memories, Dreams, Reflections*, recorded and edited by Aniela Jaffé, translated from the German by Richard and Clara Winston (New York: Pantheon Books, 1961), pp. 46, 73, 54, 55, 73, 90, 92.

2. Jung, *Letters*, 2, June 13, 1955. See also the letter of May 28, 1952, to Dorothee Hoch: "True, I didn't like theology because it set my father problems which *he* couldn't solve and which I felt unjustified."

3. Marilyn Nagy, "Jung and Kaufmann: The Father Complex," *Psychological Perspectives* 14, no. 1 (1983): 111–22.

4. Jung, "The Border Zones of Exact Science," in *Zofingia Lectures*, para. 57.

5. William Coleman, *Biology in the Nineteenth Century: Problems of Form, and Transformation* (Cambridge: Cambridge University Press, 1977), p. 150.

6. Quoted in Thomas S. Hall, *Ideas of Life and Matter: Studies in the History of General Physiology, 600 B.C.–1900 A.D.*, 2 vols., (Chicago: University of Chicago Press, 1969), pp. 277 f. See also Emil Du Bois-Reymond and Carl Ludwig, *Two Great Scientists of the Nineteenth Century: Correspondence of Emil Du Bois-Reymond and Carl Ludwig* (1927), collected by Estelle Du Bois-Reymond, Foreword, Notes, and Indexes by Paul Diepgen, trans. Sabine Lichtner-Ayed, ed. with a Foreword by Paul F. Cranefield (Baltimore: Johns Hopkins Press, 1982). In the letter of Du Bois-Reymond to Ludwig on August 29, 1872, the former complains about the press review of his speech, which criticized him for not being extemporaneous. "That's what I call a bit too much, expecting one to get up before 2000 people and speak for three-quarters of an hour on the limits of physics and metaphysics without any preparation."

7. Ernst Haeckel, *Monism as Connecting Religion and Science: The Confession of Faith of a Man of Science*, trans. J. Gilchrist (London: Adam and Charles Black, 1895), p. 110.

8. Jung, "Some Thoughts on Psychology," *Zofingia Lectures*, para. 71–72.

9. Heinz Kohut, *The Analysis of the Self* (New York: International Universities Press, 1971). See also Peter Homans, *Jung in Context: Modernity and the Making of a Psychology* (Chicago: University of Chicago Press, 1979), for an analysis of the narcissistic aspects of the relationship between Freud and Jung and the resolution of conflict after his subsequent crisis years, 1912–16.

10. Jung, "Some Thoughts on Psychology," *Zofingia Lectures*, para. 113–15.

11. Immanuel Kant, *Dreams of a Spirit Seer and Other Related Writings*, translation and commentary by John Manolesco (New York: Vantage Press, 1969).

12. Jung quotes this letter almost in its entirety in "On Spiritualistic Phenomena" (1905), CW 18, para. 708. During the period between 1900 and 1910 Jung was himself very much the skeptical young scientist. "Before we jump to the conclusion that thought flies through time and space detached from the brain, we should seek to discover by meticulous psychological investigation the hidden sources of the apparently supernatural knowledge" (para. 735). After 1910, the central themes of Jung's own epistemology began to re-emerge.

13. Kant, *Spirit Seer*, p. 45 (Edition Cassirer, pp. 344, 345).

14. Ibid., p. 47 (Edition Cassirer, pp. 346, 347).

15. Ibid., p. 42 (Edition Cassirer, p. 341), quoted by Jung in "Some Thoughts on Psychology," *Zofingia Lectures*, para. 86.

16. Ibid., pp. 68 ff. (Edition Cassirer, pp. 365–70).

17. See the discussion of Leibniz and Kant in Chapter 5, below.

18. With one exception: "Some Thoughts on Psychology," para. 103. But here Jung goes on to say that new facts on extrasensory perception and spiritualism have made Kant's doubts outdated. Even much later in his life Jung tended toward a positive view of spirits. See his letter of July 10, 1946, to Fritz Künkel regarding Stewart Edward White's book, *The Unobstructed Universe*: "In each individual case I must of necessity be sceptical, but in the long run I have to admit that the spirit hypothesis yields better results in practice than any other" (*Letters*, 2). See also Jung's Introduction to the German translation, CW 18, para. 746–56, and the Foreword to Fanny Moser's "Spuk: Irrglaube oder Wahrglaube," CW 18, para. 758. Compare Kant's own statement: "I did not dare to deny completely the truth of the various ghost tales; on the contrary, I have always maintained a certain reserve and a sense of wonder towards them, doubting each story individually, but attributing some truthfulness to all of them put together." *Spirit Seer*, p. 70 (Edition Cassirer, p. 367).

19. Ibid., para. 138.

20. "Thoughts on Speculative Inquiry" (1898), *Zofingia Lectures*, para. 172, 174, 175.

21. See Jung, *Psychological Types*, CW 6, para. 540: "Pragmatism is but a makeshift, and it can claim validity only so long as no sources are discovered, other than intellectual capacities coloured by temperament, which might reveal new elements in the formation of philosophical concepts."

22. Kant is discussed in a variety of contexts throughout this book. The most extensive treatment is in Chapter 5, following, where the theory of mind developed in the *Critique of Pure Reason* is examined at some length. The purpose of that chapter is to establish the specific historical framework of Jung's epistemological views. The concluding pages of Chapter 4 of Part II relate Jung's use of the Common Consent argument to a passage in the final section of Kant's *Prolegomena*. Chapter 3 of Part III considers two passages in the first *Critique* which refer to the regulative use of our concepts of divine order in connection with Jung's own teleological views. The present chapter has referred to Kant's early essay, the *Spirit Seer*, and now begins a brief discussion of Kant's moral philosophy. The *Foundations of the Metaphysics of Morals* and the *Critique of Practical Reason* were crucially important for Jung as a student. The evidence shows that they helped him elucidate his own philosophical orientation and they therefore receive comment here, by way of clarifying Jung's specific references to their content in the Zofingia lectures. Their appearance in Chapter 1 is however out of order for Kant's own philosophical development; they are the consequence of rather than the precursor to the first *Critique*. The reader wanting a general orientation to Kant may wish to turn immediately to Chapter 5.

23. "The title to freedom of the will claimed by common reason is based on the consciousness and the conceded presupposition of the independence of reason from merely subjectively determining causes which together constitute what belongs only to sensation, being comprehended under the general name of sensibility. Man, who in this way regards himself as intelligence, puts himself in a different order of things and in a relationship to determining grounds of an altogether different kind when he thinks of himself as intelligence with a will and thus as endowed with causality, compared with that other order of things and that other set of determining grounds which become relevant when he perceives himself as a phenomenon in the world of sense, (as he really also is) and submits his causality to external determination according to natural laws." *Foundations of the Metaphysics of Morals*, trans. with an Introduction by Lewis White Beck, Library of Liberal Arts (New York: Bobbs-Merrill Company, 1959), p. 76 (Akademie Edition 457). See also *Critique of Pure Practical Reason*: "The supersensible nature of the same [rational] beings is their existence under laws that are independent of all empirical conditions and which therefore belong to the *autonomy* of pure reason. . . . Now the law of this autonomy is moral law, which is therefore the fundamental law of a supersensible nature

and of a pure intellectual world whose counterpart must exist in the world of sense, but without interfering with its laws." Trans. Carl J. Friedrich in *The Philosophy of Kant: Moral and Political Writings* (1949) (New York: Modern Library, 1977), p. 236. Citations from Kant's 2nd *Critique* in this book are from the translation by Friedrich.

24. Kant, *Critique of Pure Practical Reason*: "Moral law is given as a fact by pure reason of which we are conscious *a priori* and which is apodictically certain, even though it is granted that no example of its exact fulfillment can be found in experience. Hence the objective reality of moral law cannot be proved through a deduction by any efforts [on the part of] theoretical reason, whether speculative or supported empirically. Therefore, even if we renounced its apodictic certainty, it could not be proved by experience *a posteriori*. Yet the objective reality of moral law is firmly established by itself" (In Friedrich, Moral and Political Writings, p. 239).

25. "There is one imperative which directly commands a certain conduct without making its condition some purpose to be reached by it. This imperative is categorical." Kant, *Foundations of the Metaphysics of Morals*, p. 33 (Akademie Edition, p. 416).

26. See Lewis White Beck, *A Commentary on Kant's Critique of Practical Reason* (Chicago: University of Chicago Press, 1960), pp. 277 ff.

27. See Part III, Chapter 1, pp. 213–19, below.

28. By the term *category of causality* Jung means the inner need to feel that there is an orderly life process and that there are explanations for things that happen. As the context of para. 171 shows, he has been reading Kant, Schopenhauer, and von Hartmann. He is aware of Hume's challenge concerning the meaning of causal terms and responds on one level by insisting that whether or not we can perceive causal sequences we nevertheless need to believe in their existence. On a second level the term *category of causality* refers to a late 19th–century usage in which "causality" was set up by the advocates of divine order over against the "chance" of the physicists and Darwinian biologists. Schopenhauer and more especially von Hartmann subsumed both teleological final causes and mechanistic causality under the higher aegis of the Will, thinking thus to solve the problem. Von Hartmann concludes: "causality is another name for logical necessity, that attains actuality through the Will...either causation and final causality have their identity in a *higher unity*, of which they form merely different aspects of the apprehension through the discursive thinking of man, or both chains stand in a *pre-established harmony*, or the present link in the chain of causation only *accidentally* agrees with the present link in the chain of final causes (as one and the same event). Chance would once and a way be possible, but not in constant repetition; the pre-established harmony is miracle or the renunciation of comprehension; thus only the first case remains....Thus and only thus are the difficulties resolved which the concept of causality has caused

from Hume to Kirchmann." Eduard von Hartmann, *Philosophy of the Uncon-scious: Speculative Results according to the Inductive Method of Physical Science* (1869), authorized translation by William Chatterton Coupland, new edition in one volume (New York: Harcourt, Brace and Company, 1931), 3: 186 f. About the same time, Gustav Fechner commented: "If it were true indeed that the efforts of the creatures to better their conditions were constantly counterbalanced by deteriorating influences on the part of unconscious nature, the betterment could not be brought about. But, on the contrary, a sublime teleology of nature (or, to content the *Zeitgeist*, let us say, a causality which in its consequences looks like teleology) works hand in hand with the efforts of men." *Religion of a Scientist: Selections from Gustav Th. Fechner,* ed. and trans. Walter Lowrie (New York: Pantheon Books, 1946), p. 235.

By "category of causality" Jung connotes also, then, a teleological world view.

29. The careful reader will have noted that the principal knowledge criterion for scientific verification for Jung is subjective personal experience; these are strange bedfellows for a period when the criteria for knowledge for experimental scientists and religionists were miles apart. Jung's reading of Eduard von Hartmann, who attempted something like a statistical verifica-tion of certain physical principles, fitting these statistics to his philosophical view of nature as purposive, may have had something to do with the views Jung expressed here. Jung later changed his mind about what kind of knowledge a subjectivist perspective yields. At the same time many "hard" scientists were moving in the opposite direction, toward a "new recognition of the fact that the account of the world which our minds afford must be taken as, in the main, and at least potentially, a trustworthy account." George Perigo Conger, *Theories of Macrocosms and Microcosms in the History of Philosophy* (New York: Columbia University Press, 1922), p. 136. Jung's sub-jectivist views and their sources will be studied in Chapters 2–7, to follow.

30. *Foundations of the Metaphysics of Morals,* p. 80 (Akademie Edition 460 f.).

31. *Critique of Pure Practical Reason,* in Friedrich, *Moral and Political Writings,* pp. 261 f. See also *Foundations of the Metaphysics of Morals,* p. 70 (Akademie Edition, p. 451). "A man may not presume to know even himself as he really is by knowing himself through inner sensation. ...But beyond the characteristic of his own subject which is compounded of these mere appearances, he necessarily assumes something else as its basis, namely, his ego as it is in itself. Thus in respect to mere perception and receptivity to sensations he must count himself as belonging to the world of sense; but in respect to that which may be pure activity in himself (i.e., in respect to that which reaches consciousness directly and not by affecting the senses) he must reckon himself as belonging to the intellectual world. But he has no further knowledge of that world."

32. Jung, *Psychology and Alchemy*, CW 12, para. 126. Jung references that comment with his own quotation from Meister Eckhart: "It is not outside, it is inside: wholly within." Franz Pfeiffer, *Meister Eckhart*, 2 vols., trans. C. De B. Evans (London, 1924), 1:8.

Chapter 2

1. C. J. Jung, *Psychology of the Unconscious: A Study of the Transformations and Symbolisms of the Libido. A Contribution to the History of the Evolution of Thought* (1912), trans. Beatrice M. Hinkle (New York: Dodd, Mead and Company, 1925), hereafter cited as *Symbols of Transformation*, 1912. The passages quoted in Chapter 5 appear, in order of their citation, on pp. 254, 255, 261, 262, 262, 262, 262, 263.

2. Ibid., p. 529: "Just as man is a dual being, having an intellectual and an animal nature, so does he appear to need two forms of reality, the reality of culture, that is, the symbolic transcendent theory, and the reality of nature which corresponds to our conception of the 'true reality.'" Compare these lines with the conclusion of Kant's 2nd Critique: "The first view of a numberless quantity of worlds destroys my importance, so to speak, since I am an *animal-like being* who must return its matter from whence it came to the planet. . . . The second view raises my value infinitely, as an *intelligence*, through my personality." Kant's vision of man as a dual being with both an intelligent and a sensuous nature has been translated by Jung into his estimation of what is *psychologically true* vs. what is *actually true*. This entire footnote is excised in the revised version.

3. Jung, *Symbols of Transformation*, CW 5, xxiii.

4. Jung had met William James personally during his Clark University lectures in 1909. He recalls their having discussed together the psychology of religious experience and para-psychology. See the letter to Virginia Payne, July 12, 1949 (Letters, 2). See also Eugene Taylor, "William James and C. G. Jung," *Spring* (1980), pp. 157–67.

5. In *Two Essays in Analytical Psychology*, CW 7. The original version of this essay was published in 1917.

6. "A Contribution to Psychological Types," in CW 6, para. 868.

7. Part III of the present essay has to do with Jung's teleology.

8. Jung, "On Psychological Understanding," CW 3, para. 398, 407.

9. Quoted by Aniela Jaffé in "The Creative Phases in Jung's Life," *Spring* (1972), pp. 175 f.

10. Jung, "The Spiritual Problem of Modern Man," CW 10, para. 159.

11. Jung, "Basic Postulates of Analytical Psychology," CW 8, para. 671–72.

12. Jung, "The Stages of Life," CW 8, para. 794.

Chapter 3

1. See "The Aims of Psychology" (1929), CW 16. "I must content myself wholly with the fact that the result means something to the patient and sets his life in motion again. I may allow myself only one criterion for the result of my labours: Does it work? As for my scientific hobby—my desire to know *why* it works—this I must reserve for my spare time." Yet, as I have already indicated, Jung was not a pragmatist. He was in these years a disciple of Kant's second *Critique*. Reason was, in Jung's understanding, the a priori inner voice. One could not explain why or how one knew something to be true, but trusting in the inner voice would not lead a person astray.

2. Jung, *Symbols of Transformation*, CW 5, para. 344.

3. Hermann von Helmholtz and scientists since his time have thought they had a way out of this dilemma. See Chap. 6 following, pp. 66 f. and Part III, Chap. 4, pp. 241 f.

4. See *Psychology and the Philosophy of Mind in the Philosophy Curriculum*. Some work has been done connecting research in mental representation and imagery with the semantics of analytic philosophy, but a content approach is completely lacking. A companion volume issued the following year, *Philosophy of Biology in the Philosophy Curriculum* (San Francisco: Council for Philosophical Studies, San Francisco University, 1982), comes nearer in its curriculum outlines to material which interested Jung. Sociobiological research comes close in one respect to Jung's concept of the archetype, while sharply differing in other respects, as will be seen. Darwinism and the history of the mind-brain problem were of deep interest to Jung, though not explicit in his writing after his student days. The "depth psychologies" lack a scientific context because their materials are individually unique and their results are not measurable by means of scientific instrumentation. Research comparing the imagery of dreams and fantasies with motifs in the history of culture has however been most successful. A vast literature has developed over the last eighty years.

5. "The language I speak must be ambiguous, must have two meanings, in order to do justice to the dual aspect of our psychic nature, I strive

quite consciously and deliberately for ambiguity of expression, because it is superior to unequivocalness and reflects the nature of life." Letter to R. J. Zwi Werblowsky, June 17, 1952, *Letters*, 2.

6. The hypostasization of religious feeling as though it might exist without referents in concepts, value judgments, or belief has recently been analyzed by Wayne Proudfoot in *Religious Experience* (Berkeley: University of California Press, 1985). With regard to Rudolf Otto's prescription that "religious experience" must not be qualified "by other forms of consciousness," Proudfoot shows that the criteria for the experience have actually been set up so as to protect against reductionism. "When Otto coins the term *numinous* to stand for 'the holy' *minus* its moral factor or 'moment,' and...minus its 'rational' aspect altogether," he seems to be saying that, like a pang, the sense of the numinous is uninformed by conceptual presuppositions and moral assessments. According to him, concepts and judgments are employed to schematize or interpret an affective experience that is independent of thought. But emotions require reference to concepts and beliefs to incorporate into the rules for the identification of an experience of the numinous the claim that the experience transcends all concepts and judgments" (p. 88). It is Otto's definition of religion as numinous feeling—as "dynamic agency or effect not caused by an arbitrary act of will"—that Jung adopts as his own. See, for example, CW 11, para. 6. "Inner feeling" is elevated to the status of religion and is thus not open to critical evaluation of content.

7. Letter to Bernhard Lang, June 8, 1957, *Letters*, 2. See Chapter 5, Part II, below, for further clarification of Jung's use of subjectivist epistemology.

8. "A Reply to Martin Buber," CW 18, para. 1499–1513.

9. A detailed discussion of what Jung meant by the empiricism of the psyche is contained in Part II of this essay, on the archetype.

10. "A Reply to Martin Buber," CW 18, para. 1506.

11. Jung is not being entirely straightforward. These very same arguments, about the empiricism and universality of a concept of God, formed the basis of his very frequent use of the Common Consent Argument *for* God. The *consensus gentium* argument was used in conjunction with the three-stage argument for the validity of inner experience. See Part II of this essay, Chapter 4.

12. Letter to Bernhard Lang, June 1957, *Letters*, 2:377. See also *Mysterium Coniunctionis*, CW 14, para. 781.

13. *Psychological Types*, CW 6, para. 533. See also para. 623, 632.

14. Ibid., para. 512. See also para. 322.

15. "On Psychic Energy," CW 8, para. 5. The early sections of this essay may have been written as early as 1912. See also "On the Nature of the Psyche," CW 8, para. 358, for a commentary on the post-Kantian rebellion against his critique of knowledge.

16. *Psychological Types*, CW 6, para. 855.

17. Jung, "The Soul and Death," CW 8, para. 814. See also "On Psychic Energy," CW 8, para. 45; *Psychological Types*, para. 279: "Psychologically we have a right on purely empirical grounds to treat the contents of the unconscious as just as *real* as the things of the outside world." And *Mysterium Coniunctionis*, CW 14, para. 667: "One should not be put off by the physical impossibilities of dogma or of the coniunctio, for they are symbols in regard to which the allurements of rationalism are entirely out of place and miss the mark...one must be content to leave things as they are, and give up trying to know anything about the symbol."

18. Letter to Bernhard Martin, Dec. 7, 1954, *Letters*, 2.

19. Letter to R. J. Zwi Werblowsky, June 17, 1952, *Letters*, 2.

20. *Psychological Types*, CW 6, para. 77. See also "Basic Postulates of Analytical Psychology," CW 8, para. 680: "The conflict between the physical and the spiritual aspects only shows that psychic life is in the last analysis an incomprehensible 'something'. Without a doubt, it is our only immediate experience."

21. C. G. Jung, Emma Jung and Toni Wolff: A Collection of Remembrances, ed. Ferne Jensen (San Francisco: Analytical Psychology Club, 1982), pp. 90–95.

22. *Psychology and Alchemy*, CW 12, para. 516.

23. "On the Nature of the Psyche," CW 8, para. 357. See also para. 423.

Chapter 4

1. I have not yet discussed Jung's concept of the self as supraordinate, unconscious center of the psyche. See Part III below.

2. See Beck, *A Commentary on Kant's Critique of Practical Reason*, p. 48. "We may and do mistake the function of theoretical reason and think that its Ideas are constitutive of an intelligible world — of the world of things as they really are and not as they appear. When we make this mistake, transcendental Ideas become transcendent, and philosophical thinking falls into

antinomies, paralogisms, and other fallacies exhibited and eradicated in the Dialectic of the first *Critique*. The same reason, following our demands for unconditional conditions for every motive and for the unity of motives in a pattern of life, is, on the contrary, an immanent reason, actually producing the objects to correspond to its Ideas. These objects, produced by us in acting in accordance with the demands of these Ideas, are not things in the outer world, which we may have or lack the power to effect; they are motives or states of mind or decisions of will which directly express in actual experience the Idea of freedom, of which the moral law is a necessary consequence.... Reason becomes practical, generating an Idea of a world that, through our actions and attitudes, may be established with immanent completeness, order, and systematic unity, whether it can be actualized in the products of human skill or not." *Critique of Pure Reason*, A 548 = B 576; *Critique of Practical Reason*, 15 (101).

3. Kant was aware that his own work stood in the tradition of Western idealism just because of its emphasis on the moral problem. *Critique of Practical Reason*, Akademie, 140: "In the history of Greek philosophy before Anaxagoras there is no definite trace of a pure rational theology. The reason for this is not that the earlier philosophers lacked the understanding and insight.... But the evils in the world appeared to them to be too important an objection for them to hold such a hypothesis to be justified.... But when this acute people had progressed far enough in their inquiries to deal philosophically even with moral subjects,...they found for the first time a new need, a practical need which gave them the definite concept of the First Being."

4. Plato, *Protagoras and Meno*, trans. W. K. C. Guthrie (Harmondsworth, Middlesex: Penguin Books, 1976).

5. *Iliad* 21.462–67, trans. by F. M. Cornford in *Greek Religious Thought from Homer to Alexander* (New York: AMS Press, 1969), pp. 5 f.

6. Hesiod, *The Works and Days. Theogony. The Shield of Herakles*, trans. Richmond Lattimore (Ann Arbor: University of Michigan Press, 1978), p. 165.

7. Herbert Weir Smyth, "Greek Conceptions of Immortality from Homer to Plato," in *Harvard Essays on Classical Subjects*, ed. Herbert Weir Smyth (Boston: Houghton Mifflin Company, 1912), pp. 231–84.

8. Richard Broxton Onians, *The Origins of European Thought about the Body, the Mind, the Soul, the World, Time and Fate* (Cambridge: Cambridge University Press, 1951), pp. 1–9; A. W. H. Adkins, *From the Many to the One* (London: Constable, 1970), pp. 28 ff.

9. Plato, *Phaedo*, trans. Hugh Tredennick, in *The Last Days of Socrates* (Harmondsworth, Middlesex: Penguin Classics, 1954), 80c–81a.

10. Speculation among scholars that Plato had within the two or three years prior to writing the *Meno* undergone a religious conversion experience of an Orphic/Pythagorean type is still heard. Plato is the main source of our knowledge of Orphism and his references to Orphic doctrine express the vitality and conviction typical of the convert.

11. W. K. C. Guthrie, *A History of Greek Philosophy* (Cambridge: Cambridge University Press, 1975), 4:195 f.

For a concise summary of the most recent evidence on Orphism see Walter Burkert, *Greek Religion*, trans. John Raffian (Cambridge: Harvard University Press, 1985), pp. 296–301. "What is most important is the transformation in the concept of the soul, *psyche*, which takes place in these [Orphic/Pythagorean] circles.... With the idea of the immortal soul the discovery of the individual had reached a goal which is only fulfilled in philosophy. It was Socratic care for the soul and Platonic metaphysics that gave it the classical form that was to predominate for thousands of years."

Guthrie's own earlier essay, *Orpheus and Greek Religion* (1934) (New York: W. W. Norton, 1966) thoroughly discusses Orphic questions from a positive point of view. Recent discoveries have largely confirmed Guthrie's position as over against the more skeptical stance of Ivan Linforth and U. von Wilamowitz.

12. C. G. Jung, "Answer to Job," in *Psychology and Religion: West and East*, CW 11, para. 553–758; *Aion: Researches into the Phenomenology of the Self*, CW 9ii, para. 68–126 (Chap. 5). Most of the published letters to Victor White contain some reference to the problem of the *privatio boni*; in some of them there is a detailed discussion of Jung's view, e.g., April 30, 1952, and June 30, 1952, *Letters*, 2. See also the letters to H. L. Philp, published in "Jung and Religious Belief," CW 18, para. 1584–1690.

Chapter 5

1. Plato's analogy of the cave in the *Republic* is actually a perceptual *analogy* of the moral and formal problematic of the Good. Plato is not discussing a theory of perception in these passages. But the cave metaphor serves to illustrate the historical tendency of metaphysical idealists to disparage sense knowledge.

2. "We must use our sensations as the foundation of all our investigations; that is, we must base investigations on the mental apprehensions, upon the purposeful use of the several senses that furnish us with knowledge, and upon our immediate feelings." Letter to Herodotus 38b, in *Epicurus: Letters, Principal Doctrines and Vatican Sayings*, Library of Liberal Arts (New York: Bobbs-Merrill Company, 1964).

3. "Whatever is false and erroneous is due to what opinion adds." Ibid., 50b.

4. Ibid., Letter to Menoeceus, 125.

5. Authority and revelation belong of course also to the epistemological criteria of scholastic philosophy/theology.

6. Galileo's discovery of the mathematical laws of falling bodies was published in 1604. In 1632 his *Dialogue Concerning the Two Chief World Systems* was published. In 1633 he was sentenced by the Inquisition to life imprisonment and his book was condemned. Johannes Kepler's *A Physics of the Sky Derived from Investigations of the Motions of the Star Mars* was published in 1609. Isaac Newton's *Principia* was published in 1687.

7. René Descartes, *The Meditations Concerning First Philosophy*, trans. Laurence J. Lafleur, Library of Liberal Arts (New York: Bobbs-Merrill Company, 1960). Sixth Meditation, p. 133: "I cannot doubt that there is in me a certain passive faculty of perceiving...but it would be valueless to me...if there were not also in me, or in something else, another active faculty capable of forming and producing these ideas. But this active faculty cannot be in me....[I]t must necessarily exist in some substance different from myself, in which all the reality that exists is formally or eminently contained....This substance is either a body...or else it is God himself....I do not see how we could clear God of the charge of deceit if these ideas did in fact come from some other source or were produced by other causes than corporeal objects. Therefore we must conclude that corporeal objects exist."

8. George Berkeley, *A Treatise Concerning the Principles of Human Knowledge* (1710), ed. and with introduction by Colin M. Turbayne, Library of Liberal Arts (New York: Bobbs-Merrill Company, 1957). No. 18: "As for our senses, by them we have the knowledge only of our sensations, ideas, or those things that are immediately perceived by sense...but they do not inform us that things exist without the mind."

9. Ibid., No. 23.

10. Ibid., No. 33.

11. Arthur Schopenhauer, *The World as Will and Representation* (1819), trans. E. F. J. Payne (New York: Dover Publications, 1969), 1:1: "The world is representation....Berkeley was the first to enunciate it positively, and he has thus rendered an immortal service to philosophy." Appendix, pp. 434 f.: "I found [in the first edition of the *Critique*] that although Kant does not use the formula, 'No object without a subject', he nevertheless, with just as much emphasis as do Berkeley and I, declares the external world lying before us in space and time to be mere representation of the subject that knows it."

12. Cf. pp. 34 f. above.

13. *Monadology* 69: "There is nothing uncultured, sterile or dead in the universe, no chaos, no disorder." *Monadology* 89: "God as the architect satisfies in all respects God as the legislator. Thus sin must entail punishment according to the order of nature and as the very result of the mechanical structure of the universe; and, analogously, good actions will attract their rewards through machinelike corporeal process." Gottfried Wilhelm Leibniz, *Monadology and Other Philosophical Essays*, trans. Paul Schrecker and Anne Martin Schrecker, Library of Liberal Arts (Indianapolis: Bobbs-Merrill Educational Publishing, 1985).

14. The principle of non-contradiction lies at the base of those propositions of reason which define analytic, or necessary truths, for Leibniz. For the way in which Leibniz sought to bring into the realm of public knowledge his secret mythical doctrine see Robert E. Butts, *Kant and the Double Government Methodology: Supersensibility and Method in Kant's Philosophy of Science* (Dordrecht: D. Reidel Publishing Company, 1984), pp. 8, 26, 29 ff., 36 f.

15. According to Aristotelian and scholastic philosophy, God is the only fully *actualized* being, all other substances being in the process of *becoming* actualized. According to Plotinus, God is the One fully good and real being. The created world is an emanation downwards from Nous and from true being, with decreasing participation in God's being the closer one approaches to pure matter, which represents the negation of both goodness and being. Leibniz borrowed elements of both systems.

16. "Thus every portion of matter can be conceived as a garden full of plants or as a pond full of fish. But every branch of the plant, every limb of the animal, every drop of its humors, is again such a garden or such a pond."

17. Cf. Aristotle's *Metaphysics* 1072b2–4.

18. Butts, *Kant and the Double Government Methodology*, pp. 44–48 and n. 7.

19. Ibid., pp. 28, 59.

20. Ibid.

21. Ibid., pp. 53 f.; Henry E. Allison, *Kant's Transcendental Idealism: An Interpretation and Defense* (New Haven: Yale University Press, 1983), p. 20.

22. Butts, *Kant and the Double Government Methodology*, pp. 142 f.

23. Allison, *Kant's Transcendental Idealism*, p. 29: "The cognitive structure of the human mind is viewed as the source of certain conditions which must be met by anything that is to be represented as an object by such a mind."

24. Immanuel Kant, *Prolegomena to Any Future Metaphysics*, with an Introduction by Lewis White Beck (New York: Liberal Arts Press, 1950), pp. 6 ff. (AK 259–60). The sentence order of the cited text has been somewhat rearranged to suit the present context, but I trust that Kant's meaning is accurately represented.

25. Allison, *Kant's Transcendental Idealism*, pp. 65 ff.

26. Ibid., p. 10.

27. Ibid., p. 89.

28. Ibid., pp. 176 f., 187.

29. Jung once remarked that the metaphysical vitality of Plato's concept of archetypes degenerated over time until it was reduced in Kant to a limited number of categories of understanding. "Instinct and the Unconscious," CW 8, para. 176. Jung was himself much more interested in the possibility that inner states actually influence or produce outer states or events, at least insofar as we experience such events, and he followed Schopenhauer in this respect, as the evidence will show. See Part II of this essay. Kant's concept of the schemata, with their image-producing capacity and their quality as a kind of innate grammar might however come close to Jung's notion of the archetype. The affective component of Jung's concept is missing in Kant's view.

30. Butts, *Kant and the Double Government Methodology*, pp. 151 f., 159, 198 f. Butts goes further. The universal grammar or the semantics is actually mathematics. "Kant's entire categorial structure (his epistemic grammar and its required semantical rules) is one complex and exotic set of expectations that reality will be the sorts of things we understand and comprehend under scientific laws."

31. Allison cites five of the best known of these passages, *Kant's Transcendental Idealism*, pp. 238 f.

32. I am grateful to Margaret Morrison for a succinct differentiation of the role of the positive and negative noumena in the first and second editions of the *Critique*, in her unpublished paper, "Kant and the Problem of the Noumena": "The limiting concept of ·the noumenon enables us to recognize our epistemic limitations so that we can correctly interpret the demands of reason as purely regulative rather than as an attempt to provide us with constitutive knowledge of an extra-phenomenal realm."

Chapter 6

1. By Eduard Zeller, in "Ueber die Bedeutung und Aufgabe der Erkenntnis Theorie," (1862) Vorträge und Abhandlungen, Zweite Sammlung

(Leipzig: Fues Verlag, 1887). See E. Cassirer, *The Problem of Knowledge: Philosophy, Science and History since Hegel*, trans. William H. Woglom and Charles W. Hendel (New Haven: Yale University Press, 1950), pp. 3 f.

2. For example, Christoph Sigwart, *Logik*, 2 vols. (Tübingen, 1873).

3. A passage at the conclusion of David Hume's *Enquiry Concerning Human Understanding* is often quoted by the positivists: "If we take in our hand any volume; of divinity or school metaphysics, for instance, let us ask; *does it contain any abstract reasoning concerning quantity or number?* No. *Does it contain any experimental reasoning concerning matter of fact and existence?* No. Commit it then to the flames, for it can contain nothing but sophistry and confusion." *Enquiries Concerning the Human Understanding and Concerning the Principles of Morals*, ed. L. A. Selby-Bigge, 2nd ed. (1902; reprint, Oxford: Clarendon Press, 1966), p. 165.

4. Otto Liebmann, *Kant und die Epigonen* (Stuttgart, 1865).

5. This paper and its consequences are discussed in Part III of this essay, pp. 238 ff.

6. Hermann von Helmholtz, "Thought in Medicine" (1877) in *Selected Writings*, ed. and with Introduction by Russell Kahl (Middletown, Conn.: Wesleyan University Press, 1971), p. 353.

7. Hermann von Helmhotz, "Recent Progress in the Theory of Vision" (1868), in *Selected Writings*, p. 184.

8. Hermann von Helmhotz, "The Facts in Perception" (1878), in *Epistemological Writings: The Paul Hertz/Moritz Schlick Centenary Edition of 1921* (Dordrecht, Holland/Boston, 1977), pp. 119 f.

9. Ibid., p. 137.

10. Ibid., p. 132; "Theory of Vision," p. 215.

11. "The Facts in Perception," p. 141.

12. "Theory of Vision," p. 197.

13. "The Facts in Perception," p. 142. See the note by Schlick.

14. See the instructive discussion by Maurice Mandelbaum, *History, Man and Reason: A Study in Nineteenth-Century Thought* (Baltimore: Johns Hopkins Press, 1971), pp. 292 ff.

15. Lewis White Beck, "Neo-Kantianism," *Encyclopedia of Philosophy*, 5:472.

16. F. A. Lange, *The History of Materialism* (1865), 3rd ed., trans. E. C. Thomas, 3 vols. in one (London: Kegan Paul, Trench, Trübner & Co., 1925), Book II, First Section, p. 158.

17. Ibid., p. 156.

18. Thomas Case, "Metaphysics," *Encyclopaedia Britannica*, 11th ed., 1911, 18:236 f. "Lange['s book]...has exercised a profound influence, which is due partly to its apparent success in answering materialism by Kantian arguments, and partly to its ingenious attempt to give to Kantism itself a consistency, which, however, has only succeeded in producing a new philosophy of neo-Kantism, differing from Kantism in itself. Lange to some extent modified the transcendentalism of Kant's theory of the origin of knowledge. A priori forms, according to Kant, are contributions of the mental powers of sense, understanding, and reason; but, according to Lange, they are rooted in 'the physico-psychical organization.' " See also Beck, "Neo-Kantianism"; Arnulf Zweig, "F. A. Lange," *Encyclopedia of Philosophy*, 4:383.

19. Case, "Metaphysics," pp. 237 f.

20. James Iverach, "Epistemology," *Hastings Encyclopedia of Religion and Ethics* (Edinburgh, 1912), 5:345 f. See also Roger Scruton, *From Descartes to Wittgenstein* (New York: Harper Collophon Books, 1981), p. 145.

21. Wilhelm Max Wundt, *Ueber den Einfluss der Philosophie auf die Erfahrungswissenschaften*, Akademische Antrittsrede Gehalten zu Leipzig, am 20 November, 1875 (Leipzig: Verlag von Wilhelm Engelmann, 1876), pp. 17 f.: "Denn so hoch die heutige Naturforschung die Erfahrung auch stellt, darüber sind doch nicht wenige Physiker einig, dass gewisse Elemente a priori sich bei unserer Naturerkenntniss wirksam erweisen, und hierhin rechnet man vor allem das Princip der Causalität. Aber es scheint mir, als wenn in dieser Anwendung des Causalprincips auf die Sinnesanschauung eine jener Begriffsvertauschungen vorliege, die für die Entwicklung unserer Erkenntniss so verhängnissvoll sind, eine Vertauschung nämlich des Begriffs der Ursache, mit dem Erkenntnissgrund. Den äusseren Gegenstand sollen wir unmittelbar als die Ursache unserer Vorstellung denken, und ebenso sollen wir bei der Wahrnehmung der Grösse, Entfernung und Anordnung der Objekte auf ursächliche Verhältnisse zurückgehen. Und doch bezieht sich der Begriff der Ursache überall auf ein Geschehen. Ursache ist nur was eine Wirkung hervorbringt.... Der Trieb, nach einem Grund der Erscheinungen zu suchen, muss zwar in uns gelegen sein, ehe auch nur der Versuch einer Naturerklärung beginnen kann. Aber dieser Trieb hat seine Wurzel in unserm stets vom Grund zur Folge oder von der Folge zum Grund fortschreitenden Denken. In diesem Sinne können wir sagen, dass das Gesetz der Causalität aus der Erfahrung stamme, und dass es doch gleichzeitig auf die ursprünglichen Eigenschaften unseres Bewusstseins sich stütze. Aus der Erfahrung kommt die besondere Form des Zusammenhangs der Erscheinungen nach Ursache und Wirkung, das Verlangen aber, diesen Zusammenhang als einen allgemeinen und nothwendigen zu begreifen, entstammt der Natur unsers erkennenden Geistes."

22. At the turn of the century he was still arguing the same point, and with even less conviction that there was more than a "tiny group" of orthodox Kantians who understood what he meant: "What one cannot give up, so long as one adheres at all to Kant's views on the nature of cognitive experience, that is the demand that those a priori functions which first lend form to experience must be brought into logical connection with each other and with the laws of thought and into relationship with sense perception." Wilhelm Wundt, "Was soll uns Kant nicht sein?" in *Kleine Schriften*, 2 vols. (Leipzig: Verlag von Wilhelm Engelmann, 1910), p. 147: "Was man nicht preisgeben kann, so lange man überhaupt an den Anschauungen Kants von dem Wesen der Erfahrungserkenntnis festhält, das ist die Forderung, dass jene Funktionen *a priori*, die aller Erfahrung erst ihre Form geben, in einen logischen Zusammenhang miteinander und mit den Gesetzen unseres Denkens und in eine Beziehung zu der sinnlichen Wahrnehmung gebracht werden müssen."

23. Ernst Haeckel, *The Riddle of the Universe at the Close of the Nineteenth Century*, trans. Joseph McCabe (New York: Harper & Brothers Publishers, 1900), p. 292.

24. Ernst Haeckel, *Der Monistenbund: Thesen zur Organisation des Monismus* (Frankfurt a. M.: Neuer Frankfurter Verlag, 1905), p. 4: "Ebenso unhaltbar und der Erfahrung widersprechend ist die Behauptung der Metaphysik (Kant), dass ein Teil der wichtigsten Erkenntnisse *a priori*, unabhängig von jeder Erfahrung, allein durch Vernunftschlüsse gewonnen werde. Tatsächlich sind die sogenannte "Erkenntnisse *a priori*" alle durch Assozion von Vorstellungen entstanden, die ursprünglich aus Ketten von Erfahrungen, *a posteriori* erlangt wurden."

25. Erich Adickes, *Kant contra Haeckel: Erkenntnistheorie gegen naturwissenschaftlichen Dogmatismus* (Berlin: Verlag von Reuther & Reichard, 1901), pp. 35 ff.

26. Ibid., p. 56: "Die Existenz des Psychischen ist der Stein des Anstosses, an dem jeder Materialist scheitert, mag er sein Schifflein wenden und drehn, wie er will. Nichts hilft über die Thatsache hinweg, dass unsere Empfindungen und Bewusstseinszustände das uns Nächstliegende und Bestbekannte, das allein direkt Gegebene sind. Der Götze des Materialisten ist ein echter Fetisch, den er selbst gemacht hat: die Materie, der das Bewusstsein entstammen soll, existiert allein innerhalb des Bewusstseins. Ein Ding an sich kann sie nicht sein; denn alle ihre Eigenschaften bestehn aus Empfindungsinhalten und deren Kombinationen. Nicht unser Geist ist von ihr: sie ist von unserm Geist abhängig; er schafft sie, nicht sie ihn." Compare Jung's poem in the *Red Book*: "I did not consider that the soul cannot be the object of my judgment and knowledge. Much more are my judgment and knowledge the object of my soul." Aniela Jaffé, "Phases in Jung's Life," *Spring* (1972). Cf. also p. 27, above.

27. C. G. Jung, *Analytical Psychology: Notes of the Seminar Given in 1925*, ed. William McGuire, Bollingen Series XCIX (Princeton: Princeton University Press, 1989), p. 4.

28. Schopenhauer, *World as Will and Representation*, 1, #1, p. 3.

29. Ibid., #1, p. 3; Bryan Magee, *The Philosophy of Schopenhauer* (Oxford: Clarendon Press, 1983), pp. 70, 84; Mandelbaum, *History, Man and Reason*, p. 316.

30. Schopenhauer, *World as Will and Representation*, 1, Appendix, pp. 434 f.

31. Ibid., Chap. 18, 2:195–97.

32. Kant's term for the phenomenal idealist is "empirical idealist," one who holds that "the mind can only have immediate access to its own ideas or representations." Allison, *Kant's Transcendental Idealism*, p. 15. Cf. *Critique of Pure Reason*, A369.

Chapter 7

1. Jung, *Psychological Types*, CW 6, para. 44.

2. Ibid., para. 54.

3. Ibid., para. 59. See Chapter 5, above, for Kant's demonstration in the first *Critique* that purely rational objects do not yield knowledge. Only synthetic processes are capable of doing so. The ontological argument is a pure analytic statement.

4. Jung, *Psychological Types*, CW 6, para. 62. Jung's own use of the Argument from Common Consent is extremely frequent. An interesting discussion of modern forms of the argument, including Jung's use of it, is found in the essay by Paul Edwards in the *Encyclopedia of Philosophy*, 2:147–55. See my own discussion of the Common Consent argument in Part II, Chap. 4, below.

5. Jung, *Psychological Types*, para. 66.

6. Ibid., para. 72.

7. Ibid., para. 77.

8. Ibid., para. 84–85. Jung claims for psychology apart from science what 19th-century religion claimed for itself as over against science. Maurice Mandelbaum remarked that 19th-century science, far from rejecting religion, delegated to it all of the non-scientific realm of ethics and feeling. The materialist Tyndall stated that "the facts of religious feeling are to me as certain as the facts of physics." *History, Man and Reason*, pp. 28 f.

9. Jung, *Psychological Types*, para. 86.

10. What is valuable is however often hidden from the conscious point of view and must be sought for as the secret treasure which will be revealed fully only at some future moment of utter self-knowledge. The individual must engage in a process of development (the individuation process) and remain open to fantasy, dreams, and other indicators which may guide the search for self and truth. Needless to say, the process is never finished, except conceivably at the moment of death.

11. "There can be no doubt that all our knowledge begins with experience." Kant, *Critique of Pure Reason*, B1.

12. Jung, "Paracelsus," CW 15, para. 1–17; *Psychology and Alchemy*, CW 12.

13. Jung, "Paracelsus as Physician," CW 15, para. 18–43; "Paracelsus as a Spiritual Phenomenon," CW 13, para. 145–238. The first portion of the latter monograph, "The Two Sources of Knowledge: The Light of Nature and the Light of Revelation," is of special interest for Jung's epistemological views.

14. Jung, "Psychology of the Transference," CW 16, para. 353–539.

15. The appearance of the Basel professor and scholar's book on Paracelsus caused some consternation among Jung's followers in Zürich, who thought Jung had not been adequately credited for his prior work on Paracelsus in the same area. Pagel's views on Jung can be found in "Jung's View on Alchemy," *Isis* 39 (1948): 44–48. My feeling is that Jung and Pagel both offer complementary and useful material on the subject.

16. Walter Pagel, *Paracelsus: An Introduction to Philosophical Medicine in the Era of the Renaissance* (Basel, Switzerland: S. Karger, 1958), p. 82.

17. Ibid., pp. 52, 56.

18. Jung, "Paracelsus as a Spiritual Phenomenon," CW 13, para. 148.

19. Hall, *Ideas of Life and Matter*, 1:173.

20. Quoted in Pagel, *Paracelsus*, p. 54 (Huser, 1, 103).

21. Quoted in Pagel, *Paracelsus*, p. 60 (Huser, 1, 272–74).

22. Ibid., p. 51.

23. Jung, "Paracelsus as a Spiritual Phenomenon," CW 13, para. 197. See also para. 229: "The *lumen naturae* is the natural spirit, whose strange and significant workings we can observe in the manifestations of the unconscious now that psychological research has come to realize that the unconscious is not just a 'subconscious' appendage or the dustbin of con-

sciousness, but is a largely autonomous psychic system for compensating the biases and aberrations of the conscious attitude, for the most part functionally, though it sometimes corrects them by force."

24. Jung, *Psychology and Alchemy*, CW 12, para. 346.

25. The reader familiar with Jung's psychology will think of his well-known "theory of opposites," which should describe dialectical development toward individuation, as possibly his single leading idea. Jung applied this idea epistemologically when he considered the human person as macrocosm and as microcosm. At least one important source of this idea for Jung was Kantian idealism. See pp. 21 f. above and n.31, p. 89. The theory of opposites was also critical for Goethe, to whom Jung felt a deep personal connection. A second application by Jung of the "theory of opposites" is more specifically in line with the doctrine of sympathy discussed here. No sooner have we fulfilled a powerful desire to be affectively engaged in life and with other persons than we experience an equally powerful need to disengage and to regain an objective stance. Following the path of inner desire (though not necessarily in overt action) leads eventually, thought Jung, to the emergence of a deeper understanding of one's own truth, or one's own character.

PART II

The Archetype:
Championing the Mind

Introduction

Jung's introduction into the psychological field of the early 1920s of the term *archetype* seemed to many professional and academic people of the period a scandalous archaicism. If Jung had been cast out of the psychoanalytic community ten years before on account of his disagreement with Freud over the libido theory he was now written off by most other Western academics as a mystic and a metaphysician. Even though Freud's subject matter (the unconscious psyche) and his theories about it (sexuality) remained suspicious hypotheses in other branches of the social sciences the Freudian establishment always maintained a certain reputation for scientific respectability. This was because Freud's model of the human psyche rested on a biological and mechanistic base, and it was these scientific theories which would bind together and guide the work of the academic establishment in the twentieth century.

Archetypes, on the other hand, were well known from the history of philosophy, even if no one had spoken seriously of them for many years. Plato had referred to nonliving, nonmoving a priori forms (archetypes) of the visible reality in which we live as the only true existents, all else being only an imitation of those eternal facts. Biology and physics could scarcely accommodate a psychological theory which posited archetypes as an explanatory factor. Neither could the new science of anthropology, with its comprehensive thesis that variations in human culture are due to environmental factors (the *nurture* theory) make sense of a psychology which emphasized a priori factors (the *nature* theory) as of primary importance in understanding human behavior.

Still, unexpectedly, the term *archetype* continued to be used. Mircea Eliade picked it up and used the word to describe the *historical development of ideas* in human culture. This was a distinctly different meaning from what Jung had in mind, but it was close enough that familiar connotations grew up around the term as it was used by students of both men.[1] In the 1960s the word *archetype* was made fashionable by the counter-culture in America. In recent years the term *archetype* seems to have passed over into the general vocabulary. *Newsweek* columnist Meg Greenfield referred to archetypal behavior patterns as "imprinted on the brain since about the days of *Homo habilis*." This is still a third distinct meaning for the word *archetype*, a meaning which equates *archetype* with *instinct* and seems to find common ground between depth psychology and ethology, the science of animal behavior for which Konrad Lorenz is celebrated as the principal founder.

It would be convenient if I could single out which of these three meanings is pertinent to Jung's intention and go on to explicate the facts concerning it. But Jung made many firm statements about what he meant which were at the same time not complete statements. He used the term over a period of more than forty years in which an enormous amount of work was produced. I think that a convincing and mostly complete answer to the question, What did Jung mean with his theory of archetypes? can be given. But in order to do so the question must be broadened. We must ask what problems Jung tried to solve with his theory. We must follow a historical and developmental line of approach.

Each of the new psychologies of the unconscious had to establish a theoretical base. It had also to establish a clinical technique which could be supported by the explanatory terms of its basic postulates. I want to set out a number of theses about Jung's concept of the archetype as an outline for the work which follows.

1. Jung took over from Freud the problem of the aetiology of psychic processes. He rejected Freud's theory. His own theory of archetypes represents an economic, structural, and dynamic alternative to Freud's theory.

2. Jung's *theory of psychic energy* must be seen as a bridge concept or middle station on the way to his theory of archetypes. Other "bridge concepts" to the archetype were his *constructive method* and his *theory of symbols*.

3. Jung acquired from Freud a biological-mechanical model and he at first expressed his modifications of libido theory in biological and energic terms. Over the years his theory of energy and of archetypes became less and less biological.

4. Finally, the archetype as expression of the "autonomy of the psyche" triumphed over the idea of archetype as "pattern of behavior." Jung's use of the phrase "pattern of behavior" in connection with archetypes must always be evaluated in the light of the formal factor of reality as it is expressed in the philosophy of Schopenhauer.

Of all the social sciences, surely none has been so bedeviled with the mind-body problem in the search for a theoretical basis as the so-called depth psychologies of the unconscious. They have for their subject matter the vagaries of fantasy and dreams, powerful affective states, intuitions of God, and symptomatic behavior. With such material, how shall they find a theoretical base? The biological sciences have had a hard enough time dealing with the realities of conscious psychic functioning without succumbing to dualism, to say nothing of the difficulties of making meaning out of the affectivity of the unconscious.[3] Though often courted by psychology, biology has not been an eager bride.[4] Philosophers of the mind since Plato, on the other hand, have equated affectivity with the black steed of wanton desire who destroys the soul's love of reason and beauty, and with the chaos of nature without intelligible mind.[5] For the philosopher, meaning will scarcely be found in the realm of the emotions.

Under the circumstances it is understandable that the two principal progenitors of depth psychology should have claimed that their new science was not to be identified with the principles of any other discipline. As early as 1900, in the difficult metaphysical Chapter 7 of his *Interpretation of Dreams*, Freud warned that the physical-mechanical explanation of mental functioning which he was suggesting was to be taken as analogical only. "We are justified, in my view, in giving free rein to our speculations so long as we retain the coolness of our judgment and do not mistake the scaffolding for the building.[6] In 1911 he was warning Jung about the danger of subordinating psychology to biology in the paper of Jung's former analysand and protégé Frl. Sabina Spielrein: "This dependency is no more acceptable than a dependency on philosophy, physiology, or brain anatomy. Ψ*A farà da se.* (Psychoanalysis goes by itself.)"[7] Jung, for his part, was also ready to claim the independence of his own field of study. In his essay "On Psychic Energy," published only in 1928 but written as early as 1912, Jung said: "Psychology as much as physics may avail itself of the right to build its own concepts." "I am purposely leaving out of account here...whether the psychic energy process exists independently of, or is included in, the physical process. In my view we know practically nothing about this....Exhaustive discussion of this question may be all very well for philosophers, but empirical psychology should confine itself to empirically accessible facts."[8] Jung then went on to develop exhaustive analogies of physical energic concepts with psychological process.

The fact is that although the data of depth psychology clearly have to do with living beings, we are not yet able to connect those data in any significant way with the "hard" data of biological process.[9] Yet we cannot interpret clinical data in a vacuum. While in a certain sense it is true that the psychology of the unconscious stands on its own, it is also and even more importantly true that we unavoidably, consciously or unconsciously, rely on philosophical presupppositions about the nature of reality to form the interpretive framework for understanding our data. Where the interpretive framework is not explicitly defined it will be contained in the language and the terms of the clinical report. In spite of their occasional disclaimers there is every evidence that both Freud and Jung spent a great deal of effort in attempting to establish a theoretical base for the psychologies. In his charming and profound little essay, "The Aims of Psychotherapy," Jung remarked in 1929:

> I must content myself wholly with the fact that the result means something to the patient and sets his life in motion again. I may allow myself only one criterion for the results of my labours: Does it work? As for my scientific hobby—my desire to know why it works—this I must reserve for my spare time.[10]

Jung is talking here about the interplay between the type of therapeutic result achieved and the technique which is applied to achieve it. Theoretical applications (in this case, a subjective, prospective approach to the data) are validated by their practical effectiveness, that is, by a particular kind of attitudinal change on the part of the patient. But Jung also knew that the interpretive framework influenced his understanding of psychic process. As early as 1914, in his essay "On Psychological Understanding," Jung wrote:

> Constructive understanding also *analyses*, but it does not *reduce*.... From the comparative analysis of many systems the typical formations can be discovered. If one can speak of reduction at all, it is simply a reduction to general types, but not to some general principle arrived at inductively or deductively, such as "sexuality" or "striving for power."[11]

The "typical formations" and "general types" of which Jung speaks here are a very early formulation of what he five years later explicitly defined as a theory of archetypes. It is clear from this passage that these "typical formations" are indeed to replace the general explanatory principle of Freud's theory of sexuality and of Adler's power motive. What one knows about one's patient has a great deal to do with the theory which is applied to clinical data.

A few years ago I sat with a small group of fellow analysts who had been assigned the task of interviewing students. After one student had left the room a senior colleague of mine remarked with great irritation: "You would think he had never in his whole life met up with an archetype!" The others of us in the room smiled and knew what our colleague had meant. The unfortunate student appeared to have a very rationalistic defense system (against his own emotional states). There was much affective dissonance. Sitting with him one felt somehow that he was not quite all there, or that there was something in the atmosphere which one could not trust, because too much was being unconsciously hidden. My colleague's use of the term *archetype* was decidedly colloquial. But the way in which it was used helps to show a number of contents which belong to Jung's definition of the concept:

1. Archetypes have to do with emotion.

2. Archetypes are experienced as autonomous agents impinging on conscious states as though they were foreign objects. It is not always clear whether the emotional state which impacts consciousness stems from within or without the organism.

3. It is a *good thing* to have experienced states of high emotion, not a bad thing.

4. Experiential knowledge of the power of "archetypal states" has something to do with normative human life.

Although the autonomous-seeming quality of the archetype was contained in my colleague's brief exclamation, what was not included is the fact that powerful affective states which Jungians call archetypal are frequently accompanied by spontaneous images which may appear in dreams, semi-conscious fantasies, or may even be projectively vested in outer objects. What is particularly important for me to show at this point is that Jung's concept of archetypes, while, as we shall see, it does partake of the innate or a priori quality of Plato's doctrine of forms, is not at all like the eternal, unmoving grounds of Plato's vision of true being. Affectivity is of the very stuff of Jung's view of archetypes. It is for him the substance of the real.

We are now in a position to make a transition backwards to the work which Freud did to construct a basis for human emotion and the unconscious psychic process.

1

Freud and the Theory of Instinct Libido

Freud reported that his hearing the beautiful essay on Nature ascribed to Goethe read aloud in a lecture towards the end of his years at the Gymnasium helped set his decision for the natural science curriculum at the University of Vienna.[1] He enrolled as a medical student in 1873, and joined the famous Physiological Institute directed by Ernst Brücke in 1876.[2] He took his medical degree in 1881 but continued on in the Physiological Institute, publishing over the course of six years five papers on the neuro-anatomy of fish, eels, and crayfish. It might well be expected that he would make a career in research biology, but when Ernst Brücke himself kindly pointed out that his income potential would be most limited, and that the two available assistantships in the Institute were held by men who were still young, Freud reluctantly began to prepare to practice medicine as a neurologist, the only branch of medicine he felt he had learned enough about to warrant a professional practice.[3] He undertook a three-year program of residency internships at Vienna General Hospital beginning in 1882, won with the help of Brücke's recommendation a six-month fellowship to study with Jean-Martin Charcot in Paris in 1885–86, and came home to a new position as director of the neurological section of Kassowitz's Institute for Children's Diseases. He opened his private practice in that same year and was finally able to marry Martha Bernays, his fiancee of four years.

The picture which emerges is that of a brilliant young man who used the freedom of his youth to pursue his heart's desire — science — and who, as the years of maturity neared, maneuvered to match as nearly as might be his true inner interests with the practical exigencies of life. To say that Freud fell accidentally and by reason of practical necessity into his profession as neurologist and psychiatrist would be going too far. There had been from the begin-

113

ning his profound interest in *neuro*-anatomical problems. Concern with the *psychic* was always present. What is probably true is that the professional practice of medicine was not something Freud would have freely chosen. His passion was for understanding the connection between mind and body.[4]

By 1895, with ten years of neurological experience behind him and with some beginning experience in a psychological approach to hysterical disturbances, there were two major works which began to show the framework of Freud's theoretical explanation of psychic functioning. One of them was his publication jointly with Josef Breuer of *Studies on Hysteria*. The second was a detailed model study of the neurological base of psychic activity which was never completed and was in fact unknown until it was discovered in a packet of letters to Wilhelm Fliess which had come into the hands of a second-hand dealer in Nazi Germany. Known simply as The Project, it was first published in 1950.

Studies on Hysteria contains clinical case studies of Breuer's patient Anna O. and of Freud's patients Frau Emmy von. N., Miss Lucy R., Katharina, and Frl. Elisabeth von R. as well as a theoretical discussion by Breuer and a discussion of the therapeutic method of catharsis by Freud. What Breuer and Freud were trying to understand was the syndrome of the conversion hysterias, which have strangely disappeared almost entirely from clinical casebooks in the late twentieth century. A hundred years ago they were the most frequently seen of the psychoneurotic disturbances. In these hysterias emotionally laden data too painful to be tolerated by consciousness are repressed and displaced onto other systems, into amnesic disturbances and frequently onto other organs, resulting for example in hysterical paralyses. The successful repression results always also in a certain secondary gain, so that the patient may gain sympathy for his/her affliction, as well as relief from the distressing pressure of the true emotional content. But this explanation was not so neatly encapsulated in the 1890s.

Hysterical disorders were much discussed among physicians of the late nineteenth century. Charcot had shown that hysterical symptoms could be reproduced artificially by hypnosis; they therefore represented something "real" that might be located in some region of the brain.[5] If so, they would be subject to lawful physiological processes and could not be classified as mere malingering. Earlier and still prevalent theories referred hysteria to a female disorder of the sexual apparatus. Clitorectomies were still being routinely prescribed for female hysterics by respectable physicians.

The cathartic "talking cure" of Breuer was indeed something new. Breuer and Freud had to try to explain the phenomena of repression and conversion. They did so by positing a model of self-regulating psychic energy which functions like the laws of thermodynamics elucidated a half-century earlier by Helmholtz.[6]

According to the Breuer-Freud theory, the organism possesses a certain amount (potential) of energy and of that, a quantum is made available for psychic functions. During sleep it is built up by the brain cells, and during waking activity that energy is discharged in work. (Note the differential relationship between the *unconscious* sleep states and the *conscious* waking states, for this is the core of Freud's later more fully developed "economic standpoint" with regard to mental functioning.) In hysteria, the energy in its form as affect is strangulated and symptoms appear, often in somatic form. When the affect is released through the catharsis of the talking cure the piled-up internal energy can be discharged in a normal way and an optimal, balanced relationship between internal potential and external discharge—a state of constancy—is re-introduced. For Breuer and Freud, the psychic activity of the waking organism had the function of using excess energy in order to equalize potentials.[7] According to this theory, the mind is like an electrical machine.

Many commentators have noted that the theory developed by Breuer typifies the reductionist ideals of Du Bois-Reymond, Helmholtz, Ludwig, and Brücke. Bernfeld called the four famous physiologists the "School of Helmholtz," and a number of later writers followed this usage. In order to show the extent of the physicalist hypothesis Bernfeld published a summary of the theoretical introduction to Brücke's *Lectures in Physiology*:

Organisms differ from dead material wholes in action— machines—in possessing the faculty of assimilation but they are all phenomena of the physical world: systems of atoms, moved by forces, according to the principle of conservation of energy formulated by Helmholtz. The sum of forces (motive forces and potential forces) remains constant in every isolated system. The real causes are symbolized in science by the word 'force'. The less we know about them, the more kinds of forces do we distinguish: mechanical, electrical, magnetic forces, light, heat. Progress in knowledge reduces them to two: attraction and repulsion. This applies as well to the organism man.[8]

Both Breuer and Freud were devoted and inculcated students of Brücke; their friendship with each other had begun in the 1880s when they were research colleagues at the Physiological Institute. Clearly the two men shared at this period the reductionist assumptions of their master. Brücke had honored Breuer by employing him as a family physician. Freud had been passionately happy in the laboratory, and never gave up his affiliative feelings for Brücke. He named his third son for him and in the last decade of his life could still affirm that Brücke had "carried more weight with me than any one else in my whole life."[9]

Other scholars, disagreeing with Bernfeld's hypothesis that the energy theory of the Hysteria Studies originated with Brücke, have pointed out that the so-called School of Helmholtz was actually led by Du Bois-Reymond and that by the 1890s the physiologists had long since given up the goal set by him fifty years before.[10] Henri Ellenberger proposed that a more likely candidate as the source of the energy theory would be Gustav Fechner, the originator of psycho-physics, whose concept of psycho-physical activity was one of the first attempts to re-work Helmholtz's law into a form in which it might be applied to organic life.[11] Freud took over from Fechner in the first place this organicized concept of energy and he then later on appropriated more precisely Fechner's law of stability as his "principle of constancy" (*Beyond the Pleasure Principle*). Breuer was an early follower of Fechner, and Freud acknowledged his influence as early as 1895 in the opening lines of the long unpublished *Project for a Scientific Psychology*, where he declared, "I was always open to the ideas of G. T. Fechner and have followed that thinker upon many important points."[12] So it may be that the physicalist reductionism which began to characterize the terms of Freud's theoretical explanations as early as the *Studies on Hysteria* must be traced most directly to Fechner and not to Brücke.

The quarrel among historians of science concerning the source of Freud's first theories is important because Freud himself has had such enormous influence on twentieth-century thought. But there are reasons why we must separate the physiological issues involved in the search for sources from the names of the men who are thought to have represented them. First, to say that the physiologists had long since given up their goal of reducing mind to matter is not to say that they had abandoned their conviction that it is in fact so, or even the terminological framework into which their research results should fit. Du Bois-Reymond had himself, in his famous 1872 *Ignorabimus* speech, declared that the task was impossible of achievement, but not that it was theoretically untrue.[13]

Secondly, Gustav Fechner, if it is he to whom we are to trace Freud's physicalist theories, was one of the most important and most deeply misunderstood of nineteenth-century figures. He was praised by Haeckel and by Oswald, who thought Fechner gave support to their materialist monist philosophy. Freud adopted his psychophysical theories as the theoretical base of his biological reductionist psychology. Yet William James, who ridiculed Fechner in his 1890 *Principles of Psychology,* afterwards read him more closely and dedicated his 1908 Hibbert Lectures (*A Pluralistic Universe*) to an exposition of Fechner's ingenious and imaginative image of reality in the *Zend-Avesta.* In modern times the pan-psychists (e.g. Charles Hartshorne) have declared Fechner for one of their own. Clearly, Fechner was not just one of those people who are many things to many men. He was in fact a deeply religious man who held a professorship in physics at the University of Leipzig, suffered a three-year-long mental crisis, and emerged from it determined to bring together the truths of his religious experience and his scientific knowledge. He spent the rest of his very long life constructing a model by which he might show, by an *inductive procedure,* how the physically observable aspects of the universe are just one facet of an identical and parallel process in which all is spiritual, and/or all is alive. Fechner's metaphysics has been compared to that of Leibniz; it is actually more Stoic in tenor, the principal thrust being to demonstrate how a natural world which is apparently unensouled is in fact "matter" only in one facet of its being. His method of demonstration was mostly by analogy and he developed many beautiful symbolic images. One of his favorite was that of the convex and the concave surfaces of a curved object. Both have to do with the identical object, but they reflect it in varying ways.

Fechner hit upon his idea of psychophysics as a way of demonstrating to a skeptical world that there is indeed a connection between psyche and soma. Using his colleague E. H. Weber's observation that there is a regular and inverse ratio between the intensity of a repeated external stimulus and the intensity of the experienced sensation, Fechner constructed an elaborate set of logarithmic computations and tables demonstrating, as he thought, his case. Fechner's *Psychophysics* finally regained him serious attention from scientists, after he had been given up as lost, even after his recovery from the long illness. We may reconstruct the reasons why this is so. 1) The Weberian thesis was plausible. It was long taught to beginning students in physiological psychology, who have regarded Fechner as the founder of their discipline. 2) It may be that people in the nineteenth century read only the first volume of the *Psycho-*

physics, just as today. The *Psychophysics* was translated into English only in 1966, and then only the first volume, the second volume being devoted to metaphysics and therefore of little interest, as the editors explained.[14] 3) Fechner maintained a reputation as an excellent physicist, and this reputation carried over into the later period of his very long life.[15] That former reputation must have encouraged the newer generation of scientists who came into prominence after 1870 or so to overlook the metaphysical assumptions that lay behind the last forty-three years of his work.

Two conclusions appear from what has been said. If Freud took from Fechner the theoretical constructs out of which his psychoanalysis was built, it was not because he understood or sympathized with Fechner's own metaphysics.[16] It was because Fechner had tried to suggest how modern discoveries in physics might be applied to understanding the mind-body connection, that Freud was interested in him.[17] Freud's own sympathies were entirely with Brücke and with the positivist philosophy associated with the Physiological Institute. It was only that the physiology of his time was, as Freud later regretfully noted, "too narrowly restricted to histology," and offered no path into the sphere of mental functioning.[18]

The evidence for a second conclusion has yet to be offered. If Jung had not known how indebted Freud felt to Fechner (there are repeated references to Fechner in Freud's writings published before 1912, the year of their break) and if Jung had not studied the version of Fechner's psychophysics taught by the experimental psychologist Wilhelm Wundt, he might have been inclined to look at Fechner's theories with a far less critical eye. Many of Jung's own theories, especially his late concepts of the psychoid, of a microcosmic/ macrocosmic universe, and of synchronicity, are very similar to the theories of Fechner in the sense that they suggest that psychic experience may be used as empirical evidence of a besouled but unseen aspect of reality.

My concern is however not yet with Jung. The aim of this chapter is to show how Freud's philosophical attitude was revealed in the development of his libido theory in the period between 1880–1910. We have reached the year 1895, when *Studies in Hysteria* was published. Within a few months of its appearance Freud was at work on a new scientific project — his plan for integrating psychology into hard science. On April 24 he wrote to Wilhelm Fliess that "I am so deep in the 'Psychology for Neurologists' that it quite consumes me, until I have to break off out of sheer exhaustion. I have never been so intensely preoccupied by anything."[19] On May 25 he wrote further about it:

I am plagued by two ambitions: to see how the theory of mental functioning takes shape in quantitative considerations, a sort of economics of nerve force are introduced into it; and secondly, to extract from psycho-pathology what may be of benefit to normal psychology. Actually a satisfactory general theory of neuropsychotic disturbances is impossible if it cannot be brought into association with clear assumptions about normal mental processes.[20]

The Project turned out to be a very tightly thought out theoretical scheme for explaining human conflict, and with it repression, resistance, and the division of the mind into conscious and unconscious spheres, and what later came to be called "primary" and "secondary" process, all in quantitative, that is, in energic terms.[21] In clinical language Freud's question was: How is it that we human beings are both *for* ourselves and against ourselves? Why can't and don't we do what we really want to do? Why do we forget? Why don't we let ourselves remember? Why do we suffer from conflict? In scientific terms Freud's question was: How can we express these psychological processes as brain function? By way of a proposed answer Freud utilized the structural concept of the 'neurone' which had been introduced by W. Waldeyer in 1891. Freud suggested an energic system in which stimuli arose both without and within the organism and were discharged through the neurones. So long as, in the primitive organism, stimuli arose only exogenously and could be immediately discharged by action (flight, e.g.), the system could function optimally, bringing the tension state back to zero. But in the case of endogenous stimuli arising from *within* the organism (instincts), immediate discharge was not possible, since needs could be met only by arrangement with the objective world. (These "exigencies of life" meant that the sexual drive could be discharged only over time, by finding and gaining the cooperation of another organism.) So the neuronic system must also learn to store or bind energy in order that tension can be maintained until discharge is possible. This means that the optimum energic state is no longer zero but a constant state. That amounts to the secondary process, and accounts for our civilized state as well as for our conflicted state as human beings, for we are always in danger of reverting to primary process functioning under the duress of pain, or in sleep when our dreams continue to reveal our wishful impulses.[22]

The Project occupied Freud for a period of several months. He was up and down about it in his letters to Fliess, sometimes believing that the whole solution was within his purview, at other times realizing that the scheme could not be realized:

> One strenuous night last week...the barriers suddenly lifted, the veils dropped, and it was possible to see from the details of neurosis all the way to the very conditioning of consciousness. Everything fell into place, the cogs meshed, the thing really seemed to be a machine which in a moment would run by itself. (October 20)

> This psychology is really an incubus—skittles and mushroom-hunting are certainly much healthier pasttimes. All I was trying to do was to explain defence, but I found myself explaining something from the very heart of nature. (August 16)

At last, on November 29, Freud had given it up:

> I no longer understand the state of mind in which I concocted the psychology; I cannot conceive how I came to inflict it on you...it seems to me to have been a kind of aberration.

The manuscript drafts which had been sent off to Fliess in Berlin were never returned, nor, apparently, requested. After Fliess's death Freud's letters to Fliess, along with the manuscripts, were sold to a second-hand dealer and were rescued only at the onset of the war by Princess Marie Bonaparte, long a colleague and close confidant of Freud. They could be posthumously printed only in 1950. The attitude of first generation Freudian analysts and scholars toward this work, and the psycho-biological philosophical stance which it reveals, has been that it represents the culmination of the period in which Freud the physiologist and neurologist was at work on the problems of the mind. It was also a turning point. Ernst Kris thought that it was Freud's own self-analysis, begun a year or so later, which "brought about a shift in his interests. Insight into the conditions in which individual conflict arose in the course of the interaction between the child and its environment...meant that the need to explain psychological processes by immediate physiological processes had lost its urgency."[23] Ernest Jones suggested that Freud was perhaps in the Project "releasing his early, and so thoroughly checked, tendency to philosophize." But he was gradually liberated from the illusion that one might bring order into "the apparent chaos of mental process" through brain physiology, and the episode was completely finished by 1897.[24] From then on, Freud might use the *language* of physiology but he really meant by it a psychological dynamics which must be understood independently of biology.[25]

Some support for this position might be taken from Freud's statement for instance in the 1900 *Interpretation of Dreams* that "we are justified, in my view, in giving free rein to our speculations so long as we retain the coolness of our judgment and do not mistake the scaffolding for the building."[26] But it is also the case that in Chapter 7 of the *Interpretation of Dreams* Freud reiterates in psychological form essentially the same theories which he had tested out five years earlier in the Project.[27]

Ernest Jones admitted, and this is the crucial point of interest, that:

Two opinions in this context...Freud held all his life. One was that there was no evidence of psychical processes occurring apart from physiological ones: that no mind could exist apart from the brain....The other was that physical processes must precede psychical ones: information reaching the mind, whether from the outer world through the sense organs or from the body through the chemical stimuli it provides, must begin as a physical excitation.[28]

In spite of the interpretive work of Freud's first pupils and colleagues to the effect that the mature theory of psychoanalysis, the metapsychology, as Freud called it, made use of terminology analogous to biology while it really described a science which should be understood on its own terms, there has been increasing insistence in recent years that Freud never abandoned the biological standpoint of his early period. I refer especially to the monumental work of science historian Frank Sulloway, whose 1979 book, *Freud, Biologist of the Mind*, has changed the face of Freud scholarship. The great mass of evidence presented by Sulloway has to do with the time period after 1910, when Freud developed his theories of phylogenetic origins and his devotion to Lamarckian evolutionary principles. What Sulloway showed is that while Freud gave up on tracing the neurological pathways of psychic activity he continued to embrace a theory of the biological and evolutionary origins of mind, utilizing for this purpose Ernst Haeckel's theory that ontogeny recapitulates phylogeny.[29] Freud was more apt as a philosopher than his pupils insofar as he realized that our interpretations of psychological functioning necessarily rest on *assumptions* about the ultimate nature of mind. At the same time, as Sulloway has pointed out, he *taught* his pupils to think psychologically, and thus effectively, if perhaps unconsciously, obscured the extent of his reliance on biological theses.[30]

The focus of this chapter is rather more on the developmental phase of Freud's theory in the period before 1910. The break between Freud and Jung at that time meant practically that Freud's influence on Jung's own thinking nearly ceased. The most important features of Freud's theory were by then however complete. What remains is to show how the neurologically formulated theory of psychic energy in the Project evolved into the sexual libido of psychoanalytic theory. We know that Freud's main experiences with neurosis had been with the hysterias, and that he was seeking to understand the conflict and the defense against it which seemed to characterize symptom formation. We also know that he was inclined from early training and from inner disposition to seek a solution resting on *physis* — on matter alone. He had gotten as far in the Project as to propose a two-phase system of mental functioning. In order to gratify the endogenous drive impulses the organism had to learn to delay activity moving toward gratification until suitable objects in the environment could be found, so that constant tension accompanied by withholding of discharge became the usual state of the organism.[31] What this amounts to is an early theory of instinct.

By 1897 it had become clear to Freud that *all* the hysterias owed their etiololgy not to early traumas in which the girl child had been actually sexually seduced by the father, but by the regularly recurring and repressed fantasy that this had been so. Freud had nearly lighted on the Oedipus complex. He wrote to Fliess on September 21:

> Let me tell you straight away the great secret which has been slowly dawning on me in recent months. I no longer believe in my *neurotica*. . . . [It seemed unreasonable to assume that parental perversion was so general a phenomenon; also, as Freud realized, there is no reality testing in the unconscious.] Now I do not know where I am, as I have failed to reach theoretical understanding of repression and its play of forces.[32]

By 1901, in the famous case of Dora, he was able to analyze a set of complex relationships down to repressed jealousy and longing for the father. In commenting on the case Freud says:

> I was . . . anxious to show that sexuality does not simply intervene like a *deus ex machina*, on one single occasion . . . but that it provides the motive power for every single symptom, and for every single manifestation of a symptom.

...I can only repeat over and over again—for I never find it otherwise—that sexuality is the key to the problem of psychoneuroses and of the neuroses in general.[33]

Freud had generalized from the clinical data of the hysterias to *all* neurotic disturbances. He had the great satisfaction of realizing that profound symptomatic disturbances can originate from things that did not happen but which the patient wishes had happened. Fantasy is something real in itself, and if its recurrence in a specific form is general, there must be some law governing its recurrence. That law was the law of instinctive sexuality. With the hypothesis that *infantile fantasy* causes *neurosis* Freud had fairly entered the realm of depth psychology, a frightening step, perhaps, for a neurobiologist.

But the theory of sexual libido was to serve still another purpose, this one philosophical. No one should mistake the significance of his discovery as a purely psychological theory, "incapable of solving a pathological problem":

It is the therapeutic technique alone that is purely psychological; the theory does not by any means fail to point out that neuroses have an organic basis.... *No one, probably, will be inclined to deny the sexual function the character of an organic factor,* and it is the sexual function that I look upon as the foundation of hysteria and that of the psychoneuroses in general.[34] (my italics)

We are now in a position to understand the extreme importance for Freud of the theory of sexual instinctual forces as the etiological factor of neurosis and the central organizing factor in normal psychic functioning. It enabled him to enter the realm of the purely psychological, while at the same time he remained firmly anchored on the philosophical base of organic derivations. Jung once many years later remarked, "I had a strong intuition that for him sexuality was a sort of numinosum."[35] That would indeed be correct. The theory of sexual libido represented for Freud his deep inner conviction that the activity of the human psyche is reducible to biological, evolutionary origins and subject finally to the same energic law that governs both organic and non-organic matter.

By the time the epoch-making "Three Essays on the Theory of Sexuality" was published in 1905 Freud was quite settled about the matter and could state with all emphasis:

I do not merely mean that the energy of the sexual instinct makes a contribution to the forces that maintain the pathological manifestations....I mean expressly to assert that that contribution is the most important and only constant source of energy of the neurosis and that in consequence the sexual life of the persons in question is expressed in these symptoms.[36]

How could this clear evidence of Freud's philosophical position have been so far overseen by a generation of pupils and interested observers? The biological ideals which lay in the background of the libido theory had been somewhat obscured. The Project had never been published. The trauma theory, which had rooted neurosis in external rather than in internal causes, had only recently been abandoned and the significance of the change was not well understood. Add to that the prurient associations which are probably never entirely absent from considerations of sexuality, and it is understandable that the theory of sexual libido should become a public scandal rather more easily than it could be understood as a profound statement about mental origins.

2

Toward a Genetic Theory of Libido

Jung was perfectly clear about the philosophical significance of Freud's concept of sexual libido. In the opening paragraphs of Part II of his 1912 *Symbols of Transformation*, the section where he begins to unveil for the first time his deep divergence from Freud's thought, Jung wrote:

> Originally taken from the sexual sphere, this word [libido] has become the most frequent technical expression of psychoanalysis. . . . It is sufficiently comprehensive and rich in meaning *to characterize the real nature of the psychical entity which it includes*. . . . It can be said that the conception of the libido as developed in the new work of Freud and of his school has functionally the same significance in the biological territory as has the conception of energy since the time of Robert Mayer in the physical realm.[1] (my italics)

We may expect to discover that Jung's separation from Freud was marked by the development of his own view on the ultimate nature of the psychic, at first with regard to the nature and origin of libido, or psychic energy, and then with regard to the ultimate *structures* to which what is psychic can be reduced, namely the archetypes. Jung's theories will have emerged gradually out of his own clinical experience with patients and out of his own self-discovery, two closely related though not identical procedures. A certain portion of every analysis is strictly technical, a matter of following known rules and guaranteeing protected boundaries in the therapeutic relationship. But the challenge presented by the patient will finally bring a moment when the analyst must speak from the heart his/her own inner truth. The healing moment when two souls are open to each other is also the moment when the true basis of one's own belief system is revealed. It will have been in the course of this process, in pursuit of his professional goals, that Jung's own philosophy emerged.

I am going to analyze the steps in which Jung's concept of the archetype developed in reverse order, beginning with philosophical conclusions, but I want to be clear that I don't think these conclusions sprang up as rational postulates. They were born out of inner meditation and clinical experience. There are passages in Jung's writing which show us that he was aware of the fact that philosophical assumptions were a necessary part of this process but that he tried not to let intellectual criticism take charge of inner intuitions and feelings. In a 1929 essay he wrote:

> All too easily does self-criticism poison one's naïveté, that priceless possession, or rather gift, which no creative person can do without. At any rate, philosophical criticism has helped me to see that every psychology—my own included—has the character of a subjective confession. And yet I must prevent my critical powers from destroying my creativeness. I know well enough that every word I utter carries with it something of myself—of my special and unique self with its particular history and its own particular world. Even when I deal with empirical data I am necessarily speaking about myself.[2]

If Jung now proposed theoretical postulates which would fly in the face of scientific fashion and even scientific knowledge, we must recognize in him a kind of stubborn faithfulness to inner experience and inner feelings and a willingness to make space in theoretical structures for those feelings.

Jung's objections to Freud's psychological theory, as they appeared in Chapter 2 of Part II of the 1912 *Symbols of Transformation* and in the third of his lectures on "The Theory of Psychoanalysis" delivered the following year at Fordham University, were as follows:[3]

1. The theory that affluxes and displacements of sexual libido account for neurotic and psychotic disturbances is inadequate. It is true for the hysterical neuroses, where the unconscious material regularly reveals repressed sexual fantasies and the transference phenomena to the analyst are also sexual in nature. But the concept of sexual libido cannot account for the complete loss of reality as it is observed in schizophrenic patients. The energy held back in the unconscious psyche by reason of repressions of sexual origin cannot be so great as to swallow up reality, as well as all capacity to connect in an affectively appropriate manner to others.

(Here Jung relied on his long experience with psychiatric patients at the famous Burghölzli Clinic under Eugen Bleuler. The bulk of his very early psychiatric experience had been with psychotic patients, whereas Freud had the greatest experience with neurotic patients of his private practice.)[4]

2. In place of what Jung called Freud's "descriptive" definition of instincts, in which, among a "bundle" of instincts which included hunger, sex, and so on, the disturbances of the sexual libido were made to account for mental illness, Jung now proposed what he termed a "genetic definition of libido."[5]

We should imagine, he said (and here Jung admitted as well as Freud finally did that we are dealing with an unknown factor and are positing a mere model or counter) that the libido must originally have been unitary in nature and has in fact basically always remained so. If the original impulse of the primal libido was sexual in nature, then along the course of its evolutionary path that libido has split off into other functions of the organism in such a way that "libido which was originally employed in the production of ova and spermatozoa is now firmly organized in the function of nest building, for instance, and can no longer be employed otherwise. We are compelled to include every striving and every desire, as well as hunger, in this conception. . . . We are seeking to replace the reciprocal action of co-ordinated psychic faculties by an energy conceived to be homogeneous."[6]

If the psychic libido is conceived as a unified, progressive force leading from the more complex organisms and dividing off from itself the tributary energies needed to maintain those complex functions, then the solution to the problem of loss of reality in the psychoses may be solved. The sense of "reality" of the so-called ego functions lies somewhere along the line of a continuum in the advanced stages of a progressing, evolutionary libido. The "loss of reality" in psychosis may then be understood as a regression on the path of that libido, a turning around or away from reality and a retreat into the unconscious realm of fantasy, that is, into a more primitive level of psychic organization. Sexuality is thus not the main thing.

Whether or not Jung's theory of psychic energy offers a more suitable clinical model than Freud's for understanding psychotic illness as well as less severe mental disturbances has been disputed over the course of the twentieth-century between adherents of the two schools. But I think this is not the main point. There are problems of fact and problems of philosophical significance bound up with Jung's interpretation of the differences between Freud and himself.

It was incorrect for Jung to describe Freud's theory as "descriptive" and his own as "genetic." Freud's theory was nothing if it was not genetic, in the sense that the term *genetic* refers to a theory of common origins. I have outlined the evidence for this in the period up to the end of Jung's relationship with Freud in the preceding pages, and for the period after 1910 the weight of evidence is overwhelming. A doubtful reader may consult Sulloway's book, *Freud: Biologist of the Mind*.

In 1911 Freud published his essay on "The Two Principles in Mental Functioning" in which he delineated the reality principle as a secondary afflux of the pleasure principle, but as early as 1900 he was describing in all clarity what he meant by primary process, as well as his conviction that "the unconscious is the true psychical reality":[7]

> All that I insist upon is the idea that the activity of the *first* Ψ-system is directed toward securing the *free discharge* of the quantities of excitation, while the *second system*, by means of the cathexes emanating from it, succeeds in *inhibiting* this discharge and in transforming the cathexis into a quiescent one, no doubt with a simultaneous raising of its level.[8]

I am certain that what was really at stake between the two men in their struggle over the nature of psychic libido was the ancient mind-body problem as it surfaces in the biological sphere. For the person who believes in a final reduction of life processes to the properties of inorganic matter it is always a problem to explain the unique facts of human consciousness ("the reality function"), human creativity, and human culture. Freud proposed that survival entails compromise and struggle and that culture and consciousness are accidents of the evolutionary process.

For the person who believes in God and in the transcendent qualities of the human mind which intuits God's existence, the problem is to explain how it happens that human beings are connected to lower life forms and to the dead matter of the earth they inhabit. The usual solution to this dilemma has been sought by declaring that life itself is unique—that there is a break-off (or a break-in) point where life forms intervene in the accidental course of activity in the universe, and that life forms themselves may be seen as developing or evolving in an unconscious but purposeful fashion toward ever higher forms of consciousness.

This is the program which has been undertaken by the vitalistic biologists (Driesch and others), by theories of emergent evolution (Morgan and Alexander) and by the process philosophers (Whitehead) in a modified form. For them, mind and purpose are present with life itself. That this is the sort of idea which Jung had in mind can be proved by comparing two identical passages in his epoch-making book, *Symbols of Transformation*, one from the 1912 edition and one from the revised 1952 edition, where what he means becomes much clearer:

> Because we have already arrived at the daring assumption that the libido, which was employed originally in the exclusive service of egg and seed production, now appears firmly organized in the function of nest building, and can no longer be employed otherwise; similarly this conception forces us to relate it to every desire, including hunger. For now we can no longer make any essential distinction between the will to build a nest and the will to eat. This view brings us to a conception of libido, which extends over the boundaries of the physical sciences into a philosophical aspect — to a conception of the will in general. I must give this bit of psychological "Voluntarismus" into the hands of the philosophers for them to manage. For the rest I refer to the words of Schopenhauer relating to this.

> Having once made the bold conjecture that the libido which was originally employed in the production of ova and spermatozoa is now firmly organized in the function of nest-building, for instance, and can no longer be employed otherwise, we are compelled to regard every striving and every desire, including hunger and instinct however understood, as equally a phenomenon of energy.
>
> This view leads to a conception of libido which expands into a conception of *intentionality* in general. As the above quotation from Freud shows [a quotation from the Schreber case] we know far too little about the nature of human instincts and their psychic dynamism to risk giving priority to any one instinct. We would be better advised, therefore, when speaking of libido, to understand it as an energy-value which is able to communicate itself to any field of activity whatsoever, be it power, hunger, hatred, sexuality, or religion, without ever being itself a specific instinct. As Schopenhauer says [WWI, Haldane & Kemp, 1:145 modified]: "The Will as a thing-in-itself is quite different from its phenomenal manifestation, and entirely free from all forms of phenomenality, which it assumes only when it becomes manifest, and which therefore affect its objectivity only, and are foreign to the Will itself."[9]

Jung continues on in this passage to draw parallels from ancient philosophy to the sense of "creative force" which is subjectively experienced by man as his will—to Hesiod's Eros, to Phanes, the "shining one" of Orphic cosmogony, to Priapus of the cult of Dionysus, to the Neoplatonic world soul. In each case there is an energic force which reigns over or governs the phenomenal or material reality.

With the theme of intentionality in the libido, and the connection between will and its manifestation in Schopenhauer I am going to break off the discussion of the quarrel over libido between Freud and Jung. Intentionality is the theme of Part III of this essay, and I shall return to it there. Here I am bent on showing what Jung meant by archetypes. We cannot talk about the structural elements of the psyche without talking about the nature of psychic interaction. Soul moves, as even Plato finally had to admit. But neither can we talk about libido or psychic energy without indicating whether those energic processes should refer to mind or to matter. By proposing a unitary, genetic concept of libido, which is progressively accumulating more complex functions on its evolutionary path, and by referring to Schopenhauer, Jung tipped his hand that the ultimate structural referent in his theory would not be material.

3

From Libido to Archetypes: Reduction to Final Cause

Jung's closest pupils have typically begun their exposition of what Jung meant by the "collective unconscious" by explaining that Freud believed only in a "personal unconscious," that is, in an unconscious psyche which consisted solely of contents which had been repressed as being unacceptable to the conscious point of view.[1] Presumably they were following Jung's own statements on the matter. What is implied by the statement is that Freud's concept of the psyche does not reach to the roots of human experience.

The statement does not, however, accord with the facts. I have shown in the foregoing pages that Freud was concerned from the beginning with a meta-psychological understanding of the human person, reaching beyond the sphere of the individual back to the earliest life forms. He continued these interests throughout his life. In 1913 he published *Totem and Taboo*, and in 1939, the last year of his life, his *Moses and Monotheism* continued to expound a scheme of human origins based on ontogeny/phylogeny with a Lamarckian theory of the inheritance of culturally acquired traits. He insisted on his theory in spite of being warned by his pupil and biographer Ernest Jones that it no longer accorded with current biological knowledge.[2]

The Jungian doctrine that Freud had a theory only of a "personal unconscious" is so manifestly false that I propose to submit it to analytical interpretation. It may be a psuedo-fact which stands in the place of a real fact which is however concealed.[3] I suggest that the real statement is at three levels: 1) Freud knew only a "personal unconscious" [means]: 2) Freud's theory did not reach the depths of the psyche, [means]: 3) A biological explanation of psychic origins is not an acceptable explanation. Another level of explanation must be sought.

Jung's *own* search for a level of explanation that would satisfy inner intuitions as well as the empirical dictates of clinical experi-

131

ence may conveniently be studied under three headings: A Phylo-genetic Viewpoint, The Constructive or Prospective Technique, and Fantasy and Symbol.

a. A Phylogenetic Viewpoint

The premise of *Symbols of Transformation* had been that there is a level of the unconscious psyche that must go beyond the realm of the individual's experience in the world, and that this realm of what is beyond the individual may be discovered by comparing the images which appear in fantasies and dreams with the motifs of our mythological and legendary heritage. The terminology which Jung initially used to describe this more ancient, more impersonal, "col-lective" part of the psyche was that of evolutionary biological theory, particularly the theories of phylogenetic heritage which had been made vastly popular in the previous generation by the work of Ernst Haeckel—his famous "biogenetic law."

According to Haeckel's theory, we may observe evolutionary history in the ontogenetic development of the individual. Ontogeny recapitulates phylogeny. For Haeckel, it was the *adult*, not the infantile forms of our evolutionary forbears that are seen in the stages of fetal development. Darwin, and most other biologists, differed sharply from Haeckel on this score. If it is only the tran-sient, infantile stages of development that are observed, then noth-ing about the principle of *chance* as the prime factor of evolutionary change is violated. If on the other hand the adult forms of an earlier evolutionary stage are thought to be recapitulated, then it means that evolution proceeds in successive stages, each change being an "addition to the end of an unaltered ancestral ontogeny."[4] We would thus quite literally carry within us the evolutionary history of the world.

Haeckel supported his belief in the ontogenetic recapitulation of adult ancestral forms with a firm faith in the selective (Lamarckian) inheritance of acquired characters. Stephen Gould has shown that the ready acceptance of Haeckel's theories in late nineteenth-century German-speaking countries was due in great part to their resem-blance to the postulates of the earlier *Naturphilosophie*. The two main postulates of this pre-Darwinian romantic biology were 1) Develop-mentalism. Nature is in flux but moving always in a hierarchy of being from lower toward ever higher forms. 2) The unity of nature and its laws. We are linked in essential, even organic, bonds of unity to all of nature.[5]

Even after the re-discovery of the Mendelian laws of inheritance in 1900 exploded all scientific justification for ontogenetic recapitulation of adult forms, and for Lamarckian inheritance of acquired characters, the idea of recapitulation has continued to exercise a powerful influence on theories of child development, criminal anthropology, racism, and not least, on theories of the unconscious. Freud remained committed to recapitulation at a psychological (not a morphological) level.[6]

With Jung the case is more complex. He used the language of recapitulation in his early writings,[7] he proposed a "genetic" theory of libido in 1912–14, and he continued to speak of phylogenetic stages or modes of thought and development. But it is unclear whether he meant to indicate his literal adherence to biological theories, that is, that historical levels of thought are connected to brain structure, or whether the term is meant as a metaphor. There is some evidence that Jung's thought developed from the former to the latter view.

Gould thinks that Jung's views of phylogenetic development lead finally to a theory of archetypes that is "static," not dynamic, and therefore irrelevant in a biological sense.[8] In philosophical language one might rephrase that conclusion as a question: does "phylogenetic" refer to physiological development or to a priori existing patterns in the mind? Good Jungians would say, both! It is a matter of the "identity of opposites." Jung himself said something like that too, but the question can nevertheless not be satisfactorily answered in these terms. His mysterious and paradoxical formulation of an underlying identity relationship between apparent polar opposites is itself an essential postulate of *Naturphilosophie*, expressing faith in the underlying unity of a "Nature" which is incompletely understood. It can be deeply satisfying as a symbolic expression of that faith, but it is not a true answer. Jung was never less precise in the explanation of his theories than with regard to his concept of the archetype. We ought, I think, to press as closely as possible toward an understanding of the ingredients which comprised his concept.

In a 1916 essay on dream psychology Jung wrote:

> I would like to emphasize that the comparison of typical dream motifs with those of mythology suggests the idea—already put forward by Nietzsche—that dream thinking should be regarded as a phylogentically older mode of thought.... Just as the body bears the traces of its phylogenetic development, so also does the human mind. Hence there is nothing

surprising about the possibility that the figurative language of dreams is a survival from an archaic mode of thought.[9]

By 1928, Jung's concept of the collective unconscious and of archetypes had already been explicitly set forth. In the 1928 edition of his essay, "The Psychology of the Unconscious," he wrote:

> The collective unconscious, being the repository of man's experience, is an image of the world which has taken aeons to form. In this image certain features, the archetypes or dominants, have crystallized out in the course of time. They are the ruling powers, the gods, images of the dominant laws and principles, and of typical, regularly occurring events in the soul's cycle of experience. In so far as these images *laid down in the brain* are more or less faithful replicas of psychic events, their archetypes, that is, their general characteristics which have been emphasized through the accumulation of similar experiences, also correspond to certain general characteristics of the physical world. Archetypal images can therefore be taken metaphorically, as intuitive concepts for physical phenomena.[10] (my italics)

In this passage there seems to be a clear, historical theory of recapitulation along mechanistic Haeckelian lines, with Lamarckian modes of inheritance implied by the phrase "accumulation of similar experience" and "in the course of time." Yet in the final fifth edition the words italicized by me, "laid down in the brain" were deleted. Jung was apparently not willing to locate psyche's activity unequivocally in the brain.

A few pages farther on in the same essay Jung commented again on the phylogenetic significance of an archetypal image:

> The animal symbol points specifically to the extra-human, the transpersonal; for the contents of the collective unconscious are not only the residues of archaic, specifically human modes of functioning, but also the residues of functions from man's animal ancestry, whose duration in time was infinitely greater than the relatively brief epoch of specifically human experience. . . . If . . . we take the figures of the unconscious as collective psychic phenomena or functions, this hypothesis in no way violates our intellectual conscience. It offers a rationally acceptable solution, and at the same time a possible method of effecting a settlement with the activated residues of our racial history.[11]

These lines offer a clue that the phylogenetic hypothesis was not adopted with a view toward biological reductionism, but rather because it was intellectually respectable (as Jung thought), plausible in terms of evolutionary theory, and seemingly, a passage over from the realm of mind to the realm of body. (It must be noted that it was not phylogeny that became scientifically disreputable with the advent of neo-Darwinian theories, but Haeckel's recapitulation theory which had accompanied his popularization of phylogeny.) Jung first adopted the theory together with Freud in the first decade of the century when the Mendelian laws may still not have been generally understood. It is doubtful whether Jung ever separated the two aspects of the ontogeny/phylogeny theory. That human beings have a phylogenetic history cannot be doubted. *In what form* we continue to possess that history may well be questioned, and it is around this question that the problem of ontogeny, as well as the theory of archetypes revolves.

One of Jung's most helpful clarifications about his thinking on the relationship between brain and psyche was offered in two letters of similar content late in his life.[12] "I am personally convinced that our mind corresponds with the physiological life of the body, but the way in which it is connected with the body is for obvious reasons unintelligible. If a certain part of the brain is excised, a certain psychic function ceases to operate. But what is it that ceases to function? It is quite possible that you have only destroyed the transmitter of that function, as if you have taken away the telephone apparatus which does not mean you have killed its owner." Again, why is it if the psyche really belongs to the body that "consciousness has so exceedingly little direct information of the body from within?...Of a psyche dwelling in its own body one should expect at least that it would be immediately and thoroughly informed of any change of conditions therein. Its not being the case demands some explanation." Perhaps, said Jung (and I remind the reader that this is late Jung, mentioning issues not yet touched on in this essay), we should give up time-space categories altogether when dealing with psychic existence. Perhaps "the brain might be a transformer station, in which the relatively infinite tension or intensity of the psyche proper is transformed into perceptible frequencies or 'extensions.'"

I have moved forty years ahead of the period between 1912 and 1920 which is the focus of attention just now. I am trying to discover the critical factors which went into Jung's concept of archetypes, as it was finally presented in 1919. A hypothesis of phylogenetic human origins is certainly one of those factors. The phylogenetic theory was a vehicle for Jung's genetic theory of libido and the basis on which he could object to Freud's "descriptive" theory, ostensibly on clinical grounds but actually on philosophical grounds. The phylogenetic theory made room for a "historical" view of the psyche. (I put the word *historical* in quotation marks because Jung's view of history was always entirely subjective; the historical psyche reached far back beyond the realm of here and now in the body and the world to a kingdom conditioned by longing dreams, heroic acts, and memories of a condition of fulfillment never to be obtained in the narrow sphere of individual existence.) The phylogenetic theory was entirely familiar to the intelligentsia of the early twentieth century and it was intellectually respectable. If, as those letters of the 1950s indicate, Jung conceived the body, and physical existence in general, as a medium into the visible world of time and space for a psyche existing independently of body, then it would be possible for him to defend the realities of body and mind simultaneously. Knowing that Jung was a devoted student of Schopenhauer in his student days we might not be surprised to find out that this was so. What would *not* be possible is a reduction of psyche to somatic drive forces along the lines which Freud proposed.

There is something more to be said about Jung's theory of instinct, as it developed from his earlier concept of phylogenetic origins. But his comments on instinct are almost always directly connected with the archetype, and I am going to delay discussion until after the final theory of the archetype has been treated. At that time I will also mention the work which Konrad Lorenz was doing during this same period to elucidate the behavioral patterns of birds, and the struggles of Adolf Portmann to be both a good biologist and a good friend to Jung.

b. Fantasy, Symbol, and the Prospective Method

From the very beginning of his depth psychoanalytic writing Jung reported views on the *meaning of fantasy* and on *analytic technique* which were in sharp contrast to those held by Freud.[13] The images which appear to us in dreams and fantasy are finally benign, believed Jung, and hold within themselves the secret intentions of the developing human person. In accordance with that belief analytic technique must proceed on a *prospective* or *constructive* course to discover the developmental intention which underlies the symptom. Jung's statements on these matters even in early writings are decidedly lacking in the diffidence one would expect with an idea that was still being explored. The prospective and symbolic approach must have been a part of his working method for several years before he was writing about it; he must in fact never have followed Freud's analytic technique even during the years when the two men felt closest to each other.

I must give prefatory notice that most of what I am going to talk about here belongs, properly, organized, in Part III of this essay, on the individuation process, because it has to do with Jung's sense of the movement of the psyche toward a goal which is present as a potential in even the earliest stages of life. However the symbolic and prospective method, together with the phylogenetic theory, are the two most important ingredients that went into Jung's theory of archetypes. If we are to understand correctly what Jung meant by archetypes we must study Jung's views on the symbolic method at this point.

1. In his 1912 *Symbols of Transformation* Jung had already developed the hypothesis that the regressing libido, activated by the symptoms of psychological crisis, or even by a let-up in the kind of directed thinking which characterizes our most concentrated work, releases a kind of fantastic or symbolic thinking which must be considered a historical or archaic level of mind:

> By means of phantastic thinking, directed thinking is connected with the oldest foundations of the human mind, which have been for a long time beneath the threshold of consciousness. . . . The products arising from the unconscious are related to the mythical . . . it may be concluded that the soul possesses in some degree historical strata.[14]

> According to my available but as yet unpublished material, a remarkably archaic and at the same time generally applicable character seems to appertain to infantile phantasy, quite comparable with the products of dementia praecox. It does not seem improbable that through regression at this age those same associations of elements and analogies are reawakened which formerly constituted the archaic idea of the world.[15]

2. At the same time as Jung spoke of *regression* of libido to a "historical" level of archaic fantasy, he began to speak of the *progression* of libido as purposive:

> I think that we should view with philosophic admiration the strange paths of the libido and should investigate the purposes of its circuitous ways.

It is not too much to say that we have herewith dug up the erotic root, and yet the problem remains unsolved. Were there not bound up with that a mysterious purpose, probably of the greatest biological meaning, then certainly twenty centuries would not have yearned for it with such intense longing.[16]

If the libido itself is purposive, then we must suppose that the psychological illness of the patient is also purposive. We must not think of neurosis as merely pathological in a negative sense:

If we do use psychoanalysis, we must go along with the regressive fantasies of our patients....No one has ever thought of seeing in the neurosis an attempt at healing, or consequently, of attributing to the neurotic formations a quite special teleological significance....From this follows the inquiring and expectant attitude of psychoanalysis towards the neurosis.[17]

3. If the libido is progressive and purposeful, and if even its regressions in times of illness, danger, or life events which are otherwise of great importance is ultimately of benign intent, then the subjective or inner point of view is the one which has to be considered above all else. Jung termed this subjective view the *symbolic approach*. At least seven years before he introduced the term *archetype* Jung was writing about the significance of the symbol:

The symbol considered from the standpoint of actual truth is misleading, indeed, but it is *psychologically true*, because it was and is the bridge to all the greatest achievements of humanity.[18]

Anyone who understands *Faust* "objectively", from the causal standpoint, is—to take a drastic example—like a man who tries to understand a Gothic cathedral under its historical, technical, and finally its mineralogical aspect. But— where is the meaning of the marvelous edifice? Where is the answer to that all-important question: what goal of redemption did the Gothic man seek in his work, and how have we to understand his work subjectively, in and through ourselves? To the scientific mind this seems an idle question... it conflicts with the causal principle, for its intention is clearly speculative and constructive....If we want to understand anything psychological, we must bear in mind that all knowledge is subjectively conditioned. The world is not "objective" only; it is also as we see it....Of course it is possible to understand Faust and Cologne Cathedral that way...[but] the main value of a work of art does not lie in its causal development but in its living effect upon ourselves.[19]

The Viennese school interprets the psychological symbol semiotically, as a sign or token of certain primitive psycho-sexual processes. Its method is analytical and causal. The Zürich school recognizes the scientific possibility of such a conception but denies its exclusive validity for it does not interpret the psychological symbol semiotically only but also symbolistically, that is, it attributes a positive value to the symbol...its chief importance lies in the fact that it has meaning for the actual present and for the future.[20]

It is in the creation of fantasies that we find the unitive function we are seeking...imagination is nevertheless the creative source of all that has made progress possible to human life....If we regard...[fantasies] as authentic symbols, then they provide the directive signs we need in order to carry on our lives in harmony with ourselves....The symbol is not a sign that veils something everybody knows...on the contrary, it represents an attempt to elucidate, by means of analogy, something that still belongs entirely to the domain of the unknown, or something that is yet to be.[21]

4. Jung very soon made use of his underlying views that the libido is purposive and that the symptom, the fantasy image, and the dream have an objective and directive significance for the individual in his *prospective* or *constructive* method. The prospective method is even today the hallmark of the Jungian analyst. In one form or another, most of the current discussion among Jungians, now often stimulated by the work of other analytical schools, has to do with the compatibility of the prospective method with other approaches. The fact is, other approaches cannot easily be combined, since their differing philosophical assumptions require a different interpretive vocabulary on the part of the analyst. The bald truth of this has, I think, scarcely been seen. Without the prospective method what is distinctively "Jungian" goes by the way. Jung's therapeutic question, "I wonder what the dream is wanting from you," or "We must discover what it is your life was meant to be" was quite apparently in use long before he made doctrinal for-

mulations about the structure of the unconscious and used the term *archetype*. As early as 1913 Jung wrote:

> Without presuming to say that dreams have prophetic fore-
> sight, it is nevertheless possible that we might find, in this
> subliminal material, combinations of future events which are
> subliminal simply because they have not yet attained the
> degree of clarity necessary for them to become conscious....
> The future tendencies of the patient are elaborated with the
> help of these teleological components of the dream. If this
> work is successful, the patient passes out of the treatment
> and out of the semi-infantile transference relationship into a
> life which has been carefully prepared within him, which he
> has chosen himself, and to which, after mature deliberation,
> he can declare himself committed.[22]

> The symbolic evaluation of sexual fantasies in the later
> stages [of analysis] necessarily leads, not to a reduction of
> the personality to primitive tendencies, but to a broadening
> and continuous development of the patient's attitude; that
> is, it tends to make his thinking richer and deeper, thus
> giving him what has always been one of man's most power-
> ful weapons in the struggle for adaptation. By following this
> new course consistently, I have come to the realization that
> the religious and philosophical driving forces—what Scho-
> penhauer calls the "metaphysical need" of man—must
> receive positive consideration during the analytical work.[23]

By the following year, in his, to my mind very important but much
neglected little essay, "On Psychological Understanding," Jung had
made a crucial transition in his thinking from pragmatic consideration of man's "metaphysical need" to the positing of actual structures in the unconscious mind which are constitutive determinants
of psychic functioning:

> The *carte blanche* which the constructive standpoint gives to
> subjective factors naturally seems to the "scientific" mind an
> utter violation of reason. But it can protest only so long as
> the construction is not admitted to be subjective. Construc-
> tive understanding also *analyses*, but it does not *reduce*. It
> breaks the system down into *typical* components....From the
> comparative analysis of many systems the typical formations
> can be discovered. If one can speak of reduction at all, it is
> simply a reduction to general types, but not to some general

principle arrived at inductively or deductively, such as "sexuality" or "striving for powers." This paralleling with other typical formations serves only to widen the basis on which the construction is to rest. At the same time, it serves the purpose of objective communication.[24]

Here we see the true function of the "typical formations" or "typical components" which Jung would a few years later call "archetypes." They are to replace Freud's reduction to "sexuality" or primary process libido and Adler's "striving for power" with an ultimate interpretive principle based on the human being's ancient and ever-present dream of transcendence. We should take the subjective view seriously. We should take the psyche on its own terms, and even in its own language.

For the time being, however, Jung admitted that he had no real theoretical basis for the kind of work he was doing. Mention of the "Zürich School" seemed to re-inforce his feeling that he was at least not alone with his methodology, even though he could give as yet no thorough account of his theory:

> The work of the Zürich School gives careful and detailed records of the individual material. There we find countless typical formations which show obvious analogies with mythological formations. . . At present all we know is that... [they] are fantasy structures which...are based essentially on the activity of the unconscious.[25]

> The Zürich School has in view the end result of analysis, and it regards the fundamental thoughts and impulses of the unconscious as symbols, indicative of future development. We must admit, however, that there is *no scientific justification* for such a procedure, because our present-day science is based wholly on causality. But causality is only one principle, because the mind lives by aims as well.[26]

c. "Instinct and the Unconscious"

In 1919 Jung overcame the dilemma resulting from having a therapeutic method without a theoretical basis. He created one by hypostatizing the "primordial images" and "typical formations" which seemed to be such powerful indicators of the psychic movement. They are, he said, archetypes.

Jung's venture, in an early twentieth-century period which glorified the rise of science and in which idealist philosophies were in steep decline, was extremely bold. In an address delivered in London at a joint meeting of the Aristotelian Society, the Mind Association, and the British Psychological Society, Jung proposed that at the deepest level of the unconscious psyche there are both formal (archetypal) and material (instinctive) causes at work.[27]

Below the more superficial level of the unconscious, where we hold lost memories and suppress painful thoughts and feelings, we come to a more collective unconscious psychic level in which the most basic precipitants of human action must be presumed to be located. If we define instinct as a "typical mode of action" occurring uniformly and regularly under set conditions, without there being any conscious motivation for the action which ensues as a result of the conditions or stimuli which provoke it, then instinct must surely arise from the collective unconscious. Human action is probably still far more instinctive than we would like to think. We have learned to rationalize so many of our actions, and to believe them caused by our willing intentions. But time and again we find ourselves involved in an "unconscious process which is released in...[us] that runs its course without the aid of reason and therefore falls short of, or exceeds the degree of rational motivation."

In the same way our perceptual modes of reaction, together with the "conventional and self-evident concepts" with which we hold them consciously in mind, surely proceed far more frequently from inherited patterns of perception than from the rationalized thinking with which we imagine we have come to our ideas. Plato and Augustine still had a clear idea of the metaphysical separation of their own thoughts from their paradigms or models in the forms. But after the scholastic period there is a steady deterioration of that differentiation, thought Jung, with the forms becoming mere a priori thoughts. With Kant the archetypes are reduced to mere categories of understanding. "Yet," said Jung, "the way in which man inwardly pictures the world is still, despite all differences of detail, as uniform and as regular as his instinctive action." The archetypes are inborn forms of perception and apprehension. "Just as his instincts compel man to a specifically human mode of existence, so the archetypes force his ways of perception and apprehension into specifically human patterns."[28] We must conceive of the collective unconscious as comprising both instincts and archetypes. They seem to be two aspects of the same vital activity, and which comes first, "apprehension of the situation or the impulse to act," it is impossible to say. The archetype is "the *instinct's perception of itself*, or "the self-portrait of the instinct." Yet, if we cannot determine the priority of instinct or archetype, Jung nevertheless leaned toward the archetype as the first of the pair. "Just as conscious apprehension gives our actions form and direction so unconscious apprehension through the archetype determines the form and direction of instinct." "Archetypes are "the necessary *a priori* determinants of all psychic processes."[29]

Jung had entered the realm of metaphysics. He further clarified the meaning of his new concept in an extended definition of the primordial image (an earlier term used by Jung, synonymous with archetype) which appeared in his new book, *Psychological Types*.[30] We may conceive of the primordial image somewhat as Semon did, as a mnemic deposit, an *imprint* or engram. From the physiological point of view it would then be a precipitate, "a condensation of innumerable, similar processes." (The *Collected Works* revision says: "a typical basic form of certain ever-recurring psychic experiences," thus avoiding Lamarckian implications but confusing the meaning of the passage by mixing physiological terms with the a priori terms belonging to the mind.) But if this is all, then why is it that our inner images do not simply repeat the images from the environment in constant and unaltered fashion? Why do we have *myths* about the sun and the moon and not just the bald images themselves? "From whence would it [the psyche] draw the capacity to adopt a standpoint outside sense perception? The engram theory does not suffice; we must suppose that there is an independent collaboration of the psyche, beyond that mechanical reproduction of environmental conditions which might be attributed to the purely physiological organism. *"We are forced to assume that the given structure of the brain does not owe its peculiar nature merely to the influence of surrounding conditions, but also and just as much to the peculiar and autonomous quality of living matter, i.e., to a law inherent in life itself."* (my italics)[31]

Beyond this, the archetype is a "self-activating organism" endowed with generative power which not only expresses the psychic procession but fuels its operation. Here is Jung's answer to Freud; libido is rooted in archetypes, not in the drive forces of the sexual libido:

> The primordial image is thus a condensation of the living process. It gives a co-ordinating and coherent meaning both to sensuous and to inner perceptions, which at first appear without order or connection, and in this way frees psychic energy from its bondage to sheer uncomprehended perception. At the same time, it links the energies released by the perception of stimuli to a definite meaning, which then guides action along paths corresponding to this meaning. It

releases unavailable, dammed up energy by leading the mind back to nature and canalizing sheer instinct into mental forms.[32]

Archetypes are thus for Jung (1) the condition of a true consciousness, one infused with meanings, as over against the "sheer, uncomprehended perception" of what must be unconscious states. They also (2) fuel the psychic process. Psychic energy stems finally from archetypes. Jung goes back and forth about this. Clearly instincts are involved. But what he has in the back of his mind is a kind of voluntaristic world view like Schopenhauer's where Will is the final cause. The Will is not a body-bound instinct but the transcendent factor of the universe. For Schopenhauer the idea and the image (manifest reality) proceed from the primal Will. For Jung the concept of the archetypes embraces both the unknown energic drive force or life force and (partially) the image by which it is expressed and perceived. All else, including ideas and the psychic process itself proceed as secondary affluxes from the primary archetype.

(The archetype is not the image itself. The image is the organ of the archetype's apprehension. Jung wanted to differentiate sharply between rationalized, ideational concepts and the primordial image, which springs, he thought, from the a-priori, non-rational, autonomous source of the psyche. This source is energic.)

Finally (3) the archetype is connected to a unique and transcendent quality which separates living matter form non-organic matter in the universe.

On all three counts Jung's description of archetypes must be judged to be metaphysical. The following chapter is directed toward further clarification of this statement.

4

Jung's Empiricism and the Common Consent Argument

It is time to attempt an important distinction between what is empirical and what is metaphysical in Jung's psychology. This vexed problem is illustrated best of all with the concept of the archetype. Complexities arise from Jung's subjectivistic epistemological views (discussed in Part I of this essay), from his understanding of the symbol, and from his insight into the nature of the living projective field which surrounds every prospective knower. (See the sub-article on Paracelsus in Part I above.) These views enabled Jung to answer to the religionist who might see in his psychology a system which corresponded to his/her own that everything we think we know is in fact mere projection of subjective contents. To the rationalist skeptic, on the other hand, Jung answered that his views were purely empirical. One must count real experience above all mere ideas in the head. Jung was enabled to make the jump from his personal and clinical experience of unconscious fantasy images to the doctrine of archetypes by his conviction that knowledge is intra-subjective in nature. The doctrine of archetypes, in turn, brought him to a belief in God which has commonly been known as the Argument from Consent (the *Consensus Gentium*). Empirical criticisms of this argument counted for very little within an epistemological belief structure which validated only the subjective view. As the years went along, Jung tended to increase the extent to which he thought the archetype should be considered the basic sub-structurant of existence.[1] In 1919–21, when the concept of the archetype was introduced, Jung meant by it that the archetype is a formative cause of psychic life. By the beginning of the 1940s, when his works on alchemy began to appear, and with an ever bolder voice over the next twenty years, Jung began to speculate on an identity between body and mind. The archetype might be the ground of all reality. At this level the problem of empirical criticism is overcome, for there exists only mind and the manifestations of mind in matter.

145

There are some things that belong to Jung's views of psychic functioning that I can confirm out of my own clinical experience as an analyst for the last twenty-five years. I believe that these things are empirically true and I offer my own corroborative witness, for what it is worth. It is true, I am convinced, that the unconscious psyche has an ability to portray the psychological situation of the dreamer in symbolic images and story-like sequences which because of their perceptive acuity and affective significance are experienced as deeply meaningful by both the dreamer and the observer. Symbolic dreaming occurs throughout life; it cannot be exhausted by the most thorough investigation of unconscious contents, although there seem to be periods in the lives of relatively mature and conscious individuals when the character of dreams is changed and their affective intensity is lessened. But the return of emotionally important life situations always brings with it an intensification of the symbolic activity of the unconscious psyche.

It is true that archaic motifs (motifs which appear in the dramatic structure of myths and fairy tales) do sometimes appear in dreams, especially in emotionally loaded moments. These motifs are frequently modified in form from the ways in which we encounter them in traditional folkloristic materials, and it takes long experience with these materials and long experience with psychological developmental patterns to recognize the similarity of these motifs. Others are so frequent as to be nearly commonplace. In the San Francisco Bay area where I live dreams of bridge crossings appear often indeed, and they tell a clear tale now as in ancient times of the difficulties involved in making a transition from one point of view to another. In Europe where I worked for ten years dreams of border crossings, at night and with great danger, with or without the necessary money and identification papers, told the same story. From my experience, what we discover most often are characteristic behavior patterns expressed in symbolic terms, not the replication of exact images.

While it is a fact that I had to be taught to understand the "symbolic language" of the psyche, and that much of that teaching occurred during the process of my own training analysis when I was emotionally open and vulnerable to suggestion, so that I may be biased in my understanding, it is also the case that this kind of knowledge, like most clinical operating assumptions in psychotherapy, is not susceptible to quantitative statistical evaluation. But many analysts trained in the method and with the materials with which I was trained believe as I do on these matters. It may be that we do possess a speciality knowledge which those not so trained do not possess. Beyond this there is the independent corroboration of specialists in comparative folkloristic studies, who agree that in spite of great differences there do seem to be widespread similarities in cultural and symbolic motifs.

What is *not* empirical about Jung's views of psychic functioning are the following conclusions: 1) The fact of the symbolic image-making capacity of the psyche or mind indicates that there is a "historical" layer of the psyche—that there are archetypes. 2) Archetypes are the sub-structurants of the psyche. 3) The image-producing, formal sources of the psyche are to be differentiated from its instinctive sources. 4) Some specific images which appear in dreams are beyond any possible personal experience or knowledge of the dreamer. They must therefore spring from the collective inherited sources of psychic life. There must be a "collective unconscious." 5) Dreams (and therefore the unconscious psyche) are sometimes "wiser" than consciousness and point toward future developments in psychic life.

Statements 1 and 2 belong to the Common Consent Argument as it is coupled with epistemological subjectivism. Statement 3 will be discussed in Chapter 6, which follows. Statement 5 is the subject of Part III of this essay. A brief comment on Statement 4 is introduced here.

As empirical evidence of the existence of the collective unconscious Jung several times mentioned an experience with an uneducated, hospitalized schizophrenic patient who told Jung that he had only to look out the window and he could see an erect phallus hanging from the sun. When he (the patient) moved his head from side to side the sun's phallus moved too, and that is where the wind came from. Four years later, in 1910, while Jung was studying a Mithraic liturgy recently published for the first time by Albrecht Dieterich he came upon an exactly analogous Alexandrian text in a Greek papyrus held at the Bibliothèque Nationale in Paris:

> The path of the visible gods will appear through the disc of the sun, who is God my father. Likewise the so-called tube, the origin of the ministering wind. For you will see hanging down from the disc of the sun something that looks like a tube. And towards the regions westward it is as though there were an infinite east wind. But if the other wind should prevail towards the regions of the east, you will in like manner see the vision veering in that direction.[2]

Such a parallel is indeed very impressive. One must not doubt
the astonishing impact of such a discovery. But the empiricist is
entitled to ask: If there is such a thing as a "historical psyche" or a
"collective unconscious" why are there not many more proofs similar
to the example of the sun phallus? Again, it is one thing to say that
typically human behavioral and feeling/thought patterns are sym-
bolically represented in unconscious material. It is quite another
thing to say that archaic motifs which are no longer relevant to
modern culture may appear unchanged in modern dreams.[3] This is a
matter which requires extreme care.

We may now let Jung himself speak, first about the empiricism
of his theoretical approach, and then about the concept of God as
archetypal. Jung's letters make especially lively and succinct reading
on this subject:

> It is exceedingly difficult to explain the nature of the arche-
> type to somebody who does not know about the empirical
> material we are dealing with in psychology. The only parallel
> I can point to outside the psychological field is the so-called
> mythological motif....Inasmuch as archetypes are found in
> the mind of the insane as well as in normal dreams quite
> outside all tradition, archetypes appear also to be contents of
> the collective unconscious and their existence in the individ-
> ual mind can only be explained by inheritance.[4]

> [in response to a review of *Aion* labelling Jung as Gnostic:]
> Now I state expressly and repeatedly in my writings that
> psychology can do no more than concern itself with asser-
> tions and anthropomorphic images. The possible metaphysical
> significance of these assertions is completely outside the
> bounds of empirical psychology as a science....The diffi-
> culty which gives rise to misunderstandings is that arche-
> types are "real." That is to say, effects can be empirically
> established whose cause is described hypothetically as *arche-
> type*, just as in physics effects can be established whose
> cause is assumed to be the *atom* (which is merely a model).
> Nobody has ever seen an archetype, and nobody has ever
> seen an atom either. But the former is known to produce
> numinous effects and the latter explosions. When I say
> "atom" I am talking of the model made of it, but never of the
> thing-in-itself, which in both cases is a transcendental
> mystery...

This is scientific gnosis, such as I also pursue. Only it is news to me that such knowledge is accounted "metaphysical." You see, for me the psyche is something real *because it works*, as can be established empirically. One must therefore assume that the effective archetypal ideas including our model of the archetype, rest on something actual even though unknowable, just as the model of the atom rests on certain unknowable qualities of matter.[5]

You chiefly deal with words and names instead of giving substance. I am thoroughly empirical and therefore I have no system at all. I try to describe facts of which you merely mention the names...

I have never claimed f.i. to know much about the nature of archetypes, how they originated or whether they originated at all, whether they are inherited or planted by the grace of God in every individual anew....But I should like to know how they [the critics] would like to explain the astounding parallelism of individual and historical symbolism not reducible to tradition.[6]

All knowledge is the result of imposing some kind of order upon the reactions of the psychic system as they flow into our consciousness—an order which reflects the behavior of a *metapsychic* reality, of that which is in itself real.[7]

The empirical material to which Jung refers in these quotations is a) the images and their mythological referents, b) the fact that people do dream them, and c) the emotional impact of the images. "The archetype has a causal or conditional effect." "The psyche is real because it works." Jung often spoke, following Rudolf Otto, of the numinosity of inner experience, that is, of the archetype. The subjective standpoint is what counts, and that is what is real. Historical or concrete truth does not matter. "It is enough [that something] has been said and believed." The letter to Haberlandt and the first of the quotations from Jung's essay, "On the Nature of the Psyche," contain ideas that are even more important. Jung suggests that while we may never know more than what the psyche itself presents to us, we must assume a transcendental reality—a thing-in-itself—which lies in back of and causes the phenomena which we experience. "One must assume that the...ideas...rest on something actual." "The reactions of the psychic system.... [reflect] the behavior of a *metapsychic* reality." Though he cannot hope to know it, Jung assumes that his dreams and feelings *do* give evidence of an invisible, that is non-material reality undergirding his subjective experience. Yet he claims not to be a metaphysician.

The next group of quotations has to do with Jung's views on the archetypal experience of God. The fact is, he thought, that we know nothing of God. What we do know is our inner experience, and the fact of our belief in God. This belief, because it is so nearly universal, may be termed archetypal. Belief ought to be taken neither more nor less seriously than all inner experience. All we have is our subjective experience. But if subjective experience is all there is, then belief in God may be the most important thing there is.

> Psychic experience has two sources: the outer world and the unconscious. *All immediate experience is psychic.* There is physically transmitted (outer world) experience and inner (spiritual) experience. The one is as valid as the other. God is not a *statistical* truth, hence it is just as stupid to try to prove the existence of God as to deny him.[8]

> The idea of immortality is a psychic phenomenon that is distributed over the whole earth. Every "idea" is, from the psychological point of view, a phenomenon, just as "'philosophy" or "theology." For modern psychology, ideas are *entities*, like animals or plants. The scientific method consists in the description of nature. All mythological ideas are *essentially real*, and far older than any philosophy.[9]

> When you ask why you so confidently believe in the existence of God, nobody can tell you why. It is just a fact, a result or a fruit of your living mind. The mind is like a tree bringing forth its characteristic blossom and fruit; it is just so. As you call something that pleases you beautiful or good, so you confess to believe in God. As an apple tree that bears no fruit would be all wrong, so you would be all wrong if you didn't confess your truth. It just grows in and through you, and this great unknown thing that makes the universe tick at all, and incidentally causes ourselves to produce such thoughts and convictions, is what man has since time immemorial called 'gods' or "God."[10]

The last of these quotations brings us to the item of Jung's psychological system for which he is most famous. That is the special form of his defense of the Argument from Common Consent for God. It is scarcely possible to read any essay of Jung's without coming upon some form of the argument.

Jung's argument has four steps. The first is them is a) simple acknowledgment of the ancient and universal belief in God and b) the corollary statement that the human individual needs to believe in God in order to be healthy. One may cite ancient authorities for this belief at will. It belongs to the core of the Stoic doctrine of Common Notions and prefaces Balbus' long discussion of proofs for God in Cicero's *Nature of the Gods*: "The main issue is agreed among all men of all nations, inasmuch as all have engraved in their minds an innate belief that the gods exist."[11] Even the Epicureans, who were the fiercest of Stoic rivals in the Hellenistic world, gave a place to the gods in their system. Without power or any influence on the lives of men, the gods must nevertheless live, since men believe in them, lodged in the interstices of space between material bodies where they lead a perfectly happy life among themselves.[12]

For Jung, we deny the gods at the cost of our mental well-being:

> The idea of God is an absolutely necessary psychological function of an irrational nature, which has nothing whatever to do with the question of God's existence. The human intellect can never answer this question, still less give any proof of God. Moreover such proof is superfluous, for the idea of an all-powerful divine Being is present everywhere, unconsciously if not consciously, because it is an archetype.[13]

> The *consensus gentium* that expresses itself through the religions is, as we saw, in sympathy with my paradoxical formula. Hence it would seem to be more in accord with the collective psyche of humanity to regard death as the fulfillment of life's meaning and its goal in the truest sense, instead of a mere meaningless cessation. Anyone who cherishes a rationalistic opinion on this score has isolated himself psychologically and stands opposed to his own basic human nature.[14]

> Just as man, as a social being, cannot in the long run exist without a tie to the community, so the individual will never find the real justification for his existence and his own spiritual and moral autonomy anywhere except in an extra-mundane principle capable of relativizing the overpowering influence of external factors. The individual who is not anchored in God can offer no resistance on his own resources to the physical and moral blandishments of the world. For this he needs the evidence of inner, transcendent experience.[15]

Step 2 acknowledges what ancient authorities did not see, but what Kant did—"that the human intellect can never answer this question." In a letter written late in his life to the Dutch theologian G. A. van der Bergh von Eysinga, Jung admitted that his image of God, though similar to other images, was merely that, and not the reality itself. "I can experience God as if he were an object, but I need not assume that it is the only image. I know that I am dealing, as Kant says, with a 'symbolical anthropomorphism' which concerns language...but *not the object itself.*"[16]

The passage from Kant to which Jung refers is the conclusion of the *Prolegomena.*[17] It contains extremely important clues to Jung's own procedures with regard to his theory of the archetype. With the risk of missing something by foreshortening, I would like to suggest that Kant's argument in the cited passage runs something like this: After having established the boundaries of knowledge in what we can experience in the world, we are still left with the questions which spring up in the mind about how things are in-themselves. If we limit our concept of reality to what we can experience of it this would be absurd, "for this would be to wish to have the principles of the possibility of experience considered universal conditions of things-in-themselves" (p. 99). We can form no definite idea of things beyond our knowledge but are "not at liberty to abstain entirely from inquiring into them" (p. 100).

> Who can satisfy himself with mere empirical knowledge.... And who does not feel himself compelled, notwithstanding all interdictions against losing himself in transcendent Ideas, to seek rest and contentment, beyond all concepts which he can vindicate by experience, in the concept of a Being the possibility of which cannot be conceived but at the same time cannot be refuted, because it relates to a mere being of the understanding and without it reason must needs remain forever dissatisfied? (pp. 100–101)[18]

What should reason think about matters which we do not know and can never know? We must imagine a Supreme Being, because only thus can "reason find that completion and satisfaction which it can never hope for in the derivation of appearances from their homogeneous grounds" (p. 103). Hume objected to all such theistic thoughts as soon as they give any specific content to the concept of deity or Divine Plan, claiming that they amount to nothing more than anthropomorphisms. We are thus condemned to skepticism. But if we limit our concept of *knowledge* to *experience* (continues Kant) then we are relieved of the onus of *dogmatic* anthropomorphism. We may continue to imagine the properties of a Supreme Being in relation to the world "and allow ourselves a *symbolical* anthropomorphism, which in fact concerns language only and not the object itself." We may then imagine the world *as if* it were the work of God much as we consider the relation between watch and watchmaker or a regiment to its commanding officer. We thus deny all knowledge of God but make use of our conceptions of a Divine Maker. "We conceive the world *as if* it came, in its existence and internal plan, from a Supreme Reason" (para. 58, p. 108).

If we translate what Kant says about the uses of the concept of a Divine Being to Jung's concept of the archetype and of God we shall arrive at Jung's exact formula. Step 3 says that although the intellect can never know God we must not be so full of pride as to limit our concept of reality to what is experienced as outer object. Step 4 then goes beyond Kant to what Kant supposed but did not insist on, namely that our thoughts about supreme reality point toward something that is really there. Jung gave even more credit to those thoughts. (To be exact: thoughts, feelings, images.) They are, he said, facts of experience, even universal facts of experience, and they have to be evaluated in that light along with other aspects of human experience.

Jung had in fact returned to a form of the ontological argument (see pp. 109 f. above). Charles Hartshorne, a student of Alfred North Whitehead and the leading American exponent of panpsychism, has made a comment on the relationship between thought and experience which parallels Jung's views:

It is often said (and with an air of great wisdom) that a "mere idea" cannot reach existence, that only experience can do that. But there is no absolute disjunction between thought and experience. A thought *is* an experience of a certain kind, it means through experience, even when it reaches only a possibility....If we have a meaning for our thought of God, we also have experience of him, whether experience of him as possible or as actual being the question. It is too late to assert the total lack of experience, once meaning has been granted. The only doubt can be whether the experience, already posited, is such as to establish possibility only, or existence also. But in the case of God no distinction between "not-impossible" and "actual" can be experienced or conceived. Hence we have only to exclude impossibility or meaninglessness to establish actuality.[19]

The criticism which an empiricist may bring to bear on the theory which has been described in this chapter may count for much or for little, depending on whether consciousness is oriented toward the priority of objective or subjective objects. It is not clear, for instance, that belief in God is universal, or even nearly so, although it is a fact that belief in God or gods is a primary component of most traditional societal structures. There are numbers of people in the field of biology, especially in the philosophy of biology where I have been reading extensively during the last two years, who argue passionately against belief in God. If one broadens the definition of God so that it becomes synonymous with "highest value" then those philosophers and scientists might also be said to believe in God. But the principles they espouse—an evolutionary universe governed entirely by chance and a progression from non-organic to organic matter without the intervention of external or supra-mundane factors—are not those principles usually associated with belief in God.

Again, not everyone would agree that a religious attitude or belief in God is necessary for mental health. Numbers of professional practitioners in the field of psychology, including followers of Freud, would argue that religious belief binds the individual in neurotic and infantile dependency attitudes. Belief in God, or yearning for God must be analytically reduced to unresolved parental complexes or inadequate socialization, which produces substitute formations in the mind.

Not every belief held by a great number of people has turned out to be true in the light of the progress of knowledge. The earth is not, as it turns out, flat, nor does the sun revolve around the earth. The philosopher Paul Edwards remarked that "there is, on the face of it, no reason why the whole of mankind should not have been as wrong on a speculative topic as it has been on some more empirical questions on which, history teaches, it has been mistaken."[20]

While acknowledging that the factual data are not complete on either side of this crucial question, it seems to me that those who would mark "do not agree" on the tally sheet of the Common Consent Argument have increased their numbers to a very great extent in the years since the end of the second World War. At the same time, the number of testable hypotheses available to biologists and physicists in support of evolutionary doctrines has also increased exponentially. Scientific knowledge has increased so greatly that no one could speak, as Jung could as late as 1952, of an atom which could be felt but not seen. Many scientists will no longer admit a boundary to what they may hope to know.

In the light of these developments it seems to me that those who champion a doctrine of the primacy of mind need to be as conscious as possible of what they in fact claim by doing so.

5

Theories of Archetypes:
Plato and Schopenhauer

a. Plato

The theory of archetypes originated in the philosophy of Plato, but archetypes are not easily recognizable in the Platonic corpus in the way in which Jung meant them. Plato had been thoroughly convinced by the arguments of Heraclitus that the entire sensible world is in eternal flux and is essentially unstable, and by the sophistic relativism of Protagoras, who insisted that "Man is the measure of all things." Nothing which moves and changes could supply the criterion for an absolute standard of truth.[1] Yet soul (or psyche) was for Plato defined as that which is not only in motion but which causes or originates that motion in itself:

> All soul is immortal, for that which is ever in motion is immortal. But that which while imparting motion is itself moved by something else can cease to be in motion, and therefore cease to live; it is only that which moves itself that never intermits its motion; inasmuch as it cannot abandon its own nature; moreover this self mover is the source and first principle of motion for all other things that are moved.[2]

Plato's doctrine of soul, although it assumed an ever increasing importance in the late dialogues, and was to be echoed in Aristotle's first cause and in the voluntarism of a later age of philosophical thought, was never integrated with his doctrine of forms. What is to be the true nature of a moral quality or of any observable object must be absolutely unchanging and therefore static and without life. Plato's problem with motion and his consequent difficulty in giving a positive value to the psyche, at any rate to those aspects of psychic life in which bodily activity takes place, are the main reason why the connection of Jung's doctrine of archetypes with their source in Plato's doctrine of forms, or archetypes, is difficult to see.

Plato was of course deeply concerned with the problem of human existence; his philosophy was devoted to establishing a moral basis for human life. But Plato considered that this moral basis could be established only if it could be shown that there are absolutely unmoving and eternally existing factors which guarantee it. These factors should be removed from the all too transitory and changeable vicissitudes of human life, but they should at an underlying level substantiate not only life, but all existence whatsoever. If these factors are not to be found in the realm of movement and change in which we live our lives on the earth—if everything that we experience here *is* in change—then they may perhaps be found at an extra-mundane level. The concept that the ultimate structure of reality lies not in the materially observable strata of the universe, but at a non-material level to which only our minds (or our feelings) are witness, may fairly be said to be the connecting theme between Jung's theory and its origin in Plato's belief in *transcendent causes*. Two brief examples of such causes in Plato's work may make the purpose of Jung's use of the notion of archetypes more clear. The first example comes from the text in which Plato first enunciated his doctrine of eternal forms. The second example, from the *Symposium*, exhibits one of Plato's variations on a doctrine of soul.

In Chapter 4 of Part I of this essay we saw that Plato prepared the ground for a theory of forms by declaring that true knowledge has its solid base in the rational mind, which remembers back to what it has always known within itself. As Plato has Socrates make clear in his demonstration of an untaught slave boy's ability to solve a geometrical problem, essential knowledge is a priori (*Meno* 81e–86b). The facts concerning it will not change by reason of outer conditions which may be imposed upon it. Because we have knowledge before the fact of experience or learning, and because the knowing soul must therefore also pre-exist our experience—be immortal (86b)—we must therefore expect that (hypothesize that) the moral law, like all true knowledge, is eternal (87a–d). In his next dialogue Plato argued back in the other direction. Because of the existence of the forms we must believe in an immortal soul.

The *Phaedo* is dramatically perhaps the most perfect of the Platonic dialogues. It is hung over with the atmosphere of tragedy. If the wisest of men can be condemned by the Athens which he so deeply loved then there is little reason indeed to trust life in this world. All hope must be vested in an eternal realm. The dialogue is situated in prison. It is the last day of Socrates' life. His friends and pupils are gathered around him in sad and fearful anxiety for the coming hour. But Socrates spends the entire day in peace and cheer, consoling his friends both by his serene mood and by a series of arguments for immortality; his life will not end, but he will enter the immortal world and the company of other good men, or in any case the presence of gods who are very good masters (63b5–c5). At the culmination of the series of arguments for immortality Socrates comes back to some points he had made earlier which had to do with how opposites exclude each other. Things are large or small by virtue of the reality of the concept of large and small. "Nothing else makes [something] beautiful except the beautiful itself" (100d5). "It was agreed [by the group] that each of the forms *was* something, and that the other things, partaking in them, took the name of the forms themselves" (102b).[3] These things that are, truly, can never be something else than what they are. Hot can never be cold, and snow can never be fire. An odd number can never be an even number. By the same token a body is alive because a soul dwells in it (105c10). But since something that truly is can never admit its opposite, neither can the soul, which is by definition alive, ever admit death. So soul is immortal. "When death attacks a man, his mortal part, it seems, dies; whereas the immortal part gets out of the way of death, departs, and goes away intact and undestroyed" (106d5). True being is to be found in the eternal forms, not in the images or things which take the name of the soul which inhabits it.[4] We must posit the separability of mind from body and the independence of the objects of thought from the phenomenal objects in which they seem to inhere, if human values are to be permanent. Beauty, as well as largeness and smallness, heat and cold, exists first of all as a concept in the mind.

In the text of the *Phaedo*, Plato crowns the argument for immortality which we have just been following by having Socrates recount a beautiful mythical vision of the life hereafter. Well-ordered souls will be accompanied by gods who guide them to their true home in a realm of jeweled color and light, whereas incurable sinners will stumble and wander alone until they are finally cast into Tartarus. It is well to note that the myth, which Socrates says we should try to believe as a "spell to pronounce over ourselves" (114d), supports the argument for immortality and the doctrine of forms—all in order that we should be persuaded to lead the moral life. The role of imagination and the function of the archetype also stand in a hierarchical relation of subservience to moral ends in Jung's clinical theory. Through imaginative attention to inner affective states of mind we become conscious of desire and conflict and have to make decisions for what we perceive as the good. This point has been too little noticed in some Jungian circles in recent years, with the result that fantasy has sometimes come to be valued as an end in itself. But it then becomes empty of all significance for human life—a truly narcissistic occupation which would be entirely antithetic to Jung's own goals.

Plato experimented in several ways with a definition of the human person as a besouled being. The *Phaedo* depicts a soul divided against itself so deeply that its one side, the Spirit, is imprisoned in its other side, the Flesh, and gains its freedom only in death. The *Republic* presents a tripartite soul corresponding to three kinds of life styles: an appetitive style based on sensual desires, a power-based style aiming at political prestige and worldly honor, and a contemplative, philosophical style directed toward true knowledge.[5] The *Symposium* and the *Phaedrus* however show Plato developing an energic concept of psyche that is surprisingly modern in feeling. It refers to the facts of inner mental conflict and proposes a solution directed at the sublimation of lower forms of Eros in favor of a higher allegiance to beauty itself and to the vision of true being.[6]

In the *Symposium* Plato has Socrates offer the concluding speech at a dinner party celebrating Agathon's prize-winning tragedy. The subject for the evening is love. Socrates begins by pointing out that Eros as the god of Love is not himself at all beautiful even though the other speakers have praised him in this vein; he is merely in search of the beautiful, or the good, or whatever it is the obtaining of which causes us to experience happiness. What Socrates knows about love he claims to have learned from Diotima, a wise woman from Mantinea. It is she who taught him that every form of the search for the beautiful may have its place in the development of the individual. It may not be wrong to fall in love with a young person who seems to embody all that we search for. "For love, that renowned and all-beguiling power, includes every kind of longing for happiness and for the good" (205d). We long for our own immortality and there is a period in our lives when the bodily act of love promises to ensure that immortality. At the physical level there is no other way in which the passion for the good may be satisfied.

But, having caught through the love of another a glimpse of what is truly beautiful we may be inspired to understand that physical beauty is nothing compared to the beauties of the soul. If we hold onto that vision, and separate beauty of soul from everything physical, even from everything that can be named, we will, mounting step by step the heavenly ladder, suddenly achieve the wondrous vision of beauty itself—an "everlasting loveliness which neither comes nor goes, which neither flowers nor fades" (211a). If we succeed in obtaining this vision then we must no longer be in continual search for the object of our love, for it has become our own forever (211e). We have become a friend of God, and whatever there is of immortality has already become our possession. F. M. Cornford expressed Plato's vision felicitously: "Man is for him the plant whose roots are not in earth but in the heavens."[7]

Plato's view in the *Symposium* of the nature of the human person and the origins of human behavior would in a later age find echoes in Jung's theory: human behavior derives ultimately from energic sources containing the essential, hidden core of character, and the natural course of life is toward realization of the potential of one's character. Attainment of the self means release from bondage to the overly personalistic concerns of the conscious ego and the development of a more objective, transcendent point of view.

b. Schopenhauer

In one way or another the moral and/or epistemological denial of phenomenal experience in favor of the reasons inside the mind is the mark of all idealist approaches to the question of reality and truth, whether or not they posit such transcendent existents as archetypes. Jung's view, though not marked by the denigration of bodily emotion which accompanied Plato's separation of true reality from phenomenal experience, and which has marked much of Western religious thinking since Plato's time, was thoroughly idealist. So far as I am able to understand Jung, his reasons for an idealist view and, above all, his reasons for positing archetypes were also thoroughly religious. Jung wanted to save a place in the modern world for the human dream of eternal life, for the human sense of an ultimate meaningfulness in life, for human moral ideals. These are things that cannot be easily argued for on a rational basis, either in ancient or in modern times, although philosophers have been loath to admit it. (Plato argued more successfully for his point of view within the drama and poetry of his dialogues than in their logical structure.) When it comes to demonstration, empiricists have much the stronger case, for religious ideals are in fact much more a matter of implicit persuasion—an insistence that against the evidences of the senses there must also be some basis in truth for an opposing inner conviction—than they are of logical force. If there is no basis within the phenomenal world then it must be found outside or beyond that world.

Jung could not embrace a rationalist idealism of the older type as a professional psychiatrist whose principal concern was the affective life of the human person. What did however seem to "fit" was the voluntarist philosophy of Schopenhauer. We know that he had read a great deal of Schopenhauer in his student years and that he continued to quote Schopenhauer throughout his life. The ontological structure of Schopenhauer's philosophy stuck in his mind as peculiarly suitable and in the years between 1910 and 1920 when he was looking for a way to say that he thought the symbolic structures produced by the mind were *not* reducible to purely instinctive causes inside the phenomenal, material world, it was Schopenhauer's solution that he adopted as his own. 1) It could accommodate an energic view of the psyche, which seemed to coincide with clinical observations of regression, progression, and displacement of energy in psychic life. At the same time it allowed for a currently fashionable scientific view (the Mayer-Helmholtz laws of energy) to lend additional credence to a psychological theory. There *might* be, even though there *must* not be, coherence between theories of matter and theories of mind. 2) It gave man, or in any case an anthropomorphically conceived life quality, primacy in the world process. 3) It gave merely secondary rank in reality to the phenomenal, material world.

Schopenhauer praised Kant as "astonishing" and next to the "divine Plato" in the importance of his philosophical insight. But he adopted a view of Kant's epistemology based on certain unclear statements in the first edition of the *Critique of Pure Reason* which Kant himself revised in the second edition of his *Critique*, and which modern scholarship finds reason to understand in a very different light (see Part I, Chapter 5, above). For Schopenhauer, reality is limited to what we can experience of it. We may not *know* anything that is beyond experience. Within the framework of that experience however we must proceed inductively and *as though* we might know, from experience to concepts. All mental concepts derive from experience of the phenomenal world, and these experiences include also our experiences of ourselves. Ideas are thus not a priori mental contents, but secondary derivatives of something more basic, something which belongs to the character of the experiencing individual:

The present philosophy . . . by no means attempts to say *whence* or *for what purpose* the world exists, but merely *what* the world is. But here the *Why* is subordinated to the *What*, for it already belongs to the world, as it springs merely from the form of its phenomenon, the principle of sufficient reason, and only to this extent has it meaning and validity. Indeed, it might be said that everyone knows without further help what the world is, for he himself is the subject of knowing of which the world is representation.[8]

Behind the abstract, discursive concept, which is to say at a more basic level of psychic functioning, and nearer to actual experience, we discover the *idea*. The idea arises directly out of perceptive experience. Not being abstracted to the level of a concept it is never fully able to be transmitted to another person, but at the same time it carries with it all the affective force of the experience itself:

> The Idea...is absolutely perceptive, and, although representing an infinite number of individual things, is yet thoroughly definite...it is communicable not absolutely, but only conditionally, since the Idea, apprehended and repeated in the work of art, appeals to everyone only according to the measure of his own intellectual worth....The *Idea* is the unity that has fallen into plurality by virtue of the temporal and spatial form of our intuitive apprehension. . . The *concept* is like a dead receptable in which whatever has been put actually lies side by side, but from which no more can be taken out (by analytical judgments) than has been put in (by synthetical reflection). The Idea, on the other hand, develops in him who has grasped it representations that are new as regards the concept of the same name; it is like a generative organism, developing itself and endowed with generative force, which brings forth that which was not previously put into it.[9]

The passage from which I have quoted is actually the same passage from which Jung quoted in an attempt to explain what he meant by the *primordial image* (Jakob Burckhardt's term which Jung replaced by the term *archetype*). If the reader replaces Schopenhauer's word *idea* with the words *primordial image*, Jung instructed, then his own meaning would be understood.[10]

We should now be much closer to understanding Jung's doctrine of archetypes. The archetypal image, that part of the experience which is at all perceptible to consciousness, and which is also entirely similar to what Jung meant by a "symbol" is what Schopenhauer described as the "idea" or "representation," which becomes further refined into a concept as it distances from the present moment of experience.

Lying still further behind even the idea, as the prime force and source of all phenomena is the individual experience of a non-rational Will, the volitional base of personal existence. If the sensible world experienced by the individual is intelligible only as Will, so must the world outside the individual also proceed from Will. Schopenhauer was emphatically not a dualist. The self and world as phenomenon is not different in kind from the experience of self as will, but is only a further emanation of it. At the same time, as it is with the individual, so must it also be in the world of nature as a whole. Man is the model, the microcosm in which the essential nature of reality in the macrocosm may be seen.

The archetype itself, in Jung's terminology, is the unknown and unknowable formative source of both perceptive and affective apprehension. He meant by it almost exactly what Schopenhauer meant by the Will, although he separated from Schopenhauer's belief that the Will is blind and without design (see Part III, below). Both the Will and the archetype "reside" in the unconscious, to use a spatial metaphor. When Jung describes the unconscious, as so often in his writings, in hypostatized language as "The unconscious wants...or says..." he is describing the force of will and desire stemming from the archetype, or as Schopenhauer would have it, from the Will.

It may be helpful to realize when we come to consider in the final chapter of this section Jung's late views of the archetype, that an idealist type of voluntarism which gives precedence to psychic qualities in its vision of reality will naturally speculate about a physical world operating with the same kinds of causes that seem to obtain with the human person. Jung shocked some readers and excited the religious imagination of other readers in his late works: *Mysterium Coniunctionis*, "Synchronicity," and "On the Nature of the Psyche." But he was actually developing the implications of his concept of the archetype in a consistent, non-dualist fashion, very much as Schopenhauer did with the Will.

We may observe the extension of Schopenhauer's doctrine of the Will from the microcosmic to the macrocosmic universe in three passages from his second book, *On the Will in Nature*, a book which Jung said had been crucial to his first thinking about psychic libido and about the image forming archetypal character of the libido:[11]

> From my proposition that the Will is what Kant calls the "thing-in-itself" or the ultimate substratum of every phenomenon, I had however not only deduced that the will is

the agent in all inner, unconscious functions of the body, but also that the organism itself is nothing but the will which has entered the region of representation, the will itself, perceived in the cognitive form of space.[12]

Knowledge...then presents itself as the *mediator of motives,* i. e. of the action of causality upon beings endowed with intellect—in other words, as that which receives the changes from outside upon which those in the inside must follow, as that which acts as mediator between both. Now upon this narrow line hovers *the world as representation*—that is to say, the whole corporeal world, stretched out in Space and Time, which *as such* can never exist anywhere but in the brain any more than dreams, which, as long as they last, exist in the same way. What the intellect does for animals and for man, as the mediator of motives, susceptibility for stimuli does for plants, and susceptibility for every sort of cause for inorganic bodies; and strictly speaking, all this differs merely in degree.[13]

I am the first who has asserted that a *will* must be attributed to all that is lifeless and inorganic. For, with me, the will is not, as has been hitherto assumed, an accident of life, and life of Matter. But Matter itself is only the perceptibility of the phenomena of the will. Therefore we are compelled to recognise *volition* in every effort or tendency which proceeds from the nature of a material body, and properly speaking constitutes that nature; and there can consequently be no Matter without manifestation of will.[14]

In spite of the fact that Schopenhauer limited knowledge to what can be subjectively experienced, it is clear that what his theory of a material reality emanating from will amounts to is nevertheless a doctrine of transcendent causes. Jung once made a psychological comment acknowledging that fact:

Wherever the spirit of God is extruded from our human calculations, an unconscious substitute takes its place. In Schopenhauer we find the unconscious Will as the new definition of God, in Carus the unconscious, and in Hegel ...the practical equation of philosophical reason with Spirit.[15]

With all respect, it is perhaps nevertheless not too wicked to point out that Jung ought to have extended that statement to include his own doctrine of archetypes. Though officially denying the metaphysical implications of his psychology, Jung's theory of archetypes as formal sources of psychic life constitutes nothing less than a God theory.

6

Instincts and Archetypes

This chapter has to do with that portion of the question of the relationship between instinct and archetype which asks onto-logical questions. In psychological language those would be such questions as: What kind of object am I, as a human being, and What is the source and nature of my behavioral activity as a human being? Artificially separated off from the problem of instinct, until Part III of this essay, are such questions as: What is the connection between organic and nonorganic processes? Is life goal-directed?

In his 1919 essay, "Instinct and the Unconscious," Jung had pro-posed a polar relationship between archetype and instinct with the formula: Instincts are impulses to carry out actions from necessity, without conscious motivation. Archetypes are the a priori, inborn forms of perception and apprehension and the "necessary a priori determinants of all psychic processes."[1] A few paragraphs farther on Jung described the primordial image (the archetype) as "the instinct's perception of itself, or as the self portrait of the instinct." "Just as conscious apprehension gives our actions form and direction, so *unconscious apprehension through the archetype determines the form and direction of instinct.*" (my italics)[2] It sounds as though Jung might be opposing spirit to matter, as conscious to unconscious, undirected drive force, until we come to that last remark, which shows that he believed perception and apprehension can also be unconscious, although they contain something more than the blind drive force of instinct. If we remember Schopenhauer's definition of the *idea,* which Jung said meant what *he* intended by the archetypal image (and Jung's book on *Types* was being written at the same time as his delivery of the lecture on instinct) then we see in what respect the archetype may also be unconscious, even though it has to do with perception and apprehension. The experience of an archetypal image is fraught with affect and with meaning even though it is not understood in conceptual terms and cannot be freely communicated to others.

I believe that the evidence points to the following conclusion. Jung's basic view of the universe was Schopenhauer's—a *unitive* reality in which phenomena are expressions of an underlying Will.[3] But Jung wanted to diverge from Schopenhauer's view that the Will is blind and purposeless, at least as regards organic life forms. His distinction between archetype and instinct allowed him to distinguish between goal-directed, meaningful experiences of affect and desire and blind, undirected experiences from which one might assume a universe without meaning. This explanation makes Jung's swing between identifying mind and body and his otherwise sharp distinction between archetype and instinct understandable. It is a problem which has mystified Jung's pupils for many years. I may present a few passages in which Jung identifies body and mind, archetype and instinct:

> If we can reconcile ourselves to the mysterious truth that the spirit is the life of the body seen from within, and the body the outward manifestation of the life of the spirit—the two being really one—then we can understand why the striving to transcend the present level of consciousness through acceptance of the unconscious must give the body its due, and why recognition of the body cannot tolerate a philosophy that denies it in the name of the spirit.[4]

> Instinct is not an isolated thing, nor can it be isolated in practice. It always brings in its train archetypal contents of a spiritual nature, which are at once its foundation and its limitation. In other words, an instinct is always and inevitably coupled with something like a philosophy of life, however archaic, unclear, and hazy this may be. Instinct stimulates thought, and if a man does not think of his own free will, then you get compulsive thinking, for the two poles of the psyche, the physiological and the mental, are indissolubly connected.[5]

> Since psyche and matter are contained in one and the same world, and moreover are in continuous contact with one another and ultimately rest on irrepresentable, transcendental factors, it is not only possible but fairly probable, even, that psyche and matter are two different aspects of one and the same thing.[6]

In 1947 Jung undertook to write an essay about the most important of the theoretical postulates in his psychology. "On the Nature

of the Psyche" is widely considered to be Jung's mature and defini-
tive statement about the nature of the unconscious psyche, the individuation process, and archetypes. Other works followed; the essay
on synchronicity, his last major book, *Mysterium Coniunctionis*, the
polemical tract, *Answer to Job,* and the autobiography, which was
written only partly by Jung, and for the rest compiled by Aniela Jaffé
out of dictation, conferences with Jung, and passages taken from
earlier works. But none of these works of his last ten years discusses
his theory with anything like a systematic attempt to cover all the
major topics. A 1954 addition to the "Nature of the Psyche" included
his later thoughts on synchronicity and the problems of the new
physics, so that the essay does indeed represent his final views.
Section 7 takes up the question of the relationship between two concepts — that of a "pattern of behavior" and that of the archetype.

The psyche, Jung reminds the reader, consists of a conscious-
unconscious whole. Freud had already demonstrated the existence
of "archaic vestiges" and "primitive modes of functioning" that refer
to the evolutionary history of the human being. Instincts are in fact
never amorphous; they always reveal a distinct *pattern of behavior* which
in its turn fulfills an *image,* whether it be that of the leaf-cutting ant,
or the weaver bird. Man too has a limited range of volitional
behavior; for the most part he functions instinctively, enacting the
patterns of behavior which arise in him as images.

Yet it is difficult to catch hold of, or become conscious of how we
function instinctively, and even harder to prove that there is such a
thing as instinct in human beings. Jung proposes that there is however a peculiar psychic process with which we can indirectly observe
the instinctive process. He reports having first observed this process
in his early clinical work with patients, who seemed "stuffed full of
fantasies." If he encouraged the patient's taking up these fantasies
and developing them in an imaginative way, through painting or
modeling or dancing or any other kind of playful, creative activity,
he began to see important therapeutic results which were reflected
in a sense of "centering." "In this method," Jung reports, "I was
witnessing the spontaneous manifestation of an unconscious process
which was merely assisted by the technical ability of the patient;
and to which I later gave the name "individuation process."[7]

If the individuation process is a naturally occurring human
"pattern of behavior" it is nevertheless quite different from the kind
of instinctive process elucidated by Freud, which leads back to phylogenetic origins and to an unconscious state. The individuation
process leads toward consciousness and a sense of meaning in life.

Jung concluded that there are "certain collective unconscious conditions which act as regulators and stimulators of creative fantasy activity." Insofar, they act like instincts. But they also have a "distinctly numinous character" which can only be described as "spiritual." The term *archetype* must be used instead.

> In spite or perhaps because of its affinity with instinct, the
> archetype represents the authentic element of spirit, but a
> spirit which is not to be identified with the human intellect,
> since it is the latter's *spiritus rector*.[8]

The relationship between instinct and archetype may be compared to a color spectrum in which the dynamism of the instinct occupies the infra-red end of the polar spectrum and the archetype takes the place of the ultra-violet color at the opposite end of the polar spectrum. The archetype might be blue, or purely spiritual, and this would fit the simile better, but ultra-violet better describes what Jung meant by the archetype. Not only is violet traditionally the mystical or spiritual color, but the archetypal image is itself numinous, fascinating and most dynamic; the color combining red and blue describes the archetype most effectively. We must not integrate the experience of the instinct/archetype at the red end of the spectrum, for that would lead only to "blank unconsciousness." We must realize it by integrating into the conscious sphere "the *image which signifies and at the same time evokes* the instinct." (my italics)[9]

> Psychologically, the archetype as an image of instinct is a
> spiritual goal toward which the whole nature of man strives;
> it is the sea to which all rivers wend, the prize which the
> hero wrests from the fight with the dragon.[10]

At the same time that Jung was developing his archetypal theory of the sources of behavior, a very different theory of behavior was being developed within the field of biology by a group of people who applied mechanistic and Darwinian hypotheses to their study of human behavior.

In 1935 Konrad Lorenz published his revolutionary essay, "Companions as Factors in the Bird's Environment."[11] Building on the preliminary work of Oskar Heinroth and Jakob von Uexküll, and sharing in the contemporaneous work of Niko Tinbergen, Erich von Holst, and Karl von Frisch, Lorenz now became the leading figure in the new field of ethology. The primary aim of ethological studies was to clarify the nature of behavior by discriminating between learned and unlearned action patterns, and thus to understand *instinct*. The result of those studies has been that the content of the word *instinct*, which had been used for centuries by philosophers and scientists without anyone being able to say exactly what was meant by it, has come within the range of scientific definition. Irenaeus Eibl-Eibesfeldt, a leading pupil of Lorenz's, summarizes: "In precisely definable areas of their behavior, animals are pre-programmed by phylogenetic adaptation."[12]

In his pioneering study, Lorenz observed and experimented with the social behavior of a flock of jackdaws who lived at his home.[13] By isolating some individuals from the flock and hand-rearing them, and then releasing them at varying stages of development he was able to observe what kinds of social behavior were exhibited in a completely normal way without the possibility of there having been any learning experience within the flock, and what kinds of social behavior may be marked out as unique by the peculiarities of social environment during a critical stage of development. As a result of these studies, Lorenz could state: "Not all acquired behavior can be equated with experience and...not all processes of acquisition can be equated with learning."[14]

What Lorenz discovered is that the motoric pattern of instinctive behavior is innate—for example the detailed rituals of mating behavior and the stratified social organization of the flock—but that the acquisition of the object which should elicit that social behavior is not:

> An instinctive behavior pattern adapted towards a conspe-cific, yet initially incorporated without an object, is fixated upon an object in the environment at a quite specific time, at a quite specific developmental stage of the young bird.[15]

The fact that Lorenz could become the father or mother and forever after the *irreversible* love object of a young bird who happened to *imprint* on him (or internalize him as object of a pattern of socially directed behavior) at a specific stage of development shows that the behavioral process has to do with the mechanics of embryogeny. It has nothing to do with learning, but rather with the process of organ development.[16] Lorenz discovered that no amount of social experience in the flock after the moment of imprinting could modify the attachment of the bird to him. In such a situation one must speak of instinctive and not of learned behavior. He pointed out that there are cases from human psychopathology where an irreversible fixation of object also seems to have taken place, regardless of the suitability of the object, and which seems to be entirely similar to the object-imprinting seen in animals.

A second feature of Lorenz's theory is that there seems to be a certain amount of specific energy bound up with an instinctive behavior pattern which demands release within a regular time period. Innate release mechanisms are bound to specific releasing stimuli, but if those stimuli do not occur, the appetitive behavior may be released with ever less and less precise stimuli. The threshold may be lowered, particularly with warning and escape response, so that finally a kind of vacuum response may occur, without the necessity of external stimulation. Lorenz thought this was further evidence of the organic origin of behavior:

> The vacuum response...convincingly demonstrates the independence of the instinctive behavior pattern from external stimuli and shows the internal relationship of the behavioral chain.[17]

If the instinctive behavior patterns have the character of demanding to be lived out, and if, as ethologists believe, human behavior is still much more governed by instinctive behavioral patterns than by culturally learned behavior, then we may rightly be concerned about the capacity of human society to avoid aggressive behavior which may, in our day, destroy our world. Both Lorenz and Eibl-Eibesfeldt have made important contributions in this area.[18]

A corollary of the demand character of instinctive behavioral patterns, and a third important feature of ethological theory is the emotional quality of instinctive behavior. One must not think of an instinct as a mere automatism, devoid of the affective components which we think of as truly "psychic." There is every evidence that a red-bellied male stickelback fighting off red-bellied rivals during courtship season is thoroughly excited. A jackdaw living in the attic of Lorenz's house and responding to signals that mean intrusion is struggling for his very life. Lorenz says, "After years of close contact with animals, one is forcibly struck with the impression that instinctive behavior patterns are correlated with subjective phenomena which correspond to feelings and passions." He quotes other biologists in support of his view. Verwey wrote: "Where reflexes and instincts are at all to be distinguished, the reflex operates in a mechanical manner whereas instinctive behavior patterns are accompanied by subjective phenomena." And Heinroth: "Animals are emotional people of extremely poor intelligence."[19] In fact, says Lorenz, we must assume that animals have "far more specific feelings and passions than are known to man," more than the vocabulary of verbal human language is able to indicate. For this reason ethologists may speak of "flight motivation," "reproductive motivation" and so on, in order to designate a multiplicity of highly specific emotional reactions. An amusing and highly instructive experiment designed to observe universally meaningful but non-verbal instinctive signals of human courtship ritual was undertaken by the human ethologist David B. Givens.[20] "Wooing signals," he says, "are 'pre-wired' in the brain." For many months, notebook surreptitiously in hand, Givens sat in singles bars and recorded the signal behavior he could observe in the body, hand, clothing and facial gestures of the bars' guests.

It is true, say the ethologists, that human beings possess what no animal has, a large brain combined with a capacity for differentiated language and the ability to transmit cultural achievements from one generation to another. Cultural evolution has thus to some extent supplanted or displaced biological evolution in the human species. But we must not deceive ourselves with the belief that cultural process is "directed" any more than the instinctive processes of other animals serve any purpose beyond adaptation and survival.[21] Neither must we suppose that the moral and social responses of human beings are different in kind from the emotions of animals. Lorenz declared:

> It is an inherent property of instinctive behavior patterns that they are coupled with governing emotions. However, the emotions coupled with the social instincts of human beings are regarded as something particularly high and noble. The last thing I wish to do is to deny that these instincts are really so, but this entirely justified high estimation of the emotions governing the social instincts of human beings has robbed many scientists of the psychological possibility of admitting that this quantity of high and noble behavior is also present in animals and has also prevented them from recognizing instinctive behavior in human beings. But this latter recognition is exactly what is needed for an understanding of our own social behavior.[22]

Thus both the ethologists and Jung claim to have encompassed the spiritual and ethical characteristics of human behavior within their respective theories. Both have made use of the term *instinct*. Jung has claimed that instinctive behavior is referable to an unknown archetypal factor which underlies behavioral expression and which lends meaning and numinosity to human experience.[23] The ethologists have criticized the older use of the word *instinct* to describe clearly unlearned behavior—the immediate flight of a newly hatched butterfly and the first web spun by a spider, the migratory flight of a bird seeking its unknown goal—as an essentially empty formula which tends to make an end of questioning but fails to improve our understanding.[24] We can and must make more exact investigations of the sources of behavior. While humans have properties which are unique, their behavioral responses must be seen as being on a continuum with that of other animals. Animals are also capable of "ethical" responses which may serve to protect the family or the group at the cost of self-sacrifice. Social inhibitions which prevent animals from destroying their own kind are sometimes more evident among animals than among humans, even though, as Lorenz remarks, "the worker in comparative ethology does well to be very careful in applying moral criteria to animal behavior.[25]

A recent book by Anthony Stevens which has received a good deal of comment in Jungian circles attempted to equate Jung's archetypal theory with the body of ethological theory.[26] Stevens reproached Jungians with having been so focused on the imaginative, mythological and "meaning" centered aspect of the archetype that they have overlooked its biological implications. Thus Jungians had become isolated in the academic and scientific world, something which is, thought Stevens, completely unnecessary, since Jung's concept of archetypes expresses exactly what the ethologists have been saying for fifty years:

> Although ethology and analytical psychology might strike one as odd bedfellows, the incompatibility is in fact more apparent than real....Where they differ, it is more a matter of observational emphasis than a fundamental contradiction, for while ethology concerns itself with behavior which is objective, 'outer' and public, analytical psychology deals with behavior which is subjective, 'inner' and private.[27]

This will not do at all. Stevens displays a fundamental misunderstanding of both ethology and analytical psychology. What the two fields do have in common is a conception that behavior is rather more unlearned than learned. There has also been interest on both sides in the role of the internalized image as a releasing stimulus for behavior. Beyond this the similarity ends. Jung's theory of archetypes was made necessary precisely because of his inability to accept the mechanistic assumptions which underlie ethological theory. Jung's theory of dreams and his theory of unconscious process as a whole would be anathema to the presuppositions of biological science. I will have something more to say about this in Part III of this essay, where the subject of purpose in psychic process comes up for discussion.

A more astute attempt to reconcile the conflicting assumptions of analytical psychology and biology was undertaken by Adolf Portmann, professor of zoology at the University of Basel and a regular speaker at the Eranos meetings held each year since 1933 in Ascona, Switzerland. These meetings were always dominated by the spirit of Jung even though the many scholars who spoke there each brought a strongly individual and occasionally a dissenting perspective.

In his 1946 Eranos Lecture, "Biology and the Phenomenon of the Spiritual,"[28] Portman undertook to explore the limits to which the word *spiritual* might acceptably be applied within the science of biology.[29] Spirit may have two meanings, he said. It may denote "that quality in man's works and in his mode of life that distinguishes him from even the highest of his animal relatives." But it may also refer in an archaic sense to a kind of transcendent order beyond nature which yet permeates the natural world—an intangible "realm of the spirit." In this latter sense biology can have nothing to do with the spirit, and must energetically defend itself against the vitalistic assumptions which have, historically, invaded the realm of biological science. It is scarcely a hundred years, Portmann noted, since the germ cell was seen by Karl Ernst von Baer, in 1827. And only since 1875 was it possible to view under the microscope the penetration of sperm into the egg cell, and thus to gain insight into the origins of human life. There is still much that is unknown about how that cell divides and multiplies and differentiates into the higher structure of the developed organism. But we must not look for a directive *outside* the cell:

> The more farsighted biologists realized long ago that such a force is already at work in the egg cell and that throughout the entire course of individual development it never ceases to exist. We must penetrate the structure of the plasma, not search for a secondary factor which orders the cells.[30]

We may however, continued Portmann, very properly explore the factors of spirituality, or as the biologist would say, inwardness, in those qualities which contribute to the unique character of man.

Great progress has been made since the turn of the century, for example, in our understanding of instinct. We no longer think of instinct as a rigid pattern of unlearned behavior such as that characterized by J. H. Fabre in his wonderful studies of the sand wasps.

That rigidly determined behavior seemed sharply different from the volitional, learning modes of human beings. But we now know that instinctive behavior is not so invariant as once supposed. Young animals may imprint on the first moving object they see after breaking out of the egg, whether or not it is a species-appropriate object. There is also an inner state of readiness *before* the release of an instinctive act—a "restless searching for something, for a something which must exist in a structure within the animal but thus far is inaccessible to us."[31] The "release signals" in the environment which activate instinctive behavior are more variable than was once believed. Animals living in an optimal state, free from need, also demonstrate genuine play activity. To put it simply, "it is not possible to differentiate out of hand between the structure of this supreme directive mechanism of animal life and that of man's highest system of motivation."[32]

At a morphological level, we also see many instances of outer form which can be understood only as expressive of inner character. Only the high forms of ruminant animals, for example, have complicated head ornaments. Together with the development of the brain there are conspicuous head characters—colored patterns, manes, hands, horns, antlers, teeth, trunk, etc., in most mammals.[33] The fact is that the internal organs change relatively much less than do the external characteristics which seem to accompany the increasing complexity of brain function.

As for human beings, it is the social quality of human life which must be emphasized as unique and characteristic from the very beginning. In proportion to brain size the human infant is born about a year too soon, in comparison with other mammals. Although the fetus develops rapidly in the womb, infant development outside the womb is decidedly retarded, so that a long period of sheltered parental care, a post-uterine development in a social matrix rather than in intra-uterine isolation, is necessary. During this time period it is possible for the human being to acquire the cultural heritage of the species. The human individual can also acquire the "instrument of controlled expression" which we call speech and which enables mastery of the environment.

These are facts which the biologist can observe; they confirm the unique spiritual activity of man but we must not rush to impose meanings on phenomena which we do not fully understand. One must be patient and await the facts, said Portmann. Man is instinctive but also spiritual. But this does not appear for the biologist as a *conflict* between spirit and nature. It may be "an inevitable clash between divergent means of mastering the environment."[34] Beyond the realm of biological science it is the proper function of psychology to explore the complex nuances of human expressive modes, always remembering the scientific principle that we must await knowledge of unknown principles of higher organization.

In 1950 Portmann again took up issues having to do with the relationship between instinct and archetype. "Das Problem der Urbilder in Biologischer Sicht" explored the evidence of recent ethological research which confirms the role of images in the release of instinctive behavior patterns.[35]

Again, Portmann begins with a paragraph of exclusions. In bringing up the subject of primordial images in connection with biology one must not imagine that this has anything to do with the kind of Lamarckian, vitalistic thinking which permeated a certain group of evolutionary thinkers around the turn of the century. (Portmann has in mind Hans Driesch and some other biologists who sympathized with him. See Part III below.) According to such Lamarckian thinking the human being is a kind of storage chamber for experiences which then accumulate in the neuronic system and gradually become inheritable in so-called engrams. This theory, as it was taken up for example by Richard Semon with his "mneme" has been especially favored by psychologists.[36] But it is purely speculative, and springs from the need to understand puzzling facts, for example the complications of psychic inheritance, before the evidence is in.

From another angle however, Portmann continues, it has become possible to understand something about the role of images in psychic life. Since the turn of the century our conception of instinct has become so differentiated that we no longer think of it as a rigid, automatized behavioral sequence. From what we now know, instinctive behavior resembles nothing so much as psychic behavior in general. Some biologists have proposed letting the word *instinct* disappear. Nevertheless our knowledge of behavior which must be termed instinctive is most exact in those areas where a "primordial image" plays a role in narrowly described stereotypic action.

Portmann then describes Niko Tinbergen's investigation of the releasing mechanisms for begging movements in young silver gulls. The spot and its placement on the yellow underbeak of the old bird was essential to release the movement. Spots of other colors did well too. But the sight of a beak without a spot failed to elicit the movement. Many investigations concerning releasing factors have shown that in some cases the stimulus situation corresponds to a very definite inborn structure. In other cases the inborn scheme seems to be much more open, for example in Lorenz's case of the young gosling following the first figure it sees after slipping out of the egg. But even here we have definite evidence of an inherent, inborn structure which awaits only to be excited.

In the pre-linguistic period of human life we have an opportunity for the psychologist to make the same kinds of experiments which the biologist does. Here the researches of R. A. Spitz and K. M. Wolfe on the infant smile response are especially important. These show that between the third and sixth month the infant does not recognize a human face through individual characteristics but through general marks of a face—smooth, rounded forehead, two symmetrical eyes, nose, and a light movement. This releases a smile response. Here, says Portmann, is exactly what Jung meant by archetypes—the image of a hidden psychic structure which can be released without the necessity of a conscious response because of an inborn readiness to do so.

The evidence which has come out of research on the nature of instinct—the recognition and reaction to what has never been observed before—is, Portmann says, for him the decisive factor in positing an inherited central structure. Nevertheless one should be careful in developing the theory, since most of the evidence for it comes from so late a period that we can never know the extent of previous experience and unconscious forgotten influences. In particular we generally underestimate the degree to which we are influenced by experiences of the first four or five years— a time which is mostly forgotten in adult life.

With regard to at least two of Jung's hypotheses—that of the spiritual nature of psychic life and that of the existence of unconscious innate images, Portmann was thus able partially to agree with Jung while modifying the fundamental premises which underlay Jung's own theory. For Portmann, the archetypal image, and psychic process in general, are aspects of instinctive life which are as yet not fully understood.

7

Late Developments of the Archetype Theory: Synchronicity

Many years before he ventured his theory of synchronicity Jung had already taken an iconoclastic view of the connection between psyche and the bodily sources of life. His theory of archetypes served the purpose of differentiating a formal, non-somatic aspect of psychic functioning from causally organized material or instinctive sources, but for the most part Jung held to the connection between mind and body. It was a connection which might not be understood, for, as he firmly believed, the spontaneous and creative activity of the human spirit can never be explained in terms of matter alone, but nevertheless one should confirm the intimate relationship between mind and body, archetype and instinct.

Occasionally, however, and this in some of his most moving essays, Jung defied all scientific convention to suggest a psyche quite independent of bodily container. As early as 1931, in his essay on "The Basic Postulates of Analytical Psychology," which became a part of *Modern Man in Search of a Soul*, Jung wrote:

> Just as formerly the assumption was unquestionable that everything that exists originates in the creative will of God who is a spirit, so the nineteenth century discovered the equally unquestionable truth that everything arises from material causes.... To allow the soul or psyche a substantiality of its own is repugnant to the spirit of the age, for that would be heresy.[1]

Jung knows full well, as he says, that no one today can found a scientific psychology "on the postulate of a psyche independent of the body." But if not a modern psychology, then perhaps one might make an old-fashioned one, for it is to the teachings of the forefathers that one must turn for the necessary assumptions. We can just perhaps "summon up courage to consider the possibility of a psychology *with* the psyche — that is, a theory of the psyche ultimately based on the postulate of an autonomous, spiritual principle."[2]

In 1934, in his wide-ranging essay, "The Soul and Death," Jung had already begun to speculate about the significance of parapsychological facts, as they relate to our understanding of the psyche:

> Whether [death] means that the continuity of the psychic process is also interrupted remains doubtful, since the psychic attachment to the brain can be affirmed with far less certitude than it could be fifty years ago.[3]

In 1948 he commented on telepathic phenomena:

> In such [cases of telepathy] one is inclined...to think of "chance." But it seems to me, unfortunately that the hypothesis of chance is always an *asylum ignorantiae*....I would not, of course, assert that the law behind them is anything "supernatural," but merely something which we cannot get at with our present knowledge. Thus even questionable telepathic contents possess a reality character that mocks all expectations of probability.[4]

By 1951 Jung's thinking had come so far that he could write to his pupil and colleague Esther Harding: "I'm inclined to believe that something of the human soul remains after death, since already in this conscious life we have evidence that the psyche exists in a relative space and in a relative time, that is in a relatively non-extended and eternal state."[5]

In the following year Jung was ready to publish his most far-reaching statement on the autonomy of psychic processes. "Synchronicity: An Acausal Connecting Principle," was published together with an essay by Nobel Prize winner W. Pauli on "The Influence of Archetypal Ideas on the Scientific Theories of Kepler" in a volume entitled *Naturerklärung und Psyche.*[6]

Two events may have provided special impetus for Jung's monograph, in addition to his ever present hope that a contribution might be made toward diminishing the gulf between propositions about mind and about body. The first of these events was the series of publications by J. B. Rhine on his experiments in extra-sensory perception, culminating in the 1948 best-seller, *The Reach of the Mind.* To this experimental series Jung added an experiment of his own.

With the help of his pupil and colleague, Liliane Frey-Rohn, an experienced astrologist as well as an analyst, Jung compared the marriage horoscopes of 483 married couples to see whether the incidence of conjunctions and oppositions traditionally thought indicative of marriage occur more frequently in married couples than among non-married random pairings.

The second of the events which influenced Jung's decision to publish his essay on synchronicity had to do with certain facts about the newer physics which were becoming better known at that time, and which Jung came to appreciate especially through his conversations with Pauli. In both instances, the experiments in extra-sensory perception together with Jung's astrological experiment, and the problems of physics, the significant facts for psychology have to do with the *effect which the percipient observer has on the data.*

From the point of view of physics, the claim of the older science that all events in the universe must stand in a mechanically causal relationship to each other has been considerably diminished by the discovery that at the atomic level we can make statistical predictions about the behavior of a group of atoms under given conditions but not about the individual atom. Max Planck had discovered that a radiating atom does not emit energy in a continuous steady stream, but intermittently, in bundles.[7] In the years that followed, quantum theory developed not as a series of completely precise mathematical formulae but as a series of statistical predictions. To use the horrific example of an atom bomb, the strength of its explosion can be given with an upper and lower limit, but not with the accuracy of a conventional bomb where the nature of the chemical constituents together with the mass of explosive material permit an exact calculation of strength. On the small scale of individual events the pure determinism of Newtonian mechanics has had to be abandoned. Werner Heisenberg states: *"The incomplete knowledge of a system must be an essential part of every formulation in quantum theory"*[8]

Our understanding of physical events is limited by a second factor: the interference of the observer in the event which is observed and the space-time boundaries of our human capacities to observe. According to relativity theory, what is "future" and what is "past" depends on the distance in space between an event and its observer. Time is thus relative to space and the present moment may not be a point without temporal extension:[9]

> Relativity theory assumes that in principle no effect can be propagated faster than the velocity of light. . . . On the other

hand, we have found that in quantum theory a clear determination of position—in other words, a sharp delimitation
of space—presupposes an infinite uncertainty of velocity
and thus also of momentum and energy. This state of affairs
has as its practical consequence the fact that in attempting to
arrive at a mathematical formulation of the interaction of the
elementary particles, we shall always encounter infinite
values for energy and momentum, preventing a satisfactory
mathematical statement.[10]

Jung thought that these developments in physics were of great
importance, for they mitigated the difference between a supposedly
objective scientific world view and the subjectivist epistemology of
his own psychology. Jung explained:

Basic to this abstract scheme of explanation is a conception
of reality that takes account of the uncontrollable effects the
observer has upon the system observed, the result being
that reality forfeits something of its objective character and a
subjective element attaches to the physicist's picture of the
world.[11]

The relative or partial identity of psyche and physical continuum is of the greatest importance theoretically because
... [it bridges] over the seeming incommensurability between
the physical world and the psychic, ... from the physical side
by means of mathematical equations, and [from] the psychological side by means of empirically derived postulates—
archetypes.[12]

Jung meant that knowledge is necessarily limited by the experience
of the subject-observer. Physics and psychology are on a par with
one another and perhaps in the end even identical. Both archetypes,
which "organize images and ideas" and physics are empirical. Both
are experienced first "as psychic entities, and are conceived as such,
with the same right with which we base the physical phenomena of
immediate perception on Euclidean space." But both our perceptions
of space and our experience of archetypes bring partial knowledge
of an underlying reality which must remain unknown.

The concept that space and time are relative and that causality
may be conditional seemed to be strengthened by the experiments
in extra-sensory perception being conducted at Duke University by
J. B. Rhine and his associates. Jung read the reports of these experiments with great interest. Neither distance in space nor distance in

time prohibited the results of the experiments from exceeding statistical probability. What did matter however, was the interest of the subject:

> One consistent experience in all these experiments is the fact that the number of hits scored tends to sink after the first attempt, and the results then become negative. But if, for some inner or outer reason, there is a freshening of interest on the subject's part, the score rises again. Lack of interest and boredom are negative factors; enthusiasm, positive expectation, hope and belief in the possibility of ESP make for good results and seem to be the real conditions which determine whether there are going to be any results at all. In this connection it is interesting to note that the well-known English medium, Mrs. Eileen Garrett, achieved bad results in the Rhine experiments because, as she herself admits, she was unable to summon up any feeling for the "soulless" text-cards.[13]

In Jung's own astrological experiment, the significance of the results computed on the basis of the first one hundred fifty horoscopes by far exceeded the probabilities of chance occurrence. But with the second and third batches of marriage horoscopes the results became less and less significant, finally achieving a negative value. Jung believed that this outcome could be referred to his own declining interest in the experiment. "I was...in the position of a subject who is at first enthusiastic, but afterwards cools off on becoming habituated to the ESP experiment. The results therefore deteriorated with the growing number of experiments."[14]

Apparently, thought Jung, human emotion plays a crucial role in those instances in which strikingly unusual and seemingly meaningful coincidences between the outer world of space-time-causality and the inner psychic "moment of meaning" occur. Just as Jung was examining with a woman patient a dream in which she had been given a golden scarab there was a tapping noise at the window. Jung turned to open it and a scarabaeid beetle (the rose Chäfer common in Switzerland) flew into the room, where Jung caught it and delivered it to the dreamer. Another woman while in Europe dreamed of the death of her friend in America the night before a telegram arrived announcing the fact. A man whose psychological treatment with Jung was just being concluded was sent by him to a heart specialist because of certain symptoms. The specialist found nothing to be alarmed about, but with the negative report in his pocket the man collapsed on the way home and died soon after. His wife in the meantime was already thoroughly alarmed. A flock of birds had gathered at a the windows of the death chamber at her grandmother's death, and again at the death of her mother. Just after her husband left for the doctor's a whole flock of birds alighted on their house.[15]

Such remarkable but seldom occurring incidents, and many others which Jung also cited in his text are things that we, in modern times, tend to pass over as amazing but accidental coincidences. Jung insisted that this is an insufficient explanation. We may not understand such events with anything like certainty, but we must not ignore them. In certain cases it must be that the psyche penetrates or breaks through the time-space-causal chain and reveals an underlying a priori, acausal orderedness:

> I am...using the general concept of synchronicity in the special sense of a coincidence in time of two or more causally unrelated events which have the same or a similar meaning....Synchronicity therefore means the simultaneous occurrence of a certain psychic state with one or more external events which appear as meaningful parallels to the momentary subjective state.[16]

A synchronistic event occurs always *in time* and since "meaning" occurs only in the mind of the subject-observer, it requires a human presence for whom the event in time is significant for a synchronistic event to happen. Jung traced the beliefs which properly belong to such a synchronistic principle back to the mantic and mystical procedures of an earlier age. The ancient Chinese were able to obtain a picture of the "total situation" with their famous oracle, the *I Ching*. Albertus Magnus knew of the power of great emotion to alter a situation:

> I discovered an instructive account [of magic] in Avicenna's *Liber sextus naturalium*, which says that a certain power to alter things indwells in the human soul and subordinates the other things to her....When therefore the soul of a man falls into a great excess of any passion, it can be proved by experiment that it [the excess] binds things [magically] and alters them in the way it wants....For the soul is then so desirous of the matter she would accomplish that of her own accord she seizes on the more significant and better astrological hour which also rules over the things suited to that matter.[17]

In Western philosophy the roots of the principle of synchronicity belong to the doctrine of the sympathy of all things whose most recent representative was Leibniz.[18] Leibniz' idea of a preestablished harmony which guarantees that monads which have no communicative relationship with each other are nevertheless in perfect synchronous accord is one way of expressing belief in a universal underlying unitive principle. Still earlier, the doctrine of the microcosm-macrocosm was propounded by Paracelsus and by his philosophical mentor Agrippa von Nettesheim. Earlier still the Hellenistic Stoic doctrine of sympathy provided the basis upon which astrological science, and with it a number of other mantic procedures, could be accepted into Western culture.[19]

Jung concluded that the occurrence of synchronistic events is a kind of window into the realm of the archetype. They exhibit an order which is not causal in any modern sense of the term but which nevertheless exists as a contingent force alongside space, time, and causality. One must not think of his view as philosophical, he thought. Synchronicity is an empirical concept, an "intellectually necessary principle" which accounts for the experience of meaning in a way that no purely physical principle can.[20] Only if we take account of synchronistic (archetypal) phenomena will there be "some possibility of getting rid of the incommensurability between the observed and the observer."

The entrance into the visible realm of time and space of archetypal processes (experienced as synchronistic events) does not mean at the same time an entrance into cause and effect sequences. Archetypal equivalences, seen from the point of view of physics, are those chance events which correspond to the spontaneous behavior of the individual atom. Archetypes transgress causal processes. They are "acts of creation in time" in which what is basically a psychic process associates itself for the time being with external process and assumes the kind of order which belongs to visible events.[21]

The archetype itself, like the synchronistic event which reveals it, is "the introspectively recognizable form of *a priori* orderedness." Synchronistic events must be regarded as "the continuous creation of a pattern that exists from all eternity...and is not derivable from any known antecedents."[22]

Such a formulation is very far from the biological "pattern of behavior." It is far, too, from the theory of phylogenetic origins which Jung associated first with his genetic theory of libido and then with his theory of archetypes. In spite of Jung's caveat against philosophical interpretation, it resembles nothing so much as Plato's vision of a universe ordered by the eternal forms, directed by the World Soul, and limited in the perpetration of divine order only by the parallel existing facts of Necessary Cause.

Notes to Part II

Introduction

1. See the letter of Jung to Mircea Eliade, Jan. 19, 1955, where he reproaches Eliade for using the term without differentiating his own usage from Jung's. Eliade acknowledged the error and corrected it in the next edition of his book. *C. G. Jung Letters*, 2 vols., trans. R. F. C. Hull, selected and edited by Gerhard Adler in collaboration with Aniela Jaffé, Bollingen Series XCV (Princeton: Princeton University Press, 1973), vol. 2. "It is now known that certain myths and symbols have circulated throughout the world, spread by certain types of culture: this means that those myths and symbols are not, as such, spontaneous discoveries of archaic man, but creations of a well-defined cultural complex, elaborated and carried on in certain human societies: such creations have been diffused very far from their original home and have been assimilated by peoples who would not otherwise have known them. . . . [But] by envisaging the study of man not only inasmuch as he is a historic being, but also as a living symbol, the history of religion could become . . . a *metapsychoanalysis*. For this would lead to an awakening, and a renewal of consciousness, of the archaic symbols and archetypes, whether still living or now fossilized in the religious traditions of all mankind. . . . History does not radically modify the structure of an "immanent" symbolism. History continually adds new meanings to it, but these do not destroy the structure of the symbol." Mircea Eliade, *Images and Symbols: Studies in Religious Symbolism* (1952) (New York: Sheed and Ward, 1969), pp. 34, 35, 161. Cf. also Mac Linscott Ricketts, "The Nature and Extent of Eliade's 'Jungianism,'" *Union Seminary Quarterly Review* 25 (Winter 1970): 211–34. After about 1950, Eliade's use of the term *archetype* approached Jung's meaning more closely, as noted by Daniel L. Pals in "Is Religion a Sui Generis Phenomenon?" *Journal of the American Academy of Religion* 55 (Summer 1987): 266.

2. Meg Greenfield is commenting on the "Miss America" contest: It is much too saccharine. Beauty contests have always been held but the winner was given immediately to the chief or the king. We have in fact flattened out the real archetypal meaning of the ritual event. "The Great Khan in Atlantic City," *Newsweek*, Sept. 23, 1985, p. 84.

3. It is an apparent incongruity that modern biology is the most

mechanistic/materialistic of the exact sciences in its explanatory systems. Mind is not understood until it is reduced to physical systems and, ultimately, to non-organic matter. As early as 1848 Emil Du˙ Bois-Reymond signaled the coming trend in the introduction to his *Untersuchungen über thierische Elektrizität*: "It cannot fail that physiology, giving up her special interests, will one day be absorbed into the great unity of the physical sciences; [physiology] will in fact dissolve into organic physics and chemistry." Cited in William Coleman, *Biology in the Nineteenth Century: Problems of Form and Transformation* (Cambridge: Cambridge University Press, 1977), p. 150. In a more recent formulation which strives to unite discoveries in cellular biology with social-biological research, Edward O. Wilson writes: "Self-knowledge is constrained and shaped by the emotional control centers in the hypothalamus and limbic system of the brain." "Only when the machinery can be torn down on paper at the level of the cell and put together again will the properties of emotion and ethical judgment come clear." *Sociobiology: The New Synthesis* (Cambridge, Mass.: Belknap Press, 1975), pp. 13, 575.

4. For an excellent history from a materialist/positivist point of view which would meet the criteria of most modern biologists see Herbert Feigl, *The "Mental" and the "Physical": The Essay and a Postscript* (Minneapolis: University of Minnesota Press, 1967).

5. *Phaedrus* 246–54; *Timaeus* 48.

6. Sigmund Freud, *The Standard Edition of the Complete Psychological Works*, 24 vols., translated from the German under the general editorship of James Strachey, in collaboration with Anna Freud, assisted by Alix Strachey and Alan Tyson (London: Hogarth Press and Institute of Psycho-analysis, 1953–74) (hereafter abbreviated as S.E.), 5:236.

7. *The Freud-Jung Letters*, ed. William McGuire, trans. Ralph Manheim and R. F. C. Hull, Bollingen Series XCIV (Princeton: Princeton University Press, 1974), Letter of Nov. 30, 1911, p. 469. Also cited in Frank J. Sulloway, *Freud: Biologist of the Mind, Beyond the Psycho-analytic Legend* (New York: Basic Books, 1983), p. 432.

8. C. G. Jung, *The Collected Works*, 20 vols., trans. R. F. C. Hull, Bollingen Series XX (Pantheon Books and Princeton University Press, 1953–79) (hereafter abbreviated as CW), vol. 8, para. 28, 33.

9. The fact for example that phases of dreaming sleep may be detected by EEG measurements is a physiological concomitant proving that dreams do happen to the organism, but we still do not know what bodily purpose may be served by dreams. Theories abound.

10. Jung, CW 16, para. 86.

11. Jung, CW 3, para. 413.

Chapter 1

1. Siegfried Bernfeld, "Freud's Earliest Theories and the School of Helmholtz," *The Psychoanalytic Quarterly* 13 (1944): 353 ff.; Freud, "An Autobiographical Study," S.E. 20.

2. Ernst Brücke, one of the four pre-eminent nineteenth-century physiologists who had determined together as friends in Berlin at midcentury to struggle for a strictly physicalist view of life forms throughout the German-speaking universities. See the Autobiography, S.E. 20:67 f.

3. Sigmund Freud, *The Origins of Psycho-analysis: Letters to Wilhelm Fliess, Drafts and Notes: 1887–1902*, ed. Marie Bonaparte, Anna Freud, and Ernst Kris, authorized translation by Eric Mosbacher and James Strachey, with Introduction by Ernst Kris (New York: Basic Books, 1954), p. 57: "To go into general practice instead of specializing...is certainly the only way which promises real satisfaction and material success; but for me that is too late now. I have not learned enough for that kind of practice; there is a gap in my medical equipment which it would be hard to close. I was able to learn just enough to become a neuropathologist."

4. Freud, "On the History of the Psycho-analytic Movement," S.E. 14:9: "I...had only unwillingly taken up the profession of medicine, but I had at that time a strong motive for helping people suffering from nervous affections or at least for wishing to understand something about their states." "Autobiography," S.E. 20: "Neither at that time [at the end of gymnasial studies] nor indeed in my later life, did I feel any particular predilection for the career of a physician. I was moved, rather, by a sort of curiosity, which was, however, directed more toward human concerns than toward natural objects." See also Ernest Jones, *The Life and Work of Sigmund Freud*, 3 vols. (New York: Basic Books, 1953–57), 1:27 f.; Sulloway, *Freud*, Chap. 2.

5. Henri F. Ellenberger, *The Discovery of the Unconscious* (New York: Basic Books, 1970), p. 91; Sulloway, *Freud*, p. 34.

6. See Sulloway, *Freud*, for a thorough discussion of the extent of the famous disagreement between Freud and Breuer at the time of the publication of the *Studies*. Sulloway concludes that the disagreement had to do neither with Breuer's reputed sexual puritanism nor with Freud's rejection of Breuer's physicalist theory. It had to do with their differing scientific styles and with Freud's new insistence that the origin of the psychoneuroses was *always* sexual.

7. Bernfeld, "Freud's Earliest Theories," p. 344.

8. Ibid., p. 349. See also the editors' Introduction to the *Studies on Hysteria*, S.E. 2:xxii.

9. Freud, S.E. 20:253. Cited also in Sulloway, *Freud*, p. 15.

10. Du Bois-Reymond wrote to Ludwig in 1842: "Brücke and I pledged a solemn oath to set in power this truth: No other forces than the common physical ones were active within the organism...." Cited by Bernfeld, "Freud's Earliest Theories," p. 348.

11. Henri F. Ellenberger, "Fechner and Freud, *Bulletin of the Menninger Clinic* 20 (1956): 201–4. See also Sulloway, *Freud*, pp. 65 f.

12. Freud, "Autobiography," S.E. 20:59.

13. See p. 13 above.

14. Gustav Fechner, *Elements of Psychophysics* (1860), vol. 1, trans. Helmut E. Adler, ed. Davis H. Howes and Edwin G. Boring (New York: Holt, Rinehart and Winston, 1966).

15. Carl Ludwig wrote to Du Bois-Reymond on April 15, 1849, after returning from a visit in Leipzig: "Fechner was kindness itself; he seems to be virtually trying to forget physics...you can simply have no idea what physical poetry he is capable of developing." Du Bois-Reymond answered on May 17: "Fechner is definitely mixed up. How can the author of the *Massbestimmungen* abandon himself to such self-delusions without having an organic defect in his brain? It is not possible....But just read his work on the Becquerel chain in volume 28 of Pogg. Ann. (1839); as if that is the work of a dilettante! He was then certainly so seriously and truly a matter-of-fact scientist that it is unquestionably in this capacity, above all, that he will be remembered by future generations." *Two Great Scientists of the Nineteenth Century: Correspondence of Emil Du Bois-Reymond and Carl Ludwig* (1937), collected by Estelle Du Bois-Reymond, Foreword, Notes and Indexes by Paul Diepgen, trans. Sabine Lichtner-Ayed, ed. with a Foreword by Paul F. Cranefield (Baltimore: Johns Hopkins Press, 1982), pp. 33, 34.

16. See the Appendix for a somewhat fuller exposition of Fechner's position in nineteenth-century physics, philosophy, and psychology.

17. Ellenberger, *Discovery of the Unconscious*, p. 218: "Freud took from Fechner the concept of mental energy, the topographical concept of the mind, the principle of pleasure-unpleasure, the principle of constancy, and the principle of repetition."

18. Cited by Jones, *Life and Works*, 1:29.

19. Freud, *Origins*, p. 118.

20. Ibid., pp. 119 f.

21. Freud, *Origins*, p. 25; Walter A. Stewart, *Psychoanalysis: The First Ten Years, 1888–1898* (New York: Macmillan Company, 1967), p. 193. "Freud felt as a result of his clinical experience that the basic problem with which the apparatus had to cope was the bodily needs as represented in the drives

and that the regulation of the flow of drive energy was the main function of the psychical apparatus." Freud, "Project for a Scientific Psychology," S.E. 1:295: "The intention is to furnish a psychology that shall be a natural science; that is, to represent psychical processes as quantitatively determinate states of specifiable material particles."

22. Stewart, *The First Ten Years*, pp. 189–90.

23. Freud, *Origins*, p. 35.

24. Jones, *Life and Work*, 1:384, 379 f.

25. Ibid., p. 383.

26. S.E. 5:536–37.

27. Ibid., p. 579: "Dreaming has taken on the task of bringing back under the control of the preconscious the excitation in the Ucs. which has been left free; in so doing, it discharges the Ucs. excitation, serves it as a safety valve and at the same time preserves the sleep of the preconscious in return for a small expenditure of waking activity." P. 599: "All that I insist upon is the idea that the activity of the first psychic system is directed towards securing the *free discharge* of the quantities of excitation, while the *second* system, by means of the cathexes emanating from it, succeeds in *inhibiting* this discharge and in transforming the cathexes into a quiescent one."

28. Jones, *Life and Work*, 1:368.

29. As early as 1914, in a note added to *The Interpretation of Dreams*, Freud said: "Dreaming is on the whole an example of regression to the dreamer's earliest condition, a revival of his childhood, of the instinctual impulses which dominated it and of the methods of expression which were then available to him. Behind this childhood of the individual we are promised a picture of a phylogenetic childhood—a picture of the development of the human race, of which the individual's development is in fact an abbreviated recapitulation influenced by the chance circumstances of life." S.E. 5:548. See also Sulloway, *Freud*, pp. 390 f.

30. Sulloway, *Freud*, pp. 440, 443.

31. See "Formulations on the Two Principles in Mental Functioning," S.E. 12.

32. Freud, *Origins*, pp. 215 f.

33. Freud, "Fragment of an Analysis of a Case of Hysteria," S.E. 7:114 f.

34. Ibid., p. 113.

35. C. G. Jung, *Memories, Dreams, Reflections* (New York: Pantheon, 1961), p. 150.

36. S.E. 7:163. See p. 164 for a re-statement of the "emotionally cathected mental processes" and the problem of their expression and discharge.

Chapter 2

1. C. G. Jung, *Psychology of the Unconscious: A Study of the Transformations and Symbolisms of the Libido. A Contribution to the History of the Evolution of Thought* (1912), trans. Beatrice M. Hinkle (New York: Dodd, Mead and Company, 1925), pp. 135 f., 138. In the following pages I refer frequently to this book, which was very substantially revised in the *Collected Works* and reissued as *Symbols of Transformation*. Hereafter the original version, published first in 1912, will be referred to as *Symbols of Transformation*, 1912. The revised version will be referred to as *Symbols of Transformation*, CW 5.

2. "Freud and Jung: Contrasts," CW 4, para. 774. See also pp. 29 ff. above for the epistemological angle on this view.

3. *Symbols of Transformation*, 1912, pp. 139 ff.; "The Theory of Psychoanalysis," CW 4, para. 251 ff., and esp. para. 271–84.

4. See Jung's 1907 monograph, "The Psychology of Dementia Praecox," CW 3.

5. *Symbols of Transformation*, 1912, pp. 150–51; "The Theory of Psychoanalysis," CW 4, para. 278, 287, 288. See also Liliane Frey-Rohn, *From Freud to Jung: A Comparative Study of the Psychology of the Unconscious*, translated from the German by Fred C. Engreen and Evelyn K. Engreen (New York: G. P. Putnam's Sons, for the C. G. Jung Foundation for Analytical Psychology, 1974), Part E., "From Libido to Psychic Energy," pp. 135–87.

6. "The Theory of Psychoanalysis," CW 4, para. 280, 281.

7. *The Interpretation of Dreams*, S.E. 5:613.

8. Ibid., p. 599.

9. *Symbols of Transformation*, 1912, pp. 146 f.=*Symbols of Transformation*, CW 5, para. 196–97.

Chapter 3

1. Jolande Jacobi, *Complex, Archetype, Symbol in the Psychology of C. G. Jung*, trans. Ralph Manheim, Bollingen Series LVII (Princeton: Princeton

University Press, 1959), p. 60: "In line with Freudian theory, the whole unconscious is taken as a mere 'reservoir of repressions' "; Aniela Jaffé, "The Creative Phases in Jung's Life," trans. Murray Stein, in *Spring* (1972), p. 169: "Attempting to interpret the images, Jung discovered to his amazement identical or analogous motifs to those he had found in classical mythology. This astonishing fact could not be explained by Freud's view of the unconscious as the receptacle of repressed contents"; Jung, "On the Nature of the Psyche," CW 8, para. 372–73; *Two Essays in Analytical Psychology*, CW 7, para. 202. Liliane Frey-Rohn, in *From Freud to Jung*, has stated that matter correctly, pointing out that neither the "super-ego" nor the "primal repressed" were in Freud's view originally repressed. However, Frey states on p. 100 that "Freud, always absorbed with surface phenomena, was most interested in the neuroses, while Jung concentrated on the deeper understanding of all phases of psychic life."

2. Jones, *Life and Work*, 3:313: "I...begged him to omit the passage where he applied...[Lamarckian theories] to the whole field of biological evolution, since no responsible biologist regarded it as tenable any longer. All he would say was that they were all wrong and the passage must stay." Sulloway, *Freud*, pp. 408, 435.

3. Conscious deception is not implied by my interpretation. Belief systems do conceal other possibilities of understanding from us, as Jungian analysis was the first to teach me.

4. Stephen Jay Gould, *Ontogeny and Phylogeny* (Cambridge: Belknap Press of Harvard University Press, 1977), pp. 80 f.

5. Ibid., p. 36.

6. Ibid., pp. 155 ff. for detailed references.

7. E.g. *Symbols of Transformation*, 1912, pp. 27–28.

8. Gould, *Ontogeny and Phylogeny*, p. 162.

9. "General Aspects of Dream Psychology," CW 8, para. 474, 475. Compare with *Symbols of Transformation*, CW 5, para. 26, 27. The quotation is from Nietzsche, *Human, All-Too Human*, trans. Zimmern and Cohn, 1:24–27, modified.

10. *Two Essays*, CW 7, para. 151. See p. 100 of 3rd ed. Baynes & Baynes, *Two Essays in Analytical Psychology* (N.Y.: Dodd & Mead, 1928).

11. CW 7, para. 159.

12. Letter to John Raymond Smythies, Feb. 29, 1952, and to D. Cappon, March 15, 1954, *Letters*, 2.

13. Prior to 1912 June had written on the subject of his association experiments, on the psychology of the psychoses and on hysteria. In the

disturbances of normal reaction patterns in the association experiments he had discovered what he called "complexes." There was not yet a specific statement that in the symptom itself we must seek the seed of the cure; neither was there as yet a statement that the subjective point of view must be favored over against the objective stance, as regards its curative value.

14. *Symbols of Transformation*, 1912, pp. 36–37. Compare the revised version, para. 39–40.

15. *Symbols of Transformation*, 1912, pp. 462 f. Compare the revised version, para. 654, 655, which have been completely rewritten to account for later theoretical developments. The 1912 original version is worth consulting in more detail. Jung considers Freud's incest theory and suggests that incest may have possessed ritual and psychological significance in past ages but that it can never have been a distinctive *biological* urge. "Originally incest probably never possessed particularly great significance as such, because cohabitation with an old woman for all possible motives could hardly be preferred to mating with a young woman." This statement is of great *philosophical* significance for it shows Jung beginning to move away from a phylogenetic, somatically rooted theory of mind to the a priori theory of mind which characterizes his theory of archetypes.

16. *Symbols of Transformation*, 1912, p. 73.

17. "The Theory of Psychoanalysis," CW 4, para. 415, 416.

18. *Symbols of Transformation*, 1912, pp. 262–63.

19. "On Psychological Understanding," CW 3, para. 396, 397, 398, 407.

20. "Preface to 'Collected Papers'" (1916),CW 4, para. 673, 674.

21. "The Structure of the Unconscious" (1916),CW 7, para. 492–94.

22. "The Theory of Psychoanalysis" (1913), CW 4, para. 453, 454.

23. "General Aspects of Psychoanalysis" (1913),CW 4, para. 554.

24. "On Psychological Understanding," (1914), CW 3, para. 413.

25. Ibid., para. 414.

26. "Prefaces to 'Collected Papers,'" CW 4, para. 679.

27. "Instinct and the Unconscious" (1919), CW 8.

28. For the epistemological implications of this statement see Part I of this essay, above.

29. "Instinct and the Unconscious," CW 8, para. 277, 270.

30. *Psychological Types* (1921), CW 6, para. 743–54. The earlier very good

translation by H. G. Baynes which was in use until 1971 contains only minor variations on the R. F. C. Hull translation of the CW, from which I quote here.

31. The vitalistic premise of the archetype which is revealed here will be fully discussed in Part III, Ch. 5, esp. p. 255, of this essay.

32. *Psychological Types*, CW 6, para. 749.

Chapter 4

1. I am introducing a term which is not in *Oxford's Unabridged Dictionary* to suggest more precisely what Jung meant: a structure whose primary meaning is verbal, a force driving toward image, form, and actual behavior.

2. CW 5, para. 149–53; CW 8, para. 317, 319; CW 9i, para. 104.

3. It is difficult to draw conclusions about images such as mandalas, which do sometimes appear spontaneously in unconscious imagery. They have an elaborate and very rich historical existence but they continue to be used in modern design as well. Combinations of circles and squares seem to have a calming, centering effect and to be felt as very attractive visual forms.

4. Letter to Swami Devatmananda, Feb. 9, 1937, *Letters*, 1.

5. Letter to H. Haberlandt, April 23, 1952, *Letters*, 2.

6. Letter to Calvin S. Hall, Oct. 6, 1954, *Letters*, 2.

7. "On the Nature of the Psyche," CW 8, para. 362. Cf. also the letter to Medard Boss, August 5, 1947, in *Letters*, 2:xlv: "I do not in the least understand why you ascribe to me exist.-phil. assumptions. Man as archetype is after all a purely empirical matter, without a tinge of philosophy. You are acquainted with the ubiquitous image of the *Anthropos*. It is also an empirical fact that the archetype has a causal or conditional effect. If this were not so, it could never have been observed at all. So it is not a theory but pure observation of facts." And the letter to Upton Sinclair, Nov. 24, 1952, in *Letters*, 2: "People mostly don't understand my empirical standpoint: I am dealing with psychic phenomena and I am not at all concerned with the naïve and, as a rule, unanswerable question whether a thing is historically, i.e. concretely, true or not. It is enough that it has been said and believed. Probably most history is made from opinions, the motives of which are factually quite questionable; that is, the psyche is a factor in history as powerful as it is unknown." The most straightforward statement about what Jung considers to be the empirical basis of his theory of archetypes is perhaps in "On the Nature of the Psyche," CW 8, para. 436: "My

method and whole outlook, therefore, begin with individual psychic facts which not I alone have established, but other observers as well. The material brought forward—folkloristic, mythological, or historical—serves in the first place to demonstrate the uniformity of psychic events in time and space. . . . A widespread prejudice reigns that the psychology of the unconscious processes is a sort of *philosophy* designed to explain mythologems. This unfortunately rather common prejudice assiduously overlooks the crucial point, namely, that our psychology starts with observable facts and not with philosophical speculations."

8. Letter to Heinrich Boltze, Feb. 13, 1951, *Letters*, 2.

9. Foreword to "Jung: 'Phenomenes Occultes'" (1939), CW 18, para. 742.

10. Letter to B. A. Snowdon, May 7, 1955, *Letters*, 2. Cf. also the letter to Pastor W. Niederer, Oct. 1, 1953, in *Letters*, 2: "I don't do anything to God at all, how could I? I have no idea what God is in himself. In my experience there are only psychic phenomena which are ultimately of unknown origin, since the psyche in itself is hopelessly unconscious. . . . The archetype is the ultimate I can know of the inner world. This knowledge denies nothing *else* that might be there." And the letter to Victor White, April 9, 1952, *Letters*, 2: "Empirically we are unable to confirm the existence of anything absolute, i.e. there are no logical means to establish an absolute truth, except a tautology. *Yet we are moved* (by archetypal motifs) *to make such statements.*" Jung stated quite early, in his essay "On Psychic Energy" (CW 8, para. 45), that "Since the psyche also possesses the final point of view, it is psychologically inadmissible to adopt the purely causal attitude to psychic phenomena." In his late responses to the queries of H. L. Philp, Jung wrote, "To make absolute statements is beyond man's reach, although it is ethically indispensable that he give all the credit to his subjective truth, which means that he admits being bound by his convictions to apply it as a principle of his actions. . . . To my mind it is more important that an idea exists than that it is true. This despite the fact that it makes a great deal of difference subjectively whether an idea seems to me to be true or not, though this is a secondary consideration since there is no way of establishing the truth or untruth of a transcendental statement other than by a subjective belief." ("Jung and Religious Belief" [1958], CW 18, para. 1584)

11. Cicero, *De Natura Deorum*, *Academia*, with an English translation by H. Rackham, Loeb Series (Cambridge: Harvard University Press), II.iv.12.

12. Ibid., II.xvii.46.

13. *Two Essays* (1928), CW 7, para. 110.

14. "The Soul and Death" (1934), CW 8, para. 807.

15. "The Undiscovered Self" (1957), CW 10, para. 511.

16. Letter to G. A. van der Bergh von Eysinga, Feb. 13, 1954, *Letters*, 2.

17. Immanuel Kant, *Prolegomena to Any Future Metaphysics*, with an Introduction by Lewis White Beck (New York: Liberal Arts Press, 1950), para. 57, p. 106.

18. Note the closely related discussion in Part III, pp. 230 f. below.

19. Charles Hartshorne, "The Necessarily Existent," from *Man's Vision of God* (1941), in Alvin Plantinga, ed. *The Ontological Argument: From St. Anselm to Contemporary Philosophers*, with an Introduction by Richard Taylor (New York: Doubleday and Company, 1965), p. 134.

20. Paul Edwards, "Common Consent Arguments for the Existence of God," *Encyclopedia of Philosophy*, 2:147–55.

Chapter 5

1. See Part I above, Ch. 4.

2. *Phaedrus*, trans. R. Hackworth (Cambridge: Cambridge University Press, 1952), 245c. See the discussion by W. K. C. Guthrie, *A History of Greek Philosophy*, vol. 4 (Cambridge: Cambridge University Press, 1975), pp. 419–21.

3. This is the first use of the word *Eide* in the dialogues. "Other things" are the images of the true forms.

4. A detailed technical exposition of these themes is found in *Republic* 500b–521b.

5. F. M. Cornford, "The Division of the Soul," *The Hibbert Journal* 28 (1929–30): 213.

6. Ibid., pp. 218–19: "The writings of Jung I find fascinating...but very hard to understand. He seems, however, to be the only one of the three modern psychologists to find a place in his scheme for some element of our nature answering to the true self, or divine Spirit of the Socratics."

7. F. M. Cornford, "The Doctrine of Eros in Plato's Symposium" (1937), in F. M. Cornford, *The Unwritten Philosophy and Other Essays* (Cambridge: Cambridge University Press, 1967), p. 78.

8. Arthur Schopenhauer, *The World as Will and Representation*, 2 vols., translated from the German by E. F. J. Payne (New York: Dover Publications, 1969), vol. 1, para. 15, p. 82.

9. Ibid., para. 49, pp. 234–35.

10. *Psychological Types*, CW 6, para. 751 f. "Feeling is impure and,

because undifferentiated, still fused with the *unconscious*. Hence the individual is unable to unite the contaminated feeling with the idea. At this juncture the primordial image appears in the inner field of vision as a *symbol*, and, by virtue of its concrete nature, embraces the undifferentiated, concretized feeling, but also, by virtue of its intrinsic significance, embraces the idea, of which it is indeed the matrix, and so unites the two. In this way the primordial image acts as a mediator, once again proving its redeeming power, a power it has always possessed in the various religions. What Schopenhauer says of the idea, therefore, I would apply rather to the primordial image, since, as I have already explained, the idea is not something absolutely *a priori*, but must also be regarded as secondary and derived."

11. C. G. Jung, *Analytical Psychology: Notes of the Seminar Given in 1925*, ed. William McGuire, Bollingen Series XCIX (Princeton: Princeton University Press, 1989), p. 4.

12. Arthur Schopenhauer, *On the Fourfold Root of the Principle of Sufficient Reason. On the Will in Nature*, trans. Mme. K. Hillebrand (London: George Bell & Sons, 1907), p. 252.

13. Ibid., pp. 294–95.

14. Ibid., p. 309.

15. "On the Nature of the Psyche," CW 8, para. 359.

Chapter 6

1. "Instinct and the Unconscious," CW 8, para. 270.

2. Ibid., para. 276.

3. "We are of the same substance as that table. Our discrimination, the 'I' awareness is the difference." In *C. G. Jung, Emma Jung and Toni Wolff: A Collection of Remembrances*, ed. Ferne Jensen (San Francisco: Analytical Psychology Club of San Francisco, 1982), p. 91.

4. "The Spiritual Problem of Modern Man" (1928), CW 10, para. 195. Note the psychophysical flavor of this passage, reminiscent of Fechner. See the Appendix.

5. "Psychotherapy and a Philosophy of Life" (1942), CW 16, para. 185. Cf. also:

"Not infrequently the dreams show that there is a remarkable inner symbolical connection between an undoubted physical illness and a definite psychic problem, so that the physical disorder appears as a direct mimetic expression of the psychic situation.... It seems to me...that a definite connection does exist between physical and psychic disturbances and that its significance is generally underrated, though on the other hand it is boundlessly exaggerated, owing to certain tendencies to regard physical disturbances merely as an expression of psychic disturbances, as is particularly the case with Christian Science." ("General Aspects of Dream Psychology" [1928], CW 8, para. 502)

Jung's theoretical considerations did not preclude a strong streak of common sense, and an "instinct" to avoid the moral problems which devolve upon an exclusively psychic/spiritual interpretation of physical illness.

6. "On the Nature of the Psyche" (1947), CW 8, para. 418. And see also:

"Archetypes have never been for me pure *causae*, but conditions [Bedingungen]. From your conclusions I find that you have completely misunderstood my concept of archetypes. You are utterly mistaken in saying that I have described the archetypes as given with the brain structure. Is the fact that the body also expresses character unknown to you, or do you believe that the pattern of behaviour familiar to biologists is not somehow expressed in the biological structure?...The body as a whole, so it seems to me, is a pattern of behaviour, and man as a whole is an archetype." (Letter to Medard Boss, June 27, 1947, *Letters*, 2:xli)

Medard Boss was one of the founders of existential analysis. This letter is an example of the kind of confusion sown by Jung's lack of clarity about presuppositions. It is understandable only in the context of a mind-body unity under the aegis of a psychic factor, namely the archetype, or the Will.

7. Ibid., para. 400. See Jung's charming essay, "The Transcendent Function," CW 8, for details of this process.

8. Ibid., para. 403, 405, 406.

9. Ibid., para. 414.

10. Ibid., para. 415.

11. Konrad Lorenz, "Companions as Factors in the Bird's Environment: The Conspecific as the Eliciting Factor for Social Behavior," in Konrad Lorenz, *Studies in Animal and Human Behaviour*, vol. 1 (Cambridge: Harvard University Press, 1970), pp. 101–258.

12. Irenaeus Eibl-Eibesfeldt, *The Biology of Peace and War* translation of *Krieg und Frieden aus der Sicht der Verhaltensforschung* (New York: Viking Press, 1979), p. 9.

13. See Konrad Lorenz, *King Solomon's Ring: New Light on Animal Ways*,

translated from the German by Marjorie Kerr Wilson (New York: New American Library, Signet Books, 1972), for a very readable account of Lorenz's observations of jackdaws and other animals of his Austrian home.

14. Lorenz, "Companions as Factors," p. 245. "A jackdaw exhibits almost all the properties and behaviour patterns which it would exhibit within the framework of normal society, even when it is barred from any relationship with conspecifics from an early age."

15. Ibid., p. 256.

16. Ibid., p. 249.

17. Ibid., p. 250.

18. Konrad Lorenz, *On Aggression*, translation by Marjorie Kerr Wilson of *Das sogennante Böse* (New York: Harcourt, Brace and World, 1966); Eibl-Eibesfeldt, *The Biology of Peace and War*.

19. Lorenz, "Companions as Factors," p. 251.

20. David B. Givens, *Love Signals: How to Attract a Mate* (New York: Crown Publishers, 1983). See also David B. Givens, "The Nonverbal Basis of Attraction: Flirtation, Courtship, and Seduction," *Psychiatry* 41 (November 1978): 346–59.

21. Eibl-Eibesfeldt, *The Biology of Peace and War*, pp. 21 ff.

22. Lorenz, "Companions as Factors, p. 157.

23. One must however not overlook several late statements of Jung, in which he seems to equate instinct with archetype: "I am not a philosopher and my concepts are not philosophical and abstract, but empirical, viz. *biological*. The concept generally misunderstood is that of the *archetype*, which covers certain biological facts and is not a hypostatized idea at all. The 'archetype' is practically synonymous with the biological concept of the *behavior pattern*." Letter to G. A. van den Bergh von Eysinga, Feb. 13, 1954, *Letters* 2. "The structure and function of the bodily organs are everywhere more or less the same, including those of the brain. And as the psyche is to a large extent dependent on this organ, presumably it will—at least in principle—everywhere produce the same forms." *Mysterium Coniunctionis*, CW 14, pp. xviii f. These comments must however be seen in the light of Jung's comment to D. Cappon, March 15, 1954, *Letters*, 2: "I am personally convinced that our mind corresponds with the physiological life of the body, but the way in which it is connected with the body is for obvious reasons unintelligible.... The question of brain localization is an extremely delicate one, because when you destroy a certain part of the brain you destroy a certain function. Yet you do not know whether you have really destroyed the function because it is quite possible that you have only destroyed the

transmitter of that function, as if you have taken away the telephone apparatus which does not mean that you have killed its owner. There is even no
absolute certainty about the psyche being definitely dependent upon the
brain since we know that there are facts proving that the mind can relativize
space and time, as the Rhine experiments and general experience have
proved sufficiently."

24. Eibl-Eibesfeldt, *Biology of Peace and War*, p. 9.

25. Lorenz, *King Solomon's Ring*, p. 208.

26. Anthony Stevens, *Archetypes: A Natural History of the Self* (New York:
Quill, 1983).

27. Ibid., p. 22.

28. Adolf Portmann, "Die Biologie und das Phänomen des Geistigen,"
in *Eranos Jahrbuch* (1946), vol. 14: *Geist und Natur* (Zürich: Rhein Verlag,
1947), pp. 521–67, trans. Ralph Manheim as "Biology and the Phenomenon
of the Spiritual," in *Spirit and Nature: Papers from the Eranos Yearbooks*, ed.
Joseph Campbell, vol. 1 of Bollingen Series XXX (New York: Pantheon
Books, 1954), pp. 342–70. I quote from the English version. The first version
of Jung's essay, "On the Nature of the Psyche," also appeared as a lecture
("The Spirit of Psychology") in the same Eranos series of 1946.

29. The German word *Geist* has a more general meaning than the
English term *spiritual*. Besides the meanings connoted by the English term,
Geist includes what in English might be called the spirited, the intellectual,
participating in cultural life.

30. Portmann, "Biology and the Spiritual," p. 345. The discovery of
DNA lay in 1946 still more than a decade in the future.

31. Ibid., p. 347.

32. Ibid., p. 350.

33. Ibid., p. 353.

34. Ibid., p. 368.

35. Adolf Portmann, "Das Problem der Urbilder in Biologischer Sicht,"
in *Eranos Jahrbuch* (1950), vol. 18: *Aus der Welt der Urbilder. Sonderband für
C. G. Jung zum Fünfundsiebzigsten Geburtstag.* (Zürich: Rhein Verlag, 1950),
pp. 413–32.

36. Richard Semon, *The Mneme*, trans. L. Semon (London, 1921) from
the German original: *Die Mneme als erhaltendes Prinzip im Wechsel des organischen Geschehens* (Leipzig, 1904). See also C. G. Jung, *Psychological Types*,
CW 6, para. 748, where Jung considered Semon's theory in relationship

with his definition of the primordial image (the archetype) and rejected it as being too organistic and lacking the *autonomous* psychic quality which he sought. "Semon's naturalistic and causalistic engram theory no longer suffices. We are forced to assume that the given structure of the brain does not owe its peculiar nature merely to the influence of surrounding conditions, but also and just as much to the peculiar and autonomous quality of living matter, i.e. to a law inherent in life itself."

Chapter 7

1. "The Basic Postulates of Analytical Psychology" (1931), CW 8, para. 653. Jung first used the term *synchronistic* in his memorial address for Richard Wilhelm, May 1930. CW 15, para. 81, 85.

2. "The Basic Postulates of Analytical Psychology," CW 8, para. 661.

3. "The Soul and Death," CW 8, para. 812.

4. "General Aspects of Dream Psychology," CW 8, para. 504.

5. Letter to Esther Harding, Dec. 5, 1951, *Letters*, 2.

6. Translated as *The Interpretation of Nature and the Psyche* (London: Routledge and Kegan Paul, 1952).

7. Werner Heisenberg, *The Physicist's Conception of Nature* (London: Hutchinson Scientific and Technical, 1958), p. 38.

8. Ibid., p. 41. But see David L. Hull, *Philosophy of Biological Science* (Englewood Cliffs, N.J.: Prentice-Hall, 1974), pp. 135–37: "The statistical nature of quantum physics has been shown to be an inherent feature of *current formulations* [my italics] of quantum theory.... The applicability of the principle of complementarity to biological phenomena is even more tenuous."

9. *The Physicist's Conception of Nature*, p. 46.

10. Ibid., p. 48.

11. "On the Nature of the Psyche," CW 8, para. 438.

12. Ibid., para. 440.

13. "Synchronicity: An Acausal Connecting Principle" (1952), CW 8, para. 838.

14. Ibid., para. 913.

15. Ibid., para. 843, 852, 844.

16. Ibid., para. 849, 850.

17. Ibid., para. 859, *De mirabilibus mundi*.

18. Jung did not apparently realize that Gustav Fechner held an entirely similar view. His reading in the field of psycho-physical parallelism seems to have been limited to secondary sources who favored a materialistic interpretation of psycho-physics. See para. 937, 938, 948, and Appendix, below.

19. The stoicizing Platonist, Philo of Alexandria, wrote of the Chaldeans: "They have set up a harmony between things on earth and things on high, between heavenly things and earthly. Following as it were the laws of musical proportion, they have exhibited the universe as a perfect concord or symphony produced by a sympathetic affinity between its parts, separated indeed in space, but housemates in kinship. These men imagined that this visible universe was the only thing in existence, either being itself God or containing God in itself as the soul of the whole." *The Migration of Abraham*, 178–81, in *Philo*, 10 vols., trans. F. H. Colson and G. H. Whitaker, Loeb Classical Library (Cambridge: Harvard University Press, 1968), IV, 235 f.

20. "Synchronicity," CW 8, para. 960.

21. Ibid., para. 964, 965.

22. Ibid., para. 965, 967.

PART III

Individuation Versus Evolution:
The Long War

Section A
Teleological Patterns in Jung
and in Aristotle

1

Individuation

a. Life as Purposive

If Jung's concept of the archetype forms the structural basis for his psychology, it is nevertheless for the sake of the concept of individuation that the entire system was built. Individuation, for Jung, means a lifelong process of coming into union with one's own being —a conscious (and very often also unconscious) striving to bring into realization a character which is mysteriously present from the very beginning as a potential embodied in the self.

Jung understood very early the challenge offered by science to a view of life as purposeful. In 1898, at the age of twenty-three, he delivered an impassioned lecture to his fellow students of the Zofingerverein called "Thoughts on the Nature and Value of Speculative Inquiry," in which he defended philosophy and the values of the mind against the materialism of the modern scientific view. At this stage Jung was still using the idiom of philosophy, but it is easy to translate the language he is using into his later psychological terminology. What is important to notice is how Jung contrasts a causal or materialistic view with the futuristic, hopeful view which he recommends.

I would remind the reader, too, of matters which were discussed in the early pages of Part I of this essay; of Jung's childhood in the parsonage, of the death of his father just two years before, and of Jung's conviction that his father's faith had not been able to withstand the encroachment of scientific truth into the realm of religious concepts, stultified as they were in a religious tradition which had lost touch with experiential reality.

It is not material success but the "world's future" and the "development and improvement of the individual" which are the true concerns of civilization.[1] The "ardent desire for truth...in every healthy, reflective person...develops into metaphysical longing, into religion."[2] And this religious drive has all the force and significance of a true instinct. It is "also absolutely purposeful."[3] We must oppose, said Jung, the obstructive passivity of externals in organic life and move toward relationships to the "inner world" for it is here that we find the "true root of our nature: unconditional activity."[4]

When we fail to do this our lives are like a "world...[hanging] in the darkness of space in an ugly lump, quiet, rigid, and dead, absolutely motionless and unchanging. [Only with the] essential elements of motion, light, heat and electricity" do we have a world of change and activity and form.[5] Therefore we must "reject the secularization of human interests...[and] shift our concern from the material to the transcendental world [for] the relation to material things is not purposeful....On the other hand," concludes Jung with heroic flourish, "we will affirm the will to personality, to individuality in the sense of the most radical diversity between an individual and everything else that exists, as the most radical diversification is consistent with the activity inherent in our nature, and thus the will to diversity is purposeful."[6]

The basic themes of Jung's own philosophy, as well as the outlines of his theory of individuation, are already visible in these lines. What is truly real is the human individual and the sense of inner purpose and striving for goals which belongs to the mental equipment of living beings. Jung compares the human being operating from within with the energically active world operating under the first law of thermodynamics. What is to be rejected is the non-purposive realm of collective life, and a science which produces only external goals which are of no value to the mind. Jung compares this pattern with an inert world under the power of the second [and fatal] law of thermodynamics.[7] We are, thought Jung, always embattled between two opposing forces of life and death. But we must believe in the existence of a "vital principle" which leads toward purposeful life.[8]

Three years later, with the completion of his medical studies, Jung entered on a period lasting about ten years in which he embraced science and seemed to reject completely the spiritual values he had defended in his student days. One has only to glance at the conclusion of his dissertation—a skeptical diagnosis of hysterical phenomena—or at the cynical tone of his 1905 paper, "On Spiritualistic Phenomena," where Jung reports on his experience that mediumistic people are mostly "slightly abnormal mentally," and recommends keeping close to the evidence which one might factually demonstrate.

But with the publication in 1912 of *Symbols of Transformation* Jung returned, cautiously, to the themes of his student days. Here, for the first time, we see evidence that something else besides scientific experimentation and assimilation to Freudian theory had been going on. Jung's innovative procedures seem to have had particularly to do with analytic technique. In retrospect it seems clear that Jung had never in fact used Freud's reductive technique, but was looking from the beginning toward what might be the creative potential of the personality as a whole. His diagnosis was concerned less with adaptation than with future goals. The theory of individuation followed closely upon Jung's practice of what he called the "prospective method." But that practice reflected Jung's even earlier philosophical views as a student defending human religious values over against the threat to values which he saw in scientific method.

In Chapter IV of *Symbols of Transformation*, entitled "The Hymn of Creation," Jung has just begun to discuss the significance of a dream with erotic overtones appearing in the journal of Miss Miller. Surely as a young woman her main problem is how to be creative, that is, how to have a child. But now Jung pauses and cautions: Still, that is not all. There may be a possibility of spiritual fruitfulness, of some kind of creative work lying far in the future which is also contained in the erotic fantasy. Here Jung launches into a long and interesting footnote:

> This time I shall hardly be spared the reproach of mysticism. But perhaps the facts should be further considered...it is one of the essential tasks of analysis to render impotent by dissolution the content of the complexes competing with the proper conduct of life. Psychoanalysis works backward like the science of history....History, however, knows nothing of two kinds of things, that which is hidden in the past and that which is hidden in the future....Insofar as tomorrow is already contained in today, and all the threads of the future are in place, so a more profound knowledge of the past might render possible a more or less far-reaching and certain knowledge of the future...there are certain very fine subliminal combinations of the future which are of the greatest significance for future happenings insofar as the future is conditioned by our own psychology. But ...psychological combinations [are not] the object of analysis; they would be much more the object of an infinitely refined psychological synthesis, which attempts to

follow the natural current of the libido. This we cannot do, but possibly this might happen in the unconscious, and it appears as if from time to time, in certain cases, significant fragments of this process come to light, at least in dreams.[9]

The concept of individuation is already nearly complete, though Jung does not yet dare to affirm it positively. What has been added to the formulation of his student days is the idea of an *unconscious psyche which somehow contains a knowledge of the future* just as it contains a knowledge of the personality as a whole. What we have to do is follow the natural flow of life energy so as to realize the purposes which are already there, as "prospective potencies," in an a priori but nascent form.

By 1916 a view of the purposive function of unconscious material had come to dominate Jung's discussions of analytic technique:

I am persuaded that the true end of analysis is attained when the patient has arrived at an adequate knowledge of the methods by which he can maintain contact with his unconscious, and at a psychological understanding broad enough for him to discern, as far as possible and whenever necessary, the direction of his life-line, for without this his conscious mind will not be able to follow the flow of the libido and consciously sustain the individuality he has achieved.[10]

Anyone sufficiently interested in the dream problem cannot have failed to observe that dreams also have [besides a backward continuity] a continuity *forwards*. . . . Considering a dream from the standpoint of finality, which I contrast with the causal standpoint of Freud, does not . . . involve a denial of the dream's causes, but rather a different interpretation of the associative material gathered round the dream. . . . The question may be formulated simply as follows: What is the purpose of this dream? What effect is it meant to have? These questions are not arbitrary inasmuch as they can be applied to every psychic activity. Everywhere the question of the "why" and the "wherefore" may be raised, because every organic structure consists of a complicated network of purposive functions, and each of these functions can be resolved into a series of individual facts with a purposive orientation.[11]

What Jung was describing was a *teleological view* of psychic functioning, but for many years he did not want to use that word. He
wanted to believe that one could conceive of a psyche which follows
an intrinsic developmental pattern without there being a mind
which intends that ordered development. Besides a "causal" view of
the psyche, one must take the "final" view, but we must stop short
of implying God, either within or without the organism:

> I use the word "final" rather than "teleological" in order to
> avoid the misunderstanding that attaches to the common
> conception of teleology, namely that it contains the idea of
> an anticipated end or goal.[12]

> I use the word finality intentionally, in order to avoid confu-
> sion with the concept of teleology. By finality I mean merely
> the immanent psychological striving for a goal.[13]

> One should not look for any moral function in this signi-
> fication of dreams...nor is the function of the dream
> "teleological" in the philosophic sense of the word—that is,
> of having a final end, still less of projecting a goal....[But]
> one not only can, but one *must* envisage it from the stand-
> point of finality...in order to discover to what purpose just
> these given elements are grouped together. This is not to say
> that the final meaning, in the sense of an end given *a priori*,
> pre-existed in the preparatory stages of the phenomenon we
> are discussing. According to the theory of knowledge it is
> evidently not possible, from the indubitably final meaning of
> biological mechanisms, to deduce the pre-existent fixation of
> a final end. But while thus legitimately abandoning a teleo-
> logical conclusion it would be weak-minded to sacrifice also
> the point of view of finality. All one can say is that things
> happen as if there were a fixed final aim. In psychology one
> ought to be as wary of believing absolutely in causality as of
> an absolute belief in teleology.[14]

It would not be until 1929 that Jung could reach a more satisfactory completion of his theory of individuation—one which
acknowledged the role of mind, albeit unconscious mind, in the
purposive functioning of the psyche.

b. The Self as Arbiter of Psyche

Jung's concept of the self was the last of the structural concepts which defined his psychology to be described. The individuation process proceeds, he said, not so much as the putting into action of instinctive drive forces, as rather the expression of an innate wholeness which serves at the beginning of life as the potential for development and at the end of life as the goal of all endeavor. This innate wholeness Jung called the "archetype of the self."

Jung had been deeply impressed with the translation of the *I Ching* which the sinologue Richard Wilhelm had brought back from his long years in China. The oracular hexagrams of the *I Ching* seemed to express the coincidence in time between an outer event and an inwardly felt sense of meaning—something indigenous to the mentality of the Orient but lost to Western consciousness, which has split science off from all sense of significant meaning. Upon being once asked why it was that China had developed no science, in spite of an ancient and advanced culture, Jung replied that this is in fact not true. China did have its own science, whose standard text book was the *I Ching*, but the principle of this science was different from the principle of Western science.[15]

It was that human experience of meaning which Jung thought was so little accounted for in Western science, and which in fact does violence to essential and universally experienced feelings of value and significance when it is not acknowledged:

> The intellect does indeed do harm to the soul when it dares
> to possess itself of the heritage of the spirit. It is in no way
> fitted to do this, for spirit is something higher than intellect
> since it embraces the latter and includes the feelings as
> well.... The Chinese... never strayed so far from the central
> psychic facts as to lose themselves in a one-sided over-
> development and over-valuation of a single psychic function.[16]

An interpretation of human action as motivated by instinct seemed to Jung to be just the kind of intellectualist, exterior approach which he wanted to avoid, since it neglected a great array of human experience—the facts, namely, of religious experience:

> Our time has committed a fatal error; we believe we can
> criticize the facts of religion intellectually. Like Laplace, we
> think God is a hypothesis that can be subjected to intellec-
> tual treatment, to be affirmed or denied. We completely
> forget that the reason mankind believes in the "daemon" has
> nothing whatever to do with external factors, but is simply
> due to a naive awareness of the tremendous inner effect of
> autonomous... systems.[17]

In contrast, Taoism understands life processes not causally, but in terms of meaning. Wilhelm translated *tao* as meaning. If we take on as a life task the discovery of meaning we shall come closer to embracing the facts of both outer and inner experience and may avoid the split in consciousness which Western science has promulgated.[18]

When now Wilhelm brought to Jung's attention an ancient Taoist-Buddhist text, the T'ai I Chin Hua Tsung Chih, it was decided to publish a translation of the text as a collaborative venture, with Wilhelm furnishing translation and commentary from the Eastern point of view and Jung a commentary which made connections to Western experience. The "Secret of the Golden Flower" is the best available record of the tenets of a religion called the Golden Elixir of Life which flourished in the T'ang period in eighth-century China.

Although it was adulterated at later periods with Buddhist themes involving the denial of the reality of life, both Wilhelm and Jung believed that the text in its original form was a series of psychological exercises aimed toward the transformation of one's attitude — toward release from bondage to unattainable material goals and the attainment of spiritual freedom. Spiritual freedom equaled eternal life and this felt sense of eternal life was symbolized as the Golden Flower — the beginning and the end of all existence.

Crucial to the process was the initiation of a metanoic, backward-flowing movement of psychic activity typical of all mystic paths:

> If ... it has been possible during life to set going the "backward-flowing," rising movement of the life-forces, if the forces of the *anima* are mastered by the *animus*, then a release from external things takes place. They are recognized but not desired. Thus the illusion is robbed of its strength. ... The ego withdraws from its entanglement in the world, and after death remains alive because "interiorization" has prevented the wasting of life forces in the world. Instead of these being dissipated, they have made within the inner rotation of the monad a centre of life which is independent of bodily existence.[19]

If this process of interiorization is not begun, the light (the Golden Flower) is dissipated and at death there is no independent subsistence left. True death occurs. Whoever however has practiced the "circulation of the Light" comes into relationship with the deep sources of inner creativity and feeling and can enter into the "yellow castle," the "central yellow dwelling place of the spirit."[20]

What has to be changed by reflection is the self-conscious heart, which has to direct itself toward that point where the formative spirit is not yet manifest. Within our 6 foot body, we must strive for the form which existed before the laying down of Heaven and Earth.[21]

If the exercise is successful one arrives at the "omnipresent center" in which everything is contained and from which all of creation is released. This is the "cave of power, where all that is miraculous returns to its roots."[22] It is from this center that all movement then begins anew.

Jung considered that the process of individuation which he had been observing in many of his patients as the final stage of development bore close resemblance to the process described in the ancient Chinese text of the Golden Flower. After all the more basic analytic work of analyzing unconscious complexes and becoming aware of the basic features of one's own character has been done, there still remains a crucial residue of inner dis-ease, either because of external barriers in life or because internal traits of character combine to prevent us from being fully what we might be. "I had learned that all the greatest and most important problems of life are fundamentally insoluble," wrote Jung.[23] But there are cases in which the course of further inner development, in the face of apparent insurmountable difficulty, brings about a change in point of view, or a new, unexpected potential, without these possibilities having been consciously anticipated. These people quietly "outgrew themselves." They did nothing, apparently, beyond letting things happen in a non-repressive spirit. That meant being open to shreds of fantasy, to wandering impulses. It meant giving credit to possibilities which the ego might heretofore have ignored. "The cramp in the conscious mind is relaxed" and gradually "a new attitude is created, an attitude that accepts the irrational and the incomprehensible simply because it is happening."[24] By this process the personality is enlarged and a new center is developed, one which is not strictly connected with the conscious mind but is located at a virtual mid-point between conscious and unconscious. This new center is stronger by far than the exclusively ego-centered orientation which it replaces:

If the unconscious can be recognized as a co-determining factor along with consciousness, and if we can live in such a way that conscious and unconscious demands are taken into account as far as possible, then the centre of gravity of the total personality shifts its position. It is then no longer in the ego, which is merely the centre of consciousness, but in the hypothetical point between conscious and unconscious. This new centre might be called the self.[25]

Partly inspired perhaps by the mystical tenor of the Chinese text, Jung continued on in the passage I have just cited: "If the transposition is successful, it does away with the *participation mystique* and results in a personality that suffers only in the lower storeys, as it were, but in its upper storeys is singularly detached from painful as well as from joyful happenings." It was not like Jung to display such ascetic separatism of attitude. The transformative power of great emotion, consciously experienced and accepted, played too great a role in his vision of the development of character. But there are occasions, in the face of insurmountable external limitations, conflicts of duty, and at the approach of death, when only the achievement of a more objective attitude of acceptance can free the person from being forever pulled by the tides of fortune. In achieving then the "diamond body," or "the holy fruit" one attains a true religious attitude, and with that a higher level of culture and consciousness.[26] Nothing, perhaps, has changed, and yet everything has changed, for the human person has changed and with that, one's experience of the reality of one's own fate.

Nevertheless, insisted Jung in the final chapter of his commentary, the notion of the self has nothing metaphysical in it. It is a purely psychological concept. "My aim as a psychologist is to dismiss without mercy the metaphysical claims of all esoteric teaching."[27] The self is something which must remain unknown because its locus is the unconscious psyche. It is not a content of the conscious ego; rather, the ego must be conceived as a content of the self. Yet even though unknown, its effects can be experienced. They are real—"a reality we can do something with, a living reality full of possibilities."[28] One need not deny the possibility of metaphysical entities beyond what is psychologically experienceable. But such transcendent realities must remain, like Kant's thing-in-itself, a negative, borderline concept.

Jung was positing a transcendent center of the psyche on account of the experiences of "centering" he was observing in some of his patients, and on account of the salutary maturational effect which seemed to accompany the symbolic process.[29] Like the Kant of the *Prolegomena* and the second *Critique* (as Jung understood him), one might make positive use of a transcendent concept, especially when it gives appropriate expression to the facts of human feeling, if only the step to assertion of knowledge is not taken.[30] If we say that we know, we become metaphysicians, thought Jung. If we say only that a concept is needed as an explanation for experience we remain on an empirical and psychological level. Nevertheless, Jung's difficulty with the terms *final* and *teleological* seemed to disappear in the years after his concept of the self had been published. From now on, Jung felt free to say that "Life is teleology *par excellence*" (1934).[31] The unconscious psyche contains *in potentia* the future development of the personality and acts as an "*a priori* factor...shaping the individual's fate" (1939).[32] The individuation process depends on being able to live in relationship to a subtle directive center beyond the ego.

In 1951 Jung published an entire book on the self.[33] *Aion* is an important contribution to the history of symbolism surrounding the idea of the God-man, with extensive chapters on the fish as symbol of Christ. It is however one of the least frequently consulted of Jung's works, and the reasons for that are clear to anyone who opens the book. The sheer mass of material is overwhelming; the archaic character of the symbolic images, in spite of their inherent fascination, feels so far separated from the experience of modern culture as to estrange rather than connect the reader to the roots of her/his cultural tradition. It is for the most part a book for a fellow scholar, or for a deeply meditative mood.

The four short chapters at the beginning of the book are however of a different character. They offer a.lively and concise summary of the basic themes of Jung's psychology. Chapter IV, on The Self, is to my mind one of the best small format descriptions of the individuation process. It offers *moral* reasons for positing a self at the center of the psyche.

One can go through the work of becoming conscious and withdrawing many of the projections that impede the expression of one's character and still get stuck with the *real* moral problems that begin to face us after we have disidentified from the collective solutions offered by church, family tradition, or cultural group. These deep *conflicts of duty* necessitating drastic and individual choice force us to make judgments about the sources of our inner desire. Is it instinct and natural law that speaks from within, or the voice of God (the self) pulling us toward a unique destiny? Much depends, not only on the choice which is made, but upon our judgment as to its source. If instinctive desire, then the choice becomes a matter which can satisfy the modern intellect but is morally an act of resignation. If the "will of God for my life" is however deemed to be the arbiter of choice then we may, if we have struggled earnestly with the problem, retain a sense of moral freedom and of the meaningfulness of fate and of individual character.[34]

A purely intellectual, scientific (or biological) approach cannot encompass the most important psychological data because it misses the facts of feeling and value which are crucial to psychic life.[35] Any sense of wholeness that we win as personal possession must include not just verbal concepts of order. Such "intellectual counters...sound full but are hollow.... The intellect is undeniably useful in its own field, but is a great cheat and illusionist outside of it whenever it tries to manipulate values."[36]

The concept of the self, on the other hand, offers a natural connection to universal psychic processes in which feeling and value are the primary components. "The self...[is]. the *eidos* behind the supreme ideas of unity and totality that are inherent in all monotheistic and monistic systems."[37]

In itself the self is no more than a psychological concept describing an experience of the "God within us." But "the beginnings of our whole psychic life seem to be inextricably rooted in this point, and all our highest and ultimate purposes seem to be striving towards it."[38]

The self is then, for Jung, the central archetype of the psyche. It is the source and goal of the individuation process. Individuation is a necessary postulate because without it the value experiences of the human person cannot be counted as real.

2

Aristotle's View of Teleology
as Act and Potency

Q uestions about natural order and process began to be clarified
only in the later phases of Greek philosophical thought. It was
Plato who first described a world order governed by divine intention
and contrasted it with a realm of unpurposed and therefore disordered events. Plato was attempting to solve religious dilemmas, and
it is largely because of the way in which Plato set and solved those
problems that Western thought developed as it did.[1] The religious
dilemmas of ancient Greece are like those of every age for which we
have records of human culture. They have to do with the reliability
of knowledge and with issues of chance vs. purpose in nature. Plato
believed that relativist answers to these questions must mean moral
abnegation. He had long sought an absolute standard from which
the changing perspectives of human experience might be viewed as
morally significant. In his late dialogue, the *Timaeus*, Plato now
declared that the world is for the most part ordered for the good
because the Demiurge (the Divine Craftsman) himself is good, and
wants the world to be *in order*, and good. So we should take care to
put the inner, ordered parts of ourselves, that is, the mind or soul,
at the service of the ordered purpose of the god. Otherwise we will
be like the chaff flying out of the winnowing basket into the winds
of a meaningless fate. For Plato, matter = chaos; mind = order and
God:

> Let us therefore state the reason why the framer of this uni-
> verse of change framed it at all. He was good, and...wished
> all things to be as like himself as possible....God therefore,
> wishing that all things should be good, and so far as pos-
> sible nothing be imperfect, and finding the visible universe
> in a state not of rest but of inharmonious and disorderly
> motion, reduced it to order from disorder, as he judged that

order was in every way better....When he considered, therefore, that...nothing without intelligence is to be found that
is superior to anything with it, and that intelligence is
impossible without soul, in fashioning the universe he
implanted reason in soul and soul in body, and so ensured
that his work should be by nature highest and best.[2]

Goodness is equivalent to reason, and if it is only in human
beings that we discover the capacity for reason then we may assume
that the ordering purposes of the human mind correspond to the
ordering purposes of a transcendent Being. Evidences of divine
order are present everywhere in the regular and recurrent movement
of the heavenly bodies. (The astronomer Eudoxus of Cnidus was at
that time active in Athens and associated with the Academy.) Just as
we observe order in the stars, we observe order, or *telos* in the
human being. For example, a person's most divine part, the head
(as seat of reason), imitates the shape of the heavenly spheres. The
eyes, too, like the light they receive from the divine sun, are round.
For Plato, order and regularity signify pattern and purpose. It is only
when we come to consider the disordered, irregular, and unbal-
anced movements of a world in "becoming" and in "change" that we
encounter the realm of indeterminate Necessary Cause—those
events in the universe which remain inaccessible to the "reasonable
persuasion" of ordered purpose. Before God touched the universe,
bringing definite pattern and shape to it, the world was in chaos.
The elements of a world might be there, but they were without
meaning:

> The nurse of becoming [the Receptacle; matter without the
> imprint of form] was characterized by the qualities of water
> and fire, of earth and air,...and its visual appearance was
> therefore varied; but as there was no homogeneity or bal-
> ance in the forces that filled it, no part of it was in equil-
> ibrium, but it swayed unevenly under the impact of their
> motion, and in turn communicated its motion to them. And
> its contents were in constant process of movement and sepa-
> ration, rather like the contents of a winnowing basket...they
> were all without proportion or measure.[3]

It remained for Aristotle to overcome the gulf between reason
and nature which Plato had observed by interpreting natural change
as purposive action. Change itself became for him not an instance of
chaos and a proof of the world's unreliability; it was rather the evi-

dence of continual progress toward goals which are hidden as nascent potential in the beginnings of every process, and which reveal their aims only as the process nears its final stages. Aristotle's version of teleology is that which has most often been used in theological formulations of Western Christendom. It was Aristotle's formulation which Jung also used.

What we know of Aristotle's own life reflects the nearly equally strong influences of philosophical and physiological mentors. He grew up as the son of a physician in the court of King Amyntas II of Macedonia,[4] but went at the age of eighteen to Athens and studied with Plato for nearly twenty years. After Plato's death Aristotle spent several years on the islands of Assos and Lesbos in the eastern Mediterranean. It was here that his passion for knowledge turned more specifically to biology. He made extremely detailed and accurate studies of the life cycles of many species of marine life indigenous to the coast line. When he finally returned to Athens to found his own school (after a further interval in Macedonia as tutor to the future King Alexander) Aristotle developed a *teleological view of nature* which sought to bring under one roof his observations of natural, biological process and the moral problematic of human life.

His system embedded Plato's concept of rational purpose into the changing process of nature. The Four Causes, like Plato's World Soul, subverts causal mechanistic explanations to anthropomorphically conceived goals. Unlike Plato, the natural world is not the villain of the piece.

Take any object (substance), a table for instance, he said, and consider its course. Before it was a table, it was a piece of lumber, or a tree, and before that cellulose fiber and water. These are all the *material causes* or the *material constituents* of the table, and they contain the *potentiality* for any number of developments. The wood might become a ship's helm, or the tree from which it derives might be allowed to grow into a great shade tree, or it might be cut down as a sapling and used as kindling wood for a fire, or, finally, the wood may be harvested to build the table. The material cause does not in itself cause anything, but it describes the conditions which are necessary before anything can exist (hypothetical necessity). When now the sunlight and water make the tree grow, or the carpenter comes to the wood with an order from his customer to shape a table we have the second or the *moving cause*. The third or the *formal cause* is the table itself—or the shade tree itself—the thing which we identify and call by name. It is the general concept by which the mind orders and recognizes the objects of its universe. We may say that the potential of the cellulose fiber and water to become a great shade tree, or to become a table, has now been actualized, and this is the fourth, or *final cause*—the goal to which the process has been leading.

The causal sequence just described continues. We arbitrarily choose out of the temporal process a segment which can be conceptually described with the terms just used. The table will eventually grow old and no longer be usable as a table so that it is chopped apart to be used as firewood. It is then in *privation* of its form as a table but has the *potential* for becoming fuel for the fire, after which still more elemental forms of being set the stage for new goal-directed segments of the ongoing process. Each change represents the actualization of a potential which preceded it. The water in my pot is in privation of its form as boiling water so long as it has not yet reached the boiling point. When I later set it off the stove it will gradually be deprived of its form as hot water but will not for some time reach the form of cold water.

Yet, though change is admitted to be continuous, it is not change in itself which is the centerpiece of the system, but rather the final cause to which change is directed:

> Since nature is twofold, nature as matter and nature as form, and the latter is an end, and everything else is for the end, the cause as that for which must be the latter.[5]

> We commonly say that 'this is for the sake of that' wherever there is apparent some end which the movement reaches if nothing stands in the way. So it is evident that something of this sort exists (and it is precisely what we call *nature*).[6]

> Now those who in ancient times were the first to philosophize about nature were thinking about the material origin of that sort of cause—what and what kind of thing is matter, how does the universe come to be out of it, and with what cause of movement....But if the existence of man and the animals and their parts is natural, we must have to say of each part—of flesh, bone, blood,...and of face, foot, in virtue of what, and in respect of what sort of capability, each is such as it is....If we were speaking of a bed or some such thing, we should be trying to define its form rather than its matter such as the metal or timber....For its nature in respect of conformation is more important than its material.[7]

To describe the functional operation of natural processes in terms of final goals or final causes seems easily possible. Thus: a house is built in stages toward a fixed goal, spiders spin webs, plants produce leaves to protect fruit and swallows build nests, all toward an end.[8] The analysis of motion as goal-directed leads however in Aristotle's philosophy toward a hierarchy of being culminating in an unmoving Mover who serves as ultimate goal and ultimate support for the entire system.

At the crown of the universe, as the highest of the series, the Unmoved Mover circles the universe in the outermost heaven, eternally maintaining the world as the only fully actualized substance:

> That the final cause exists in immovable things is clear by distinguishing the two meanings of "final cause." For the final cause may be (a) for some thing or (b) that for the sake of which, and of these the one may exist but the other may not; and it [the final cause] causes motion as something which is loved, and that which is moved moves the others.[9]

The final cause of movement in all of nature is thus the longing desire for the full consummation of being. Love for God—or love for the Self—is the ultimate purpose of temporal life.

If the goal of change in nature is directed toward non-moving, transcendent Being, it is also the case (to reverse the movement) that the natural world is supported by what Aristotle and all other Greeks of his time believed to be the absolute necessity of eternal things. By that they meant the eternity of the stars and the everlasting regularity of the sun, the eternal recurrence of night and day, spring and summer, fall and winter. For Aristotle it meant not only the rotation of the heavenly bodies but that of the Unmoved Mover as well. What is absolutely necessary admits of no change whatsoever. Since events which occur with absolute necessity must be cyclical, they must "return upon themselves," and must have an originative source in their pattern of movement, rectilinear movements not affording an eternal succession of antecedent causes without infinite regress:

> Then are all the things that come-to-be of this contingent character? Or, on the contrary, is it absolutely necessary for some of them to come-to-be?...For instance, is it necessary that solstices come-to-be, i.e. impossible that they should fail to be able to occur?...what is 'of necessity', coincides with what is 'always', since that which 'must-be' cannot possibly 'not-be'. Hence a thing is eternal if its being is necessary.... It

is in circular movement, therefore, and in cyclical coming-to-be that the absolutely necessary is to be found.[10]

With the concept of the absolutely necessary we are in the realm of fully actualized potential—of things that are forever—on which the contingent world depends as the source of its stability and being, as the ground of secure knowledge and as the end of aspiration. Actual being is ontologically prior to potential being. Aristotle's world is a non-evolutionary universe; the chicken always comes before the egg. Horses produce horses and men generate men. Marjorie Grene has remarked that "this is the ultimate metaphysical significance of the priority of the actual over the potential, the fully over the partly real. Even in things that change it is the *entelecheia*, the immanent goal of change, that *is* their being....Everywhere the actual *before* the possible, the fully developed before the embryonic and immature, the end of the road, as present goal, before the road that leads to it."[11]

For so long as modern science had not yet invaded the Greek conception of time Aristotle's teleology was however a perfectly suitable explanation of nature. It was taken up by the scholastics in the twelfth century and remained for nearly seven hundred years the dominant and dogmatic view in the Western world, sustaining a hopeful view of the meaning of human life. The achievement of the teleological view is this: the meaningless materiality, the matter of the universe, is seen as transformed by the presence within it of order and form and goals.

By setting out Aristotle's system in parallel format next to Jung's views I hope that I have been able to make my first point, which is to show how Jung's concept of individuation and its corollary, the self, is an example of the kind of teleological religious thinking which found its first expression in Aristotle.

My second goal will be now to trace this idea, and the fate which befell it, down through the nineteenth century and into the early part of the twentieth century so that one can observe the intellectual climate of the world in which Jung's ideas were formed.

Section B
The Nineteenth-Century Challenge
to Final Cause

3

Goals in Nature:
Kant, Schopenhauer, von Hartmann

The teleological edifice erected by Plato and by Aristotle—a world view which regarded all of nature as a developmental process headed toward the final goals of a transcendent Being—remained in its main structure unchallenged until the end of the eighteenth century.[1] Over the next seventy-five years it was however dealt three mighty blows from which it never recovered; the Greek views of time, motion, and mind upon which a teleological philosophy depended could no longer be sustained.

The first blow to the structure was delivered by Immanuel Kant's evaluation of the role of reason as a guide to truth.[2] We must be mindful that the intellectual criticism of a powerful idea, fueled as it was by authoritative cultural tradition and by an ability to satisfy ethical and religious aspirations, came about not only because of the unique genius of Kant, but also because he lived in a period in which real scientific progress had begun to make it possible to think in new ways. Developments in practical mechanics surely helped suggest a machine theory of life.[3] Improved water mills in the eleventh century, windmills in the twelfth century, the spinning wheel in the thirteenth century, mechanical clocks in the fourteenth century, movable type in the fifteenth century and matchlock and wheel-lock firearms in the sixteenth century were a part of the cultural change that accompanied new ideas. Over the course of the previous century the principles of Newtonian physics had spread throughout Europe, the microscope had been invented, the new science of paleontology had been identified. When now in 1781 Kant proved that no conception of reality and certainly no theory of transcendent principles can ever be demonstrated using pure logic or pure reason alone, he challenged the rationalistic idiom of philosophical discourse. In respectable scientific discussions people could no longer talk about "God" as though this was a matter of fact thing which one could just assume.

But Kant was nevertheless open to ways in which thought may aid both the philosophic search for unitive principles *and* the scientific effort to discriminate between various causes. A passage toward the end of the first *Critique* makes this clear. On the one hand, reason must be free to observe the world, not imposing artificially unitive criteria on what is observed. On the other hand, following the dictates of its own nature *as* reason, it is proper to seek understanding. It is a fact that we understand only in genera:

> With what right can reason, in its logical employment, call upon us to treat the multiplicity of powers exhibited in nature as simply a disguised unity, and to derive this unity, so far as may be possible, from a fundamental power—how can reason do this, if it be free to admit as likewise possible that all powers may be heterogeneous, and that such systematic unity of derivation may not be in conformity with nature?...The law of reason which requires us to seek for this unity is a necessary law, since without it we should have no reason at all, and without reason no coherent employment of the understanding, and in the absence of this no sufficient criterion of empirical truth...we have no option save to presuppose the systematic unity of nature as objectively valid and necessary. (A651/B679)[4]

Kant proposed that there are actually subjective maxims of reason which allow us to pursue any one of a variety of courses in our attempt to understand the environment in which we live. We may seek to understand a particular field in terms of ever higher degrees of unity (the principle of homogeneity) or we may discriminate ever lower degrees of unity (the principle of variety), or we may observe that the more fully we specify differences the closer we approach to elements of continuity with other species (the principle of affinity) (A666-7/B694-5).

At an underlying level however all thought reaches toward a first principle, toward a systematic, unified explanation. We have no choice about that; for it is simply the case that our minds think in this manner. Kant had already shown that the application of reason as though it might be a constitutive determinant of objects or of an Object (God) of which we can have no experience leads to serious mistakes about the nature of human knowledge. We may more properly accept the (psychological, cosmological, and theological) transcendental ideas as objective in their own right, as regulative principles which serve our effort to understand nature:

The concept of a highest intelligence is a mere idea...it is only a scheme constructed in accordance with the conditions of the greatest possible unity of reason....[But] the things of the world must be viewed *as if* they received their existence from a highest intelligence. The idea is thus really only a heuristic, not an ostensive concept. It does not show us how an object is constituted, but how, under its guidance, we should *seek* to determine the constitution and connection of the objects of experience. (A671/B699)

The principles adumbrated by reason regulate the parameters of possible experience but cannot prove its truth. The concept of Final Cause is a regulative principle belonging to the nature of thought. Its actual application is in science and in all other kinds of interpretive work where we seek unitive explanations of natural phenomena.

In the century which followed Kant, philosophers and scientists worked many variations of this theme, exploring the meaning of empirical inquiry, the place of mind and of reason, and the necessity of transcendent principles in an explanation of nature.

Arthur Schopenhauer was pleased to share with Kant in the dethronement of reason from its position as supreme arbiter of truth in nature.[5] But he could not agree with Kant that we therefore know nothing about why things are as they are. Our basic motives spring from a psychological, or volitional source, the Will. The world is a phenomenal expression of that Will.[6] As it is in the human being, so is it in the universe as a whole. Schopenhauer's philosophy was thus at two levels anthropomorphic. He claimed that what Kant had shown is a regulative principle of human reason is in fact a constitutive Primal Cause. Secondly, he projected a human cause (in an extended sense, a character of organic nature), the Will, into the universe as generally applicable in the macrocosm.

It is easily understandable that a man like Jung, schooled in the epistemological subjectivity of a certain kind of neo-Kantianism[7] and following a profession in which human affectivity is the main subject, would find Schopenhauer's voluntaristic philosophy most attractive. He first used Schopenhauer as an advocate in his battle against belief in material causes of life. In his 1897 lecture to fellow members of the Zofingia Verein Jung argued against physiologists who are "struggling to explain life in terms of natural laws, when all the time it is clear that life exists *despite* these laws."[8] He cited Schopenhauer in support for his position:

We see more and more clearly that what is chemical can never be referred to what is mechanical, and that what is

organic can never be referred to what is chemical or electrical. But those who today once more take this old misleading path will soon slink back silent and ashamed, as all
their predecessors have done.[9]

Having once discovered in Schopenhauer the Will as First Cause
in Nature, Jung thought he found the Will described also as Final
Cause. I refer once again to the important comments in Jung's 1925
Seminar Notes:

> In *Will in Nature* he drifts into a teleological attitude, though
> this is in direct opposition to his original thesis....In this
> latter work he assumes that there is direction in the creating
> will, and *this point of view I took as mine.* (my italics)

> From Schopenhauer I first got the idea of the universal urge
> of will, and the notion that this might be purposive.[10]

Jung actually misread Schopenhauer's intention in the *Will in
Nature*, but the teleological flavoring of the book is so heavily suggestive that this would be easy to do.[11] Schopenhauer quotes from
Aristotle's works (*De partibus, Physica, De Caelo, Eth. Mag.*) more frequently than from any other source, and the pages of his text resem-
ble nothing so much as an Aristotelian exercise in natural teleology:

> As the will has equipped itself with every organ and every
> weapon, offensive as well as defensive, so has it likewise
> provided itself in every animal shape with an *intellect*, as a
> means of preservation for the individual and the species.[12]

> The manifest adaptation of each animal for its mode of life
> and outward means of subsistence, even down to the
> smallest detail, together with the exceeding perfection of its
> organization, form abundant material for teleological con-
> templation, which has always been a favourite occupation of
> the human mind....The universal fitness for their ends...in
> all parts of the organisms of the lower animals without
> exception, proclaim too distinctly for it ever to have been
> seriously questioned, that here no forces of Nature acting by
> chance and without plan have been at work, but a will.[13]

Schopenhauer nevertheless did not mean to assert a teleological
demonstration of purpose in nature.[14] He utilized Aristotle's format
in describing what things are "for the purpose of." But he would not
have agreed that things develop toward a goal.

Schopenhauer also used Chevalier de Lamarck's pre-Darwinian evolutionary theory, that organisms change over time, developing structures in order to adapt to environmental needs, as a model description of the activity of the Will. Lamarck's theory, like Aristotle's, is fully teleological because it proposes that mind is at work in effecting a transition between first and final cause. For Schopenhauer this is not the case. He calls Lamarck "immortal," but objects to Lamarck's view of mind as cause: "Long before the organs necessary for its preservation could have been produced by means of such endeavors as these through countless generations, the whole species must have died out from the want of them."[15]

Schopenhauer's second objection to Lamarck was his view of evolution *in time*:

> The thought could never enter into De Lamarck's head, that the animal's will, as a thing in itself, might lie outside Time, and in this sense be prior to the animal itself.[16]

What Lamarck ought to have seen, thought Schopenhauer, is that his primary animal (if conceived in time, as a fully potential being) must once have had neither shape nor organs and must then over time have transformed itself into a myriad of animal shapes. But the primary animal (Aristotle's prime matter) is rather, thought Schopenhauer, the Will. What we see is the will to live in all extant being. But whereas for Lamarck "it is the will which arises out of knowledge," in fact, the Will is blind. No knowledge or conscious intention guides the expression of the Will in the phenomenal world:

> The physico-theological thought, that Nature must have been regulated and fashioned by an intellect, however well it may suit the untutored mind, is nevertheless fundamentally wrong. For the intellect is only known to us in animal nature, consequently as an absolutely secondary and subordinate principle in the world, a product of the latest origin; it can never therefore have been the condition of the existence of that world.... Now the will on the contrary, being that which fills everything and manifests itself immediately in each... appears everywhere as that which is primary. It is just for this reason, that the explanation of all teleological facts is to be found in the will of the being itself in which they are observed.[17]

For the purposes of this study it is as important to know what Jung discovered through Schopenhauer as it is to know what Schopenhauer actually argued. I propose the following: I think that Jung found Aristotle through Schopenhauer. (His second source of Aristotelian thought will have been in Hans Driesch; see Chapter 5, below.) The resemblance of pattern between Aristotelian teleology and Jung's concept of the individuation process is too marked for there not to have been a literary source, and there is no evidence that Jung ever read Aristotle at first hand. Jung's favored philosophical reading was all Platonic in texture. Beyond this, we have Jung's specific reference to the *Will in Nature* in the 1925 "Seminar Notes."

I think, too, that Jung got his idea of an unconscious source and center of psychic life from Schopenhauer. He borrowed however from Eduard von Hartmann the factor of *directionality* in unconscious psychic life which is implied in Schopenhauer's Aristotelian and Lamarckian references, but explicitly denied in the details of his exposition of Will.

Eduard von Hartmann brought over to a late nineteenth-century, post-Darwinian generation the metaphysical ambitions of the early part of the century. He united the voluntaristic Will of Schopenhauer with the unconscious Idea of Schelling to form a teleological philosophy which according to von Hartmann made its point on the basis of an inductive procedure. Utilizing the new, empirical facts of biology and physics, von Hartmann computed the statistical chances for there being no divine plan to account for the order displayed in nature, and came out with overwhelming probabilities against a materialistic view. In the light of present-day knowledge von Hartmann's speculative statistical inductions have become unreadable, but in his own day von Hartmann's major work, *The Philosophy of the Unconscious*, was the most widely read of philosophical books.[18] First published in 1869, it went through eight editions within ten years.[19] Looking back, one can see that its great appeal must have been to educated intellectuals who hoped to be able to embrace the inductive procedures of the new scientific heroes and yet be faithful to the ancient hope in a divine order.[20]

Schopenhauer's concept of the blind Will, thought von Hartmann, certainly provides an opening through which we can conceive of an unconscious impulse as the "moulding principle of Nature and History," but without the formulation of that willing impulse as also ideational in character there is no possibility of understanding the order which we perceive in the world:

It does not occur to...[Schopenhauer] to bring forward the *Idea* to explain the adaptation of means to end in Nature, which rather in genuine idealistic fashion he regards as a merely subjective appearance....He altogether fails to perceive that the unconscious Will of Nature *eo ipso* presupposes an unconscious Idea as goal, content, or object of itself, without which it would be empty, indefinite, and objectless.[21]

On the contrary, said von Hartmann, we can gain insight into the real nature of causes by observing our own conscious mental activity. We will an end in our minds, we conceive how it may be obtained, we take steps to realize it, and we finally obtain the desired end. These four steps do not obviate the scientific law of causality, they even presuppose it, but they do arrange the causal sequence in such a way that mind is included. "The union of willed and realised end, or final causation, is by no means something existing by the side of or even despite causality, but it is only a particular combination of different kinds of causality, such that the first and last terms are identical, only the one ideal and the other real, the one presented in the willed idea, and the other in reality."[22] We don't have to overthrow science; we must only include ideal, or mental terms within our descriptive frame.

We may observe what von Hartmann thought was "the existence of a spiritual cause" in the easy example of the brooding behavior of birds. How is it possible that the "cheerful and lively bird" suddenly abandons its customary habits and begins a "wearisome brooding over its eggs"? Even if we suppose that material causes—the existence of the egg, the existence of the bird, and the temperature of the egg—should account for nearly all of the brooding behavior, the chances that material causes account totally for this change of behavior (and here von Hartmann presents two pages of statistical calculations as evidence) are practically nil. Or take the case of normal vision. There are fully thirteen physiological conditions which must coincide (von Hartmann may have borrowed from von Helmholtz's recently published *Physiological Optics*, 1856, 1860, 1867) in order for vision to occur. Even assuming a probability of 9/10 that the material conditions of embryonic life cause normal vision to develop in the child, "still the probability that *all* these conditions follow from the material relations of the embryonic life is only $0.9^{13} = 0.254$. The probability, therefore, of a spiritual cause being required for the sum of conditions = 0.746, i.e. almost 3/4." The weight of these statistics is such that we are justified, thought von Hartmann, in concluding "the co-operation of spiritual causes, without the latter being open to immediate inspection."[23]

The advent of modern biogenetics and the development of improved knowledge about the phylogenetic sources of instinctive behavior (see Part II, Chap. 6 above) makes it painful to review such "proofs" of design, even without the statistics. But it is well to remember the painful dilemma of the educated class at the turn of the century. Its members stood at the forefront of cultural change which was to affect the personal, inner view of life of the individual more drastically than any other change in the history of Western culture. They must not only resolve their own hearts concerning the ultimate facts but they must shape through their teaching the generation to come. Jung's psychology of individuation must be seen *not only* on its practical merits as a theory of psychic process, but *also* in its historical context as one kind of attempt at resolution of the dilemma between science and religion which formed the major issue for turn-of-the-century intellectuals. In his student days Jung defended von Hartmann's demonstration of purpose in nature using the method of calculation of probability.[24] In his later years Jung referred to von Hartmann mostly as the author of a philosophy which posited the unconscious as real. Jung never attempted an inductive proof of purpose in nature using statistical calculus. He did however, as I hope to have demonstrated in this essay, using a subjectivist epistemological base, claim inductive, empirical evidence (the evidence of personal feeling) for his theory of archetypes and for his theory of individuation. The pattern for such proofs of non-material formative and directive agents is to be found in late nineteenth-century intellectual life.[25]

4

The Struggle with Vitalism: From Stahl to Haeckel

Within the sciences themselves, rationalist theological assumptions began to seem like a precarious basis for the advance of knowledge as early as the eighteenth century. Scientists who held to a belief in divine purpose began to seek other grounds for their conviction. The laws of mechanics might hold for the entire universe, but besides the laws of physics, some other principles must be at work in the living organism. Georg Ernest Stahl (1660–1734), a prominent German chemist and medical scientist, proposed that this principle is invisible soul.

When we examine the chemical properties of the organism, he said, everything about it seems to work toward destruction and disintegration. Yet there is something in all that lives, and for as long as it lives, which causes the organism to be maintained, and not destroyed. This something is a separate substance not found in inorganic matter. When rational soul enters into a body life begins, and when it departs life ends.

The doctrine that organic life is essentially different from inorganic matter *by reason of an organizational and directive principle within it* is known as vitalism. Vitalistic theories were to be the main polemic focus of nineteenth-century physicists and biologists who sought an autonomous basis for their science. Vitalism became the main line of defense for those who believed in the unique character of human life and in the transcendent purposes of a divine creator. Combatants on both sides of the war brought empirical facts and inductive reasoning to bear in favor of their respective cases.

In Stahl's view the empirical facts which formed the basis of his argument had to do with the incredible organizational complexity of the living body and the impossibility that the energic forces which sustain life could have their source in simple chemical elements. One must believe that a rational, intelligent substance (namely rational soul), not identified with the bodily substances, inhabits the body and sets its various parts in motion and directs their activity for as long as corporal life lasts.[1]

Stahl's theory was not in fact successful. The notion of a soul-substance passing in and out of material bodies, lending to them the power of movement and development, was too primitive for the scientific imagination of even the eighteenth century. Too little scope was allowed in Stahl's theory for understanding the organism in terms of its own internal development.

A modified version of Stahl's theory was however adopted by the medical faculty of the University of Montpellier and it passed thus, through the writings of the German nature-philosophers, into the nineteenth century. Two related vitalist principles became the subject of intense discussion: 1) Life cannot be reduced to non-life. 1a) Organisms cannot finally be explained in terms of their chemical properties. 1b) Living creatures did not evolve from non-living substances. 2) Life cannot be created in the laboratory from inanimate matter.[2]

Early in the nineteenth century it seemed that the chemical hypothesis might well be successfully defended. Two chemists, Justus von Liebig and Jöns-Jakob Berzelius, maintained that organic and inorganic elements are basically dissimilar.[3] But in 1828 another chemist, Friedrich Wöhler, synthesized an organic compound, urea, thus exploding at least one tenet of the vitalist theory.

Hard on the heels of this achievement in chemistry, the second great blow, after Kant's *Critique*, to a teleological view of nature in general, and to vitalism in particular, was struck—first in 1842 by Robert Mayer, and then, five years later, by Hermann von Helmholtz, who first stated the laws of thermodynamics.

Some of the earlier vitalists had conceived of the transcendent substance which is present in the organism as a kind of vital fluid. But others thought of it as a *vis vitalis*—a kind of vital force. It was in its form as a postulated force that Helmholtz's meditations about the meaning of vitalism led him to the discovery of the laws of energy. It seems to be the fate of young people, he later recounted, always to be "eager to attack at once the most profound problems."[4] He took up for himself the problem of vital force. "I had the feeling that there was something contrary to nature in...[Stahl's] explanation," he said, but for a time he could not say exactly what that was. It finally occurred to him that the idea of vital force made of every living body a *perpetuum mobile*. He had heard the problems of perpetual motion being discussed by his father and by the mathematics teachers during his school days. Now, in his last year as a student at the Friedrich-Wilhelm Institute, he was working in the library and in his spare moments turned to the eighteenth-century mathematical texts of Daniel Bernoulli and d'Alembert. He was then able to phrase his question about vitalism as a question about the necessary conditions of motion: "What relations must exist among the various natural forces for perpetual motion to be possible and do these relations actually exist?" Helmholtz's 1848 essay, "On the Conservation of Energy," brought the mathematical equations which apply to the problem of energy and motion to the attention of physiologists. In a later lecture Helmholtz described his discovery and what it meant for the theory of vitalism:

> No matter what it was called—the *archeus* [of Paracelsus], the anima inscia [of Stahl], the vital force, the healing force of nature, or whatever—the power to develop the body according to plan and to accommodate it suitably to external conditions remained the most basic property of this hypothetical controlling principle postulated by vitalistic theory.
>
> It is apparent, however, that this notion runs directly counter to the law of the conservation of force. If a vital force were to suspend for a time the action of gravity on a body, it could be raised without work to any height desired, and if the action of gravity were subsequently restored, it would perform work of any amount desired. Thus work could be obtained without expense out of nothing....
>
> In reality, however, there is no evidence that the living organism can perform the slightest trace of work without a corresponding consumption of energy. If we consider the work done by animals, we find it similar in every respect to that done by a steam engine. Animals, like machines, can move and do work only if they are continuously supplied with fuel (that is to say, food) and air containing oxygen. Both animals and machines give off this material again in a burned state, and both produce simultaneously heat and work....
>
> If, then, the law of the conservation of force holds good for living beings too, it follows that the physical and chemical forces of the material employed in building up the body are in continuous action without interruption....Physiologists should thus expect an unconditional conformity of the forces of nature to laws.[5]

"Continuous action!" "Unconditional conformity of nature to laws!" Therefore a deterministic universe, even for human beings! No freedom of the will, no principle of mind to transcend the endless series of causes, no purpose, and most of all, no hope of a good end, of immortality! These are the themes of the conflict which resonated down through the next fifty years. Helmholtz's call for a reduction of the organism to a machine and for a reduction of body to chemical elements was eagerly taken up by the physiologists of his Berlin group. (See Part I above, pp. 64 f.)

Du Bois-Reymond was just completing his major book, *Untersuchungen über Thierische Elektricität* (1848), and he confided in a letter to Ludwig the contents of its prologue: "I have attempted in it to convince physiologists of the foolishness of their notion of a vital force; this passage is written with loving care, and I hope you will be in agreement with it."[6]

The reductionist goals toward which Ludwig, Brücke, Helmholtz, and Du Bois-Reymond were actually directing their research were succinctly stated by Ludwig's pupil, Adolf Fick, in 1874. "Vital phenomena," he said, "are caused by the forces inherent in the material bases of the living organism....In so far...as all forces are in final analysis nothing other than motive forces determined by the interaction of material atoms and in so far as the general science of motion and its causal forces is called mechanics, we must designate the direction of physiological research as truly 'mechanical.' "[7]

What Jung thought of the work of these men of science is recorded in his turn-of-the-century *Zofingia Lectures*. "Hidebound, educated philistines!" he said. "One day people will laugh and weep at the same time over the disgraceful way in which highly praised German scholars have gone astray. They will build monuments to Schopenhauer...but they will curse Carl Vogt, Ludwig Büchner, Moleschott, Du Bois-Reymond, and many others, for having stuffed a passel of materialist rubbish into the gaping mouths of those guttersnipes, the educated proletariat."[8] (I remind the reader that these are student lectures, surely never intended for serious publication. But they faithfully record the convictions which Jung was to defend throughout his life.)

So great was the pressure among nineteenth-century scientists to assume a mechanistic-materialist philosophical stance that the great French experimental physiologist Claude Bernard (1813–78), who denied the relevance of every philosophical view to scientific work, was himself accused of being a new kind of vitalist.[9] He regarded metaphysical hypotheses as empty terms which cover our lack of knowledge; even the word *life* is such a word. "Life is nothing but a word which means ignorance, and when we characterize a phenomenon as vital, it amounts to saying that we do not know its immediate cause or its condition."[10] If we do not understand "life" or "vital," we also have no way of ascertaining the First Cause of any phenomenon. So materialist hypotheses also will not do; they are just as speculative as those of the vitalist.

To be sure, said Bernard, we may agree with the vitalists that "living beings exhibit phenomena peculiar to themselves and unknown in inorganic nature. I admit," he said, "that manifestations of life cannot be wholly elucidated by physico-chemical sciences."[11] But this means that living things have a complex organization and differ in appearance from inorganic bodies. It does not mean that the scientific method with which we approach them is different in kind from that with which we study non-living phenomena. The concept of finality makes sense if we mean observing the organism, its growth and the interrelation of body organs.[12] But when we use the term *Final Cause*, we necessarily assume also a First Cause, and "First causes are outside the realm of science."[13]

Bernard's overriding concern was not with philosophy, but with excluding philosophical assumptions in order to arrive at a correct scientific methodology:

> When a man of science takes a philosophic system as his base in pursuing a scientific investigation, he goes astray in regions that are too far from reality, or else the system gives his mind a sort of false confidence and an inflexibility out of harmony with the freedom and suppleness that experimenters should always maintain in their researches.[14]

The role of empirical facts in science, said Bernard (and here one sees the great difference between his approach and that of the Berlin group), is in demonstrating hypotheses about the behavior of phenomena, not in proving *either* a chemical or a divine origin for organic life. It is not that we should try to exclude the mind from science. On the contrary, within the realm of scientific work the imagination finds its true place as the framer of hypotheses:

> We must give free rein to our imagination; the idea is the essence of all reasoning and all invention. All progress depends on that. It cannot be smothered or driven away on the pretense that it may do harm; it must only be regulated and given a criterion.[15]

Bernard described this inductive reasoning process as it operates in science. The scientist notes a fact. As a result of the observation an idea is born in his/her mind. Then reason takes over and devises an experiment which might demonstrate the hypothesis. As a result of the experiment which is then performed new facts emerge which must in turn be observed and which serve as starting points for new hypotheses. "Ideas, given form by facts, embody science."[16]

For seeking to limit his scientific ambitions to the discovery of proximate causes for phenomena, and for denying the relevance of First and Final cause Bernard became fairly isolated in the midst of nineteenth-century turmoil over the nature of reality. It is only in recent years that the modernity of his thought has been re-recognized and appreciated.[17]

In the meantime, while the quarrel over the scope of scientific inquiry and the provability of vitalist hypotheses was at its height, still a third great blow was struck against teleology. In 1859, Charles Darwin published his *Origin of Species*. If Darwin's theory of evolution should be true, it would demolish the connection between First and Final Cause which must hold in order for a teleological view of nature to be valid.

The Aristotelian concept of an ordered universe depends on a view of time as eternal; change occurs only within the patterned round of yearly seasons, of the sun's revolutions, of the moon's phases, of rainfall and drought, and of the shifting positions of the heavenly bodies. (See pp. 225 f. above.) The Biblical creationist view of a universe originating some few thousand years ago is merely a variation on the Greek concept, for it too sets the events of time within the near purview of an eternal principle, which sustains and secures the purposed order. Yet now, as Loren Eiseley noted, man must adjust himself, "not just to time in unlimited quantities, but rather *to complete historicity, to the emergence of the endlessly new*."[18] On the level of empirical fact, which was, as we remember, the level on which teleological views were being tested in mid-nineteenth century, following the demise of the rationalistic theological defense, it now seemed impossible to believe in a divinely intentioned world order. The theory of natural selection demonstrated the past rather than the future, causal relationship rather than future propensities, in a chain reaching back to the beginnings of organic life.

More than that, and in spite of the marvelous adaptation to environment exhibited in many organic species, there is more evidence in the paleontological record of accident than of design. The reversing bond between potential and actual is thus broken.

Evolutionary theory does not maintain that only those features of an organism which are the most fit for their environment will be selected to survive. It says only that features which are positively harmful will be selected out. It is thus *chance* which rules the world of evolutionary biology; concepts of purpose survive only as an expression of adaptation to a specific environment. For example, teeth serve the purpose of apprehending food and of mastication; legs serve the purpose of locomotion.

The atmosphere in intellectual circles in the years following the publication of the *Origin of Species* was thoroughly politicized. Du Bois-Reymond recorded with glee that Darwin's *Origin* had finally persuaded the last of the scientific diehards. Lamarck had dared too early to break open the system. But now the grounds on which one might argue against the creation of new species by crossing of old ones were recognized as untenable. The objections based on an incomplete paleontological record had been countered by Lyell's geological achievement, and Darwin's arguments in favor of natural selection seemed completely satisfactory. The purposeful adaptation of living organisms was now understandable, for that which was unsuitable to environment had with few exceptions been destroyed in the struggle for existence.

> Thus Vitalism was driven out of its most powerful entrench-
> ment into flight. Surely, a scientific text of purely theoretical
> interest has never yet, so quickly and in such wide circles,
> seized and uprooted the entire educated world. It celebrated
> a triumph in England itself, and in Germany, with its
> powerful church influences, a success which must be rated
> twice as great. Even a political party among us saw itself
> necessitated to take notice of the dangerous seeming revolu-
> tion in thought, and in this very hall a memorial service for
> Darwin became the object of such hateful criticism that it
> reached the speaker's rostrum of the house of Parliament.[19]

Of all those who acclaimed the new theories of evolution none came so close to making a career out of discipleship to Darwin as Ernst Haeckel.[20] His *Generelle Morphologie der Organismen* (1866) and his *Natürliche Schöpfungsgeschichte* (1868) followed close upon the publication of the *Origin of Species*, and intended to spread the news to fellow German scientists. Darwin's own work was carefully critical, and he only with great hesitation concluded that the results of his research allowed for no more than an agnostic stand with regard to the existence of transcendent Being. Haeckel, by contrast, was from the beginning a missionary: Darwin's theories were thoroughly proven, and no doubt could be accepted as respectable. All of nature may be reduced to mechanical and causal effects. Traditional religious views have been totally discredited.[21]

Haeckel founded his own Monistic League in order to further religious values in a non-theistic world, and wanted a religion, as his follower Heinrich Schmidt declared, "on the sure ground of modern science, a religion that overcomes all previous religions because it builds beyond them—a new religion for the new man."[22] Darwin's theory became an article of faith. Article 9 of Haeckel's *Theses for the Organization of Monism* reads:

> The whole of nature is in causal connection with a unitary process of development and that cosmogenesis consists in an unbroken chain of formations through change. That goes just as much for the processes of anorganic nature as for the process of organic beings....Modern science must completely reject any so called "creation" of the world....An anthropological "Creator" exists just as little as any divinely ordered "moral" world order.[23]

Haeckel fervently believed that Darwin's great achievement was to overcome every last vestige of teleological thinking. His popular book, *The Riddle of the Universe*, was published in 1899, immediately translated, and became a worldwide best seller. "The older view of idealistic dualism is breaking up," he wrote. "But upon the vast field of ruins rises, majestic and brilliant, the new sun of our realistic monism, which reveals to us the wonderful temple of nature in all its beauty."[24]

Now the uproar began in earnest. The Reverend Adolf Stöcker accused Haeckel in his *Deutschen evangelischen Kirchenzeitung* (March 31, 1900) of "sovereign disregard of the boundaries given to the natural scientist," and of "passing judgment on the invisible world and the world beyond, which has led countless human beings to disbelief."[25] Professor Paulsen of Berlin accused him of being "purely negative...of filling the world of his mechanistic physics with needy, empty words."[26] Such famous names as Harnack, Rade, and Troeltsch joined in what became, according to Schmidt, a witch-hunt against Haeckel.

Criticism of Haeckel was not limited to European voices. William Cheney, a California lawyer, offered a defensive brief:

> I have read the work and am one of those for whose benefit it may be presumed it was written. I am one of the human

beings whom he would turn adrift on the sea of profound despondency, with the cables of their vessels slipped, and the sails idly slapping the yards and masts.[27]

"The struggle of life is for the individual!" he argued. "There is something more to a human individual than the 'chemical activities' of the cells of the cerebrum."[28]

Was there now no more hope that human values might have a transcendent source? There was, and this new hope came in the person of Hans Driesch, and the scientifically based doctrines of neo-vitalism which he developed. Driesch's neo-vitalism was for many years extraordinarily important in the philosophy of biology. Even today, Driesch continues to be mentioned in the literature. His theories were also, as I hope to show, critically important for Jung.

5

Neo-Vitalism: Driesch and Jung

Hans Driesch began his career as a student of zoology under August Weismann at Freiburg, then moved to Münich, and finally received his doctorate in biology in 1889 as a student of Ernst Haeckel at Jena.

He was at first completely committed to the mechanistic principles of his famous teacher. But while he was experimenting with the eggs of sea urchins he discovered something which startlingly contradicted the prevalent theory of morphogenetic development.[1] If the fertilized ovum is divided at the stage of the first two or four blastomeres, then two or four complete organisms, though smaller in size than a normal size sea urchin, can be reared from those divided cells. Driesch continued to work with modifications of this fact during ten years at the Marine Biological Station at Naples. The conclusions he drew as a result of his experimental work led him far from the laboratory, into the field of philosophy where he finally made his career. A professorship at Heidelberg in 1911 was followed by a post at Cologne and finally at Leipzig.

Driesch realized that no current theory of the development of organisms could account for his discovery of the behavior of sea urchins. If each of the cells of the embryo is destined to play a specific function in the developed organism then the creature ought to fall apart if crucial, functioning elements are removed from it. A machine would do this. But an organism is evidently not a machine. Each of the parts of the divided ovum reconstituted itself as a whole and developed in an integrated way. The organism must somehow have *intended* or *known how* to do this.

Since nothing could be observed which might account for the unity and for the development of the functioning organism, Driesch proposed that there must be an unknown, non-material factor operating to produce and regulate the life process. This factor must not

247

in any way interfere with the chemical or energic properties operating in the organism, for that would mean to confess disbelief in that visible world which was presently the most exciting object of scientific discovery. Driesch always believed that the laws of energy operate in the physical universe.[2] But though nothing might interfere with the quantitative factors at work in a mechanistic universe, there might be, indeed Driesch thought there must be something which might change the *direction* of energic movement, and which does in certain cases thus effect change in the world of objects. Anorganic nature follows the mechanistic laws of nature. In the case of organic nature, however, we must postulate a *non-material ordering entity* to account for the fact of life and for the goal-directed patterning which we see in life. We have to believe in a dualistic explanation of nature.[3] In order for life to occur, some non-material substance is added into the physical, inanimate elements that comprise a living body.

In honor of what he had learned from his reading of Aristotle, Driesch named his non-material agent "entelechy." He meant by that, he said, something different from what Aristotle meant. For Aristotle, entelechy (*entelecheia*) is a term practically synonymous with actuality (*energeia*), and it has to do with the final stage in a sequence of development described by the Four Causes, in which potential has been realized, form has been actualized, and optimal functioning is taking place.[4] Driesch meant by his use of the term *entelechy* to indicate the existence of a specific non-material substance which is responsible for, and enables life to exist.

In fact, the two usages come down to the same thing. The unity of first and final cause in the Aristotelian system cannot be conceptualized without imagining a mind-like movement which seeks form, and it was in order to describe life as purposeful that Aristotle devised his teleological views. Purposes imply always an intending mind. For Driesch, too, the problem was how to describe life if it is in truth *developmental*, and not a machine.

Driesch rejected terminology which compared his entelechy to traditional philosophical postulates. It was neither energy nor force, nor causality nor substance, nor soul, nor God. But it was a kind of whole-making causality:

> There is something in the organism's behaviour—in the widest sense of the word—which is opposed to an inorganic resolution of the same and which shows that the living organism is more than a sum or an aggregate of its parts, that it is

insufficient to call the organism a "typically combined body" without further explanation. This something we call entelechy. Entelechy—being not an extensive but an intensive manifoldness—is neither causality nor substance in the true sense of those words. But entelechy is a factor in nature, though it only relates to nature in space and is not itself anywhere in space. Entelechy's role in spatial nature may be formulated both mechanically and energetically. Introspective analysis shows that human reason possesses a special kind of category—individuality—by the aid of which it is able to understand to its own satisfaction what entelechy is; the category of individuality thus completing the concept of ideal nature in a positive way.[5]

In spite of the elaborate system of negative definitions it is clear that what Driesch has in mind is a God concept based upon the experience of the individual as an organized and purposing being.

Conceived as the property which organizes and develops objects imbued with life, Driesch thought of entelechy as a substance "handed down from generation to generation" and existing since the beginning of time.[6] In its activity within the individual, however, he named this substance the "psychoid," or soul-like, again circumscribing his definition with a number of analogies which attempted to exclude traditional philosophical concepts while describing properties entirely similar to them:

It appears better to distinguish also in terminology the natural agent which *forms* the body from the elemental agent which *directs* it. The words "soul," "mind" or "psyche" present themselves, but one of them would lead us into what we have so carefully avoided all along, viz., pseudo-psychology.... I therefore propose the very neutral name of "Psychoid" for the elemental agent discovered in action. "Psychoid"— that is, a something which though not a "psyche" can only be described in terms analogous to those of psychology.[7]

The impact of Darwinism with its vision of unending time reaching back in a causal sequence to a chaos of chemical elements, and of the discovery of the laws of thermodynamics with their implication of a purely mechanical universe was thus balanced ideologically with a purportedly scientific biological view which described life and mind as uniquely constitutive factors of the world, not reducible to matter. The facts concerning vitalist theses became the great weapon of religionists and the greatest object of scorn for those of materialist and positivist convictions. Ernst Cassirer commented: "At the turn of the century it dominated virtually all biological thinking, and both philosophy and specialized research became more and more deeply drawn into its circle."[8] The views of Driesch became so well known that he was invited to give the 1907–1908 Gifford Lectures in Aberdeen. The published lectures, *The Science and Philosophy of the Organism*, were reviewed with careful and lively interest.

J. W. Jenkinson, an embryologist at Oxford, examined the scientific premises of Driesch's work in *The Hibbert Journal*.[9] On empirical grounds one must doubt the efficacy of Driesch's whole-making entelechy, he noted. A segmented ovum will regenerate "only so long as each cell contains a sample of each substance" in the original ovum; after the time when greater cell differentiation has occurred a new organism will not develop. Again, the idea of an autonomous, holistic organism may be questioned when a worm, "bisected in a certain way, regenerates a tail instead of a head or a frog, after a particular injury, develops six legs instead of two."

T. H. Morgan praised Driesch for focusing attention on the difficult problems of epigenesis but thought his attempt to control the material basis of life with a theory of entelechy would be regarded by most readers as too near mysticism.[10]

O. W. Griffith criticized the attempt to gain understanding of a whole with any array of empirical facts. "No theory of order, or even of the autonomy of life, can be absolutely proved by the facts of embryology, or by any amount of experimental investigation."[11]

Hilda Oakeley, finally, appreciated the "great freshness and individuality" with which Driesch approached a problem as old as philosophy itself, but considered that his theory was really a remnant of the past, not a lead into the future:

> There is some relation between a philosophy and the time to which it belongs. . . . [Driesch's work] appears as if conceived in the spirit of a Stoic of the latter days of the Roman Empire, who might feel himself to be thinking in an age of civilization which is possibly passing away.[12]

I have offered a fairly substantial review of the vitalist controversies of this period because I want now to offer evidence for my judgment that the immediate philosophical source for Jung's theory of individuation and the self is in vitalism. I submit that it is fruitful to consider Jung's constantly reiterated insistence on the "autonomy of the psyche" in the light of the vitalist hypotheses. Beyond that, I want to consider specific texts which reveal Jung's vitalist assumptions.

a. Since the publication of the *Zofingia Lectures* we know that Jung was a passionate exponent of vitalism in his student days. The lectures are peppered with exhortations not to accept a mechanistic view of life, and the first two of the lectures, "On the Border Zones of Exact Science," and "Some Thoughts on Psychology," are devoted to the theme of vitalism. Two examples will suffice:

> Is life perhaps a function of matter?...But it is a fact, veri-fied by a hundred thousand cases, that organic beings never develop out of inorganic matter, but only through contact with life...it is impossible that this pre-existent life was linked to matter, and thus it must have existed indepen-dently of matter, i.e. immaterially.[13]

The second passage may be fruitfully compared with the concept of the psychoid which Jung elucidated fifty years later, at the crown of his career, in his essay "On the Nature of the Psyche." It is a pro-found example of the fact that the leading themes in our lives come to us very early and remain constant, although they may be forgot-ten for a time, or undergo superficial changes. This text dates from 1897:

> The vital principle extends far beyond our consciousness in that it also maintains the vegetative functions of the body which, as we know, are not under our conscious control. Our consciousness is dependent on the functions of the brain, but these are in turn dependent on the vital principle, and accordingly the vital principle represents a substance, whereas consciousness represents a contingent phenom-enon. Or as Schopenhauer says: "Consciousness is the object of a transcendental idea." Thus we see that animal and vegetative functions are embraced in a common root, the actual subject. Let us boldly assign to this transcendental subject the name of "soul." What do we mean by "soul"? *The soul is an intelligence independent of space and time.*[14]

b. Jung's essay "On Psychic Energy" (CW 8), published only in 1928 but partly written as early as 1912, just after the publication of his *Symbols of Transformation*, reveals how he struggled with science and vitalism in the years when his psychology was being formed. The early part of the essay attempts to work out a rationale for a theory of libido which differed from Freud's in representing a pro-gressive, goal-oriented view of psychic process.[15] Jung had broken with Freud on account of the materialistic overtones of his theory of libido. (See Part II, Chapters 2 and 3, above.) Later portions of the essay, written after the theory of archetypes and the theory of types had been announced, deal with the application of energic theory to symbol formation and typology.

The general image of psychic energy which Jung describes in the essay is easy enough to follow. One should think of energy as being somehow the core of the psyche, like a soul or inner god which suffuses life and which we have to learn to follow in order to keep life on track.

It is not so easy however to understand the basis on which Jung intends to establish his theory. He proposes that psychology, like other disciplines, has the right to establish its own independent hypotheses, but he also makes extensive references to thermodynamic laws. He refers approvingly to the philosophical view of Busse and Külpe, but doesn't tell us what they believed. It may be that their philosophical views were so well known that educated readers needed no further reference. It may also be that a psychology too obviously connected with philosophy was an embarrassment for Jung, who intended to build theory on the basis of inductively won hypotheses. I suspect some of both factors are responsible for the incomprehensibility of those passages. In any case, the names of Jung's authorities and the problems they fought over are nearly forgotten now, though Jung's own psychology lives on. It was actually partly as a result of being frustrated in my attempts to understand the essay "On Psychic Energy" that this essay came to be written. I guessed that certain ideas crucial to Jung's theory were hidden in these brief references, but I could not follow them. Only after a good deal of research did I come to realize that Jung's psychology must be seen in terms of its origins in nineteenth-century issues.

To my great surprise, I discovered that the works to which Jung refers in the early pages of his essay on energy all have to do with the problem of vitalism, together with psychophysics. In the light of the proofs of a mechanistic universe produced by the discoverers of thermodynamic laws the question became: how do we understand mind? What alternatives to a view of mind or psyche as an epiphenomenon of matter can be found? Fechner's theory of psychophysics proposed that mind and matter are identical, revealing themselves in different ways from different perspectives.[16] But while Fechner assigned priority to mind as the formative substance in reality, other psychophysicists altered that ratio, giving priority to the body. Nicolas von Grot, whom Jung cites in the energy essay, believed in the convertibility of psychic and physical energies by the agency of physiological processes.[17] Driesch thought of the psychophysicists as his philosophical enemies, for by linking mind and body they tie the mind to mechanistic laws. The belief that "conscious experience runs parallel with the mechanism of the brain—that it is this same mechanism seen 'from the other side'...is absurd....The brain is not a mere mechanism."[18] He greeted the work of Ludwig Busse with pleasure, as confirming his own views.[19]

Busse was professor of philosophy at Königsberg. He joined with Christoph Sigwart and other idealist philosophers in objecting to the psychophysical solution on the grounds that it took away from the soul or mind everything that we actually know to be true of it—its inner liveliness, its freedom, its power to be actively alert. Further, the capacity of the soul/mind would always be limited by the amount of physical energy available at any given moment. The kind of achievement which we know in times of inspired striving, where one is near to the World Spirit, would be completely impossible.[20]

One must understand the laws of energy properly as a transformation formula which describes the process of exchange of energy in the realm of matter, argued Busse.[21] But the question is, do we live in a *completely* closed system in which everything that happens is necessarily bound to the causal-mechanistic sequence? It must be remembered that the energy laws are mere empirically discovered laws whose validity for the whole of nature has not been proved. They do not reach the level of a priori necessary rules of thought. We need not disagree with the laws of energy in the realm in which they apply in order to suggest that we live only in a *relatively closed* system. There may be arenas in which the laws do not apply, namely when the psychic influences the physical, or when the physical influences the psychic.[22] Or it may also be, as Külpe proposed, that the sum of energy in the universe remains constant but that a relationship of equivalence obtains between spiritual and material processes. "The quantum of energy that must be lost on one side in order that a corresponding quantum of spiritual energy could be generated could then be once again converted back to a new form of material energy. It would thus make no difference whether a quantum of mental energy inserts itself into the course of the material process or not; the law of the conservation of energy as formulated hitherto would not be impaired."[23]

The final two sentences, quoted by Busse from Külpe's *Einleitung in die Philosophie* (1895) (p. 150), were also quoted by Jung in his essay on psychic energy. This was evidently the most important point—to be able to support science while at the same time insisting on a realm of psyche not constrained by the laws of matter. This was also the formula of Driesch's vitalism: a universe where the laws of energy apply, but where entelechy may "insert itself into the course of the material process," in the case of living organisms.

The best-known advocate of psychophysics at the beginning of the twentieth century was Wilhelm Wundt. He took over from Gustav Fechner at the University of Leipzig the inheritance of the Weberian experiments on sensation and perception which had formed the basis for calculations in Fechner's *Psychophysics*. Wundt's Institut für Experimentelle Psychologie was founded in 1879, the first of its kind in the world, and became the model for a new discipline. At the same time Wundt published voluminously in both psychology and philosophy—an incredible fifty-three thousand pages, all told. It was from the chapter entitled "Mechanism and Vitalism" in Wundt's major work, *Grundzüge der physiologischen Psychologie* that Jung quoted four times in setting up the framework for his essay on energy.[24]

Wundt argued in that chapter that although there was much good to be said about the neo-vitalist position on purpose and development in life processes, the trouble with the vitalists and their idealist supporters was that they did not recognize the epistemological limits set on *all* knowledge, and kept getting mixed up with metaphysics. We may well regard one and the same event from two points of view, from a causal and from a teleological aspect, and our understanding may be enriched by both views. But beyond that we may not go, since the principles of knowledge forbid it. We must accept the fact of our two viewpoints but we need not go further than that. In the case of Driesch's sea urchin eggs, for example, Driesch depends for his conclusion of "vital" causes on the supposition that every element of the blastoderm is pre-dispositioned to only one kind of physical-chemical process. If the morphological elements can be consistently thought of as independent in relation to each other, and independent of the surrounding elements in the environment, then it would scarcely be conceivable how they could at the same time stand teleologically under the influence of the other elements in the blastoderm, and in reverse, if a purposeful relationship of the germinal parts to each other is confirmed, one cannot resist the conclusion that the single parts also stand in a physical-chemical relationship. In other words, elements that belong to each other teleologically must necessarily also form a whole in causal relationship, which does not exclude a reciprocal relationship of parts, but includes it . . . "The difference between the teleological and the causal view of things is not a real one dividing the contents of experience into two disparate realms. The sole difference between the two views is the formal one that a causal connection belongs as a complement to every final relationship, and conversely, every causal connection can be given, if need be, a teleological form."[25]

The last two sentences are cited by Jung (para. 5 n.) at the beginning of the essay on energy. Jung retained the psychophysical doctrine of two points of view for the same event in his later theory of polar opposites in psychic life. But he chose the alternatives favored by vitalism—an energic or final view of the psyche, a relatively closed system, and the possibility of a causal relationship between psyche and soma—for his concept of libido or psychic energy.

My goal here has been to set Jung's references back into the context of the discussions from which they were taken and thus to reveal his philosophic sources and concerns. Two more passages from Jung's middle years show that he had not given up his belief in vitalist hypotheses. The first of them is in Jung's definition of the *primordial image* in *Psychological Types*.[26] This passage has been discussed before (Part II, p. 143, above), in connection with archetypes. If I now repeat that passage we may see how the concept of the archetype sprang not only from the idealist volunturism of Schopenhauer and von Hartmann but also from vitalist convictions:

> We are forced to assume that the given structure of the brain does not owe its peculiar nature merely to the influence of surrounding conditions, but also and just as much to the peculiar and *autonomous quality of living matter*, i.e. to *a law inherent in life itself*. The given constitution of the organism, therefore, is on the one hand a product of external conditions, while on the other it is determined by the intrinsic nature of living matter. Accordingly, the primordial image is related just as much to certain palpable, self-perpetuating, and continually operative natural processes as it is to certain inner determinants of psychic life and of life in general. (my italics)

A third unambiguous affirmation of vitalism appears at the conclusion of Jung's essay, "General Aspects of Dream Psychology":

> The dogma that "mental diseases are diseases of the brain" is a hangover from the materialism of the 1870's. It has become a prejudice which hinders all progress, with nothing to justify it.... *Life can never be thought of as a function of mat-*

ter, but only as a process existing in and for itself, to which
energy and matter are subordinate....We have no more
justification for understanding the psyche as a brain-process
than we have for understanding life in general from a one-
sided arbitrarily materialistic point of view that can never be
proved, quite apart from the fact that the very attempt to
imagine such a thing is crazy in itself and has always engen-
dered craziness whenever it was taken seriously. (my italics)[27]

c. In 1947, in his essay, "On the Nature of the Psyche," Jung
proposed the term *psychoid* to describe a concept bridging psychic
with non-psychic realms.[28] Though not directly psychic, that is, not
psychic in the sense of having a potential for becoming conscious,
nor directly instinctive in the sense of being connected to the drive
forces, there may be "psychoid processes at both ends of the psychic
scale" (para. 367). He cites Hans Driesch and Eugen Bleuler as his
predecessors in the use of the term, but says he means something
different from what they mean. Driesch's concept is too philosophical in denoting a directive principle for life processes, and Bleuler's
concept, while scientific in nature, is too rooted in the organological
standpoint. Bleuler's *Psychoide* has to do with the maintenance and
development of life functions in purposeful fashion, but it seats
purpose in physical organs.

(A note on Eugen Bleuler is in order. He was Jung's former chief
at the famous Burghölzli Clinic in Zürich, co-pioneer with Jung of
the psychoanalytic movement in Switzerland, and a close colleague
for many years. It was Bleuler's achievement to first describe dementia praecox as schizophrenia. The two men were present together at
parapsychological experiments (seances) which took place both at
the Burghölzli and at the home of Professor Rudolf Bernoulli.[29] In
late years Bleuler became a vitalist. Two books describe his views.[30]
Bleuler thought that the line between material functions having no
purpose and an intending, non-material psyche had been too sharply
drawn. One might correct the airborne speculations of the philosophical vitalists by basing the psychoid in a neurological function
which furnished the possibility of a true explanation, namely the
memory. Memory operates both on a psychic and on a non-psychic
level in directing life processes on the basis of past experience.[31]
Only Mnemismus [the concept of memory as a transcendent regulative function] can make the relationship between psychic and
organic purpose understandable, as two operations and two ways of
regarding a basic function whose peculiarity lies in its capacity for
memory.[32])

As a psychologist, said Jung, his interest was more in the "total-ity of these experiences that constitute the object of investigation," that is, with psychic *and* with non-psychic functions (para. 368). Perhaps the whole of these functions beyond both the upper and lower limits of spirit and of instinct possesses a subject. There may be a "second psychic system" operating as subject of the whole (para. 369).

The question I find myself asking is: why did Jung want to borrow a term with such distinct connection to vitalist doctrines only to distinguish his own meaning from theirs? Actually, all three men meant almost the same thing with their use of the term *psychoid*. They sought to describe an *immaterial, autonomous psychic factor oper-ating in organic nature according to teleological principles.*[33]

d. Very late in his life Jung was quoting Driesch's early book, *On the Soul as an Elementary Factor in Nature.*[34] In "On the Nature of the Psyche" he says that the psyche, as will and consciousness, must have a "supraordinate authority, something like a consciousness of itself" if it is to be differentiated from the compulsive force of instinc-tive function. As Driesch rightly says, "There is no willing without knowing" (Kein Wollen ohne Wissen).[35]

In his essay on "Synchronicity" Jung realized that "psychic final-ity rests on a 'pre-existent' meaning which becomes problematical only when it is an unconscious arrangement. In that case we have to suppose a 'knowledge' prior to all consciousness," as did Hans Driesch.[36] Later on in the essay Jung cited those same passages once more. "Final causes," said Jung, "twist them how we will, postulate a *foreknowledge of some kind.*"[37] This is God talk. That, at least, is the term most usually applied in Western philosophical thought to indi-cate supraordinate, intending mind.

A Postscript on Vitalism

This book has been about the philosophical and historical background of Jung's psychology, particularly in the nineteenth century. The face of philosophical issues has naturally changed over the course of the twentieth century. Scientific knowledge has increased so dramatically that the problems of nineteenth-century science might seem antiquarian. Jung's psychology, however, continues to be practiced, among some professionals with changes which reflect the influence of newer psychological theories and among others in very much the same way as Jung first taught it. The terms *archetype, self,* and *invididuation process* belong to the common goods of all Jungians. Since these terms, as we have seen, refer to the theory of a non-material substrate of life, it may be useful to discuss briefly the fate of vitalistic ideas in this century.

Hans Driesch found a support for the dualist aspect of his hypothesis (but not for the existence of an entelechy as old as time itself) in the emergence philosophies of C. Lloyd Morgan, Samuel Alexander, and C. D. Broad, who were joined in the 1920s by Arthur O. Lovejoy. It is possible to accept the facts of evolution and be bound neither to vitalism on the one hand nor to materialism on the other, they said. What must be called into question is the still medieval belief that causal factors produce only quantitative changes in phenomena. It is possible that wholly novel, qualitatively different entities are introduced into the universe in the course of its evolutionary development, things or processes which might not have been predicted on the basis of antecedent causes. There is no valid, a priori reason why this might not be so, argued Lovejoy. Emergence is "the assertion on empirical grounds of the occurrence, among the phenomena investigable by science, of events which are not mere rearrangements of pre-existent natural entities in accordance with laws identical for all arrangements of those entities."[1] If this view be accepted one can look with equanimity on whatever the future of our planet may bring. If it has brought forth life out of a once lifeless planet we may, in the thousand million years left for our solar system, believe that "out of the latent generative potencies of matter" still new forms of being may emerge in a way that our present circumstances cannot allow us to foresee.

The Whiteheadians and their close relatives, the pan-psychists, headed by Charles Hartshorne, argued against the emergence philosophers that their theory was not only too physical, too rooted in matter, but that it posed unresolvable epistemological problems. If things are indeed qualitatively different from each other then we have no means of understanding. It is much better to think of the whole of nature as being in some degree imbued with the same quality of life or mind which we experience in ourselves. This idea of "organic sympathy" solves in one stroke the mind-body relation, the subject-object relation, and the problem of causal order. "In a faint degree the whole world is our body," said Hartshorne.[2]

Process thought is thus a kind of non-dualistic vitalism, which focuses, as did Driesch, on the unique quality of life. Instead of an entelechy which intervenes to sustain and regulate organisms, life itself, together with the order and process which we experience as characteristic of life, is seen as permeating inorganic as well as organic nature. Even a stone possesses some of the cohesion and structural organization which higher forms exemplify.

Utilizing these hypotheses, W. H. Thorpe, a process philosopher, commented on recent work in molecular biology and in ethology.[3] We must begin to re-evaluate, he believes, the extent to which pure chance is responsible for evolution. We may consider for example the laws of Mendelism in genetic inheritance. It is well to remember that natural selection operates not on the genotype (the genetic information stored in the ovum) but on the phenotype (the mature organism). While it is true that acquired characteristics are not individually inherited, it is also true that the survival of a specific population, together with the gene pool of that population, depends on the adaptability of the population to its environment. "Behavior is always a jump ahead of structure."

Again, in considering the facts developed by ethology concerning the similarities between human and animal behavior, for example, the language structure which has been proved in chimpanzees, we are brought to the perennial problem of where to draw the line in defining "mind." How far back in evolutionary history must we go in order to exclude mind? Perhaps it is not possible to separate wholly from the realm of mind even those "occasions of experience" in which non-living bodies achieve form. A subjective or mental factor may be identical with natural process.

The physicist Michael Polanyi has defended vitalistic premises on the basis of complex morphogenesis and emergence. "All physiology is teleological," he says.[4] In terms of physics and chemistry alone we cannot even imagine what it would be like to state that chickens are hatched from eggs, a fact of organization and form which ordinary insight makes available to us. Reversing Helmholtz's challenge to the metaphysicians to find better reasons for believing in transcendent causes, Polanyi challenged science to find a better explanation for believing in the evolution of man:

> The rise of man can be accounted for only by other principles than those known today to physics and chemistry. If this be vitalism, then vitalism is mere common sense, which can be ignored only by a truculently bigotted mechanistic outlook. And so long as we can form no idea of the way a material system may become a conscious, responsible person, it is an empty pretense to suggest that we have an explanation for the descent of man.[5]

Defenses of vitalism among biologists have been rare. W. E. Agar, professor of biology at the University of Melbourne, produced in 1951 arguments that, even at the cellular level, organisms are feeling and purposive agents, experimenting and responding to their environment. While proof that the organism is part of some larger planned development in the universe cannot be offered, neither can such a theory be disproved. The evidence of organic life is rather more persuasive in favor of such a thesis than otherwise. It seemed to Agar that mental factors or a Central Agent was the most appropriate explanation for variations in behavior and development which may be observed in the simplest of organisms.[6] He found the insights of Whitehead and Hartshorne instructive in this regard.

A traditional re-statement of Driesch's vitalist position was made in 1962 by Rainer Schubert-Soldern of Vienna. We are obliged to conclude, he thought, that a kind of *striving for wholeness* characterizes living beings and distinguishes them qualitatively from non-living matter. "The laws governing animate things are different from those governing inanimate matter....The difference implies a difference of nature."[7]

Against the arguments of vitalists favoring purpose and supporting therefore the unique properties of life and mind in which purposes seem evident, most biologists, and the great majority of philosophers of biology, insist on a universe in which chance is the primary factor in evolutionary development.

The classic refutation of vitalism was offered in 1925 by Moritz Schlick.[8] Scientific knowledge, noted Schlick, depends on the explanation of one set of phenomena in terms of another. This means that we must ask whether it is possible to reduce organic life to non-living matter. The reverse procedure, attempted by Schelling (and the pan-psychists) is too mystically anthropomorphic to fulfill the requirements of science. Today we must either believe that life can be reduced to non-life (the mechanistic position) or that this is impossible (the vitalist position). In examining this question we must exclude from the beginning the connection of organic life with consciousness since a) we know only our own conscious states and cannot make inferences about consciousness in animals or in lower life forms, b) life and consciousness are not necessarily bound together in the empirical world, and c) physical processes of life and psychologically determined states of consciousness are two different kinds of things which since they may not stand in causal relation with each other cannot meaningfully be connected in scientific discussion.

If consciousness is to be eliminated then the concept of purpose, which is the center of discussions of this type, must be redefined to designate simply the terminal effect of action. Clearly, this changes the meaning of the word. However, we might still speak of purposiveness when a group of processes or organs generally or normally co-operate to produce a definite effect. In this sense, the co-operative operation of organs or processes results in an effect which is similarly produced each time those processes are repeated in the same way. Yet this description of purpose is not different from the description of causes which we might apply to inorganic processes.

In general, argued Schlick, the concept of finality is wrong-headed. Causality means nothing more than the laws of nature; unless we wish to deny those the term *finality* is superfluous.

Driesch's assertion of non-physical processes operating within organic life may be examined under the terms he proposed, said Schlick. If we are to describe a physical process we must stick to the *spatial* characteristics which mark everything that is physical. It is up to the proponent of a vitalist hypothesis to demonstrate that something non-spatial has occurred in a physical object. What does the case of Driesch's sea-urchin eggs prove? He would have to show us that no physical changes had occurred in two exactly similar eggs, known in the last detail, and that then two different animals emerged, in order for us to be constrained to accept non-spatial causes for life. Until that is achieved the evidence favors a materialistic hypothesis.

Modern evolutionary theory is a combination of Darwin's principle of natural selection and genetic knowledge won since 1900 when Mendel's principles of heredity were re-discovered. Evolution, according to recent thought, depends on change in the gene pool which may occur through "mutation, random fluctuation of genetic frequencies, migration of individuals in and out of the population, and natural selection."[9] It is believed to be a *purely mechanistic process*.

The fright at having so nearly and so recently escaped the coils of metaphysical and vitalist assumptions led biologists in the first half of the present century to avoid all terminology which hinted at "Purpose" in their descriptions of the objects of their study. Not only words like *teleology* and *finality* but the idea of adaptation, and the phrase "for the purpose of" became anathema. Colin Pittendrigh, chairman of the biology department at Princeton University, commented that it went so far that "biologists for a while were prepared to say a turtle came ashore *and* laid its eggs, but they refused to say it came ashore *to* lay its eggs."[10] Yet the concept of adaptation obviously has its place in describing the organism's adjustment to its environment, in describing the features enabling an organism to obtain goods for survival (hands are for grasping and eyes are for vision), and in describing somatic changes which respond to environmental changes (antibody formation, learning).

All of these uses of the concept of adaptation can be applied to biological studies without endangering the mechanistic base of evolutionary theory. Pittendrigh proposed that the term *teleonomy* be substituted for *teleology* to denote goal-directed processes without implying Aristotle or God or any autonomous soul agent. Many biologists have since then adopted this term, including Nobel Prize winner Jacques Monod, whose 1971 essay, *Chance and Necessity* has become the most frequently quoted reference (both by supporters and by adversaries) in current discussions of purpose in nature.

Since Mendel defined the gene as the bearer of hereditary traits, Avery and Hershey were able to define it chemically, and Watson and Crick described the structural basis of DNA, we know that *invariance* (the machine) is the fundamental fact of biological inheritance. Once a chance mutation has entered the DNA structure a secondary factor, *teleonomy*, is involved in the process of natural selection as the organism attempts to adapt to the given environment. Because less-suitable organisms are rejected we have the appearance of an upwardly progressive evolution, each new mutation having to demonstrate a coherence at least as strong as that of the already viable system in which it appears.[11] Scientific understanding of the factors involved in biological evolution has reached a level of unarguable certainty, says Monod:

> Since [mutation] constitutes the *only* possible source of modifications in the genetic text, itself the *sole* repository of the organism's hereditary structures, it necessarily follows that chance *alone* is at the source of every innovation, of all creation in the biosphere. Pure chance, absolutely free but blind, at the very root of the stupendous edifice of evolution: this central concept of modern biology is no longer one among other possible or even conceivable hypotheses: It is today the *sole* conceivable hypothesis, the only one that squares with observed and tested fact. And nothing warrants the supposition—or the hope—that on this score our position is likely ever to be revised.[12]

The conviction of modern biologists that blind chance governs all life processes stands therefore in sharpest contradiction to Jung's insistence on a "supraordinate authority" and a "pre-existent meaning" in life.

Conclusion

This essay has shown that the conceptual structure of Jung's psychology is based on philosophical postulates which express an idealist and a metaphysical view of reality. Analytical psychology is a position-taking on philosophical issues of the nineteenth century. It embodies views, however, which are rooted in the search for moral values in ancient Greece and which have guided Western philosophical thinking ever since.

Because he found a *psychological* format for idealism which could lead into the twentieth century, Jung himself became the latest in a tradition of great idealist philosophers to have a powerful influence in the culture of their times.

Though Jung never delineated a formal epistemological position it is possible, by following a developmental time line, and by studying a large number of his statements about what we know, to obtain a consistent picture of his views. Then, by examining the history of epistemological disputes, and particularly the moral issues which lay at the base of Plato's decision that true knowledge comes from within the mind, Jung's position can be matched with what philosophers have generally termed "metaphysical idealism." The immediate background of Jung's epistemology lies in nineteenth-century reaction to the new sciences, and the materialistic and positivist philosophies which accompanied the upswing of scientific influence. A certain type of radically subjectivistic neo-Kantianism was much favored at the end of the century, particularly by religionists who hoped thus to defend religious truths from the reductionist conclusions of scientists. Jung's views were entirely similar to those expressed by the subjectivist interpreters of Kant. Using this understanding of Jung's theory of knowledge we can then observe how it was applied by him in two specific cases: 1) Introversion, and the proposed resolution of conflict between inner and outer views through the subjectivized *esse in anima* are the underlying foci of Jung's theory of types. 2) Jung's study of Paracelsus' doctrine of the *lumen naturae*, of knowledge through inner identity between subject and object, became the springboard for Jung's vast studies of the psychology of alchemistic thought.

Jung's metaphysics is well expressed in his theory of the archetype. Here again we must approach an understanding of what Jung meant by archetypes by studying the developmental stages through which he established a theoretical basis for his psychology. The grounds on which Jung broke with Freud must be counted as primarily philosophical; that is to say, they had more to do with profoundly differing belief systems than with the psychological dynamic of the personal relationship between the two men. Insight into Freud's own philosophical process enables us to follow the steps through which Jung dissociated himself from Freud's views, at first by means of a radical alteration of the libido theory, then in the development of a prospective analytical method which viewed dreams and fantasies as purposive, and finally in the differentiation of formal (archetypal) from material (instinctive) causes in the psyche.

The philosophical antecedents of Jung's theory of archetypes are to be found first in Plato's doctrine of transcendent causes, and secondly and more directly in Schopenhauer's dynamic theory of the Will. Nearly all the qualities of Schopenhauer's Will are found reproduced in Jung's theory of archetypes except that, unlike Schopenhauer, Jung insisted that the archetype is directive and form seeking. For this reason he continued to differentiate blindly instinctive from formal, meaning-giving archetypal activity in the psyche, even during the years when the results of experimental studies gave biologists increasing confidence in a phylogenetic source of behavior. In the speculations of his late years Jung extended his theory of non-material, archetypal causes beyond the sphere of individual psychic life to the realm of conjunction with the material world, in his theory of synchronicity.

Jung's theory of individuation and its corollary doctrine of the self can be shown to exactly parallel the classic teleological scheme set out by Aristotle in his doctrine of the Four Causes, operating in a universe sustained by the Unmoved Mover. Aristotle's teleology, expressed in Christian theology as divine intentionality operating throughout creation, became standard doctrine in Western thought until it was challenged in the seventeenth and eighteenth centuries by the development of technical machinery, discoveries in astronomy and physics, and by Kant's challenge to rational theology, and in the nineteenth century by the discovery of the thermodynamic laws and by Darwin's theory of evolution. The primary defense against the reduction of life to chance or to a machine was undertaken by the vitalists, who insisted that life cannot be understood as matter, and that some kind of intentionality, or mental factor, is present in all living processes, as distinct from non-organic processes. It can be proved that the influence of vitalistic theories on Jung was much greater than has heretofore been recognized. He maintained vitalist convictions throughout his life, in flat opposition to the view of organic process which forms the basis of biological studies.

The aim of this analysis has been to contribute from a philosophical and historical perspective to the ever urgent task of becoming conscious. The principal doctrines of Jung's psychology, and the habits of interpretation which accompany belief in those doctrines, are embedded in the structures of Western religious thought. Realizing that this is so releases the believer from unconscious identification with those doctrines to a more objective point of view. It should also assist the student of the history of ideas to order Jung's work in a more general scheme. The psychological value of the historical view lies just here, in its potential for objectivizing and relativizing every particular system of belief. At the moment when an individual gains distance, or freedom, from the particularities of collective belief, he/she also wins an open attitude and adaptive potential for future events.

The objective approach does not however free us from the equally urgent need to understand the nature of the human person. This need is fueled not by rational scientific goals, although it may well be accompanied by scientific endeavor. Persistent affective states — the individual's longing to understand the significance of his/her own life — are the primary driving forces behind our search for general truths. Around these fires those who loved Jung and those who love religion will continue to gather.

A Personal Note

History is in one sense a cruel teacher. I will not conceal the fact that during the years while I have been working on this project I suffered greatly, seeing the concepts which once were able to contain all that I knew of the depth and mystery of human experience reduced to their place in a historical series.

Strangely enough, my work as a Jungian analyst has not been affected, or only minimally so, although I feared that would happen. Reflection on why this might be so led me to the realization that nothing which is truly real can be changed by a merely ego-bound concept of it. What is real in the work I do seems to be, first, the symbolic process—the mystery of the dream and the sense of "meaningfulness" by which it is apprehended by the dreamer. Secondly, and above all, what is real is the human relationship in which maturity and highest value are sought. This is not affected by the language which may be used to describe experience, although we may be hard put to find language to indicate highest value in an age which has found God contrary to nature.

It may be that neither the terms which have traditionally been used in Western philosophical/theological thought nor the analogous terms which Jung used in his psychology will survive encounter with the facts that life in the modern world entails. We must beware of a subjectivistic epistemology which obtains unity in mental perspective at the cost of denial of the facts by which we after all live in the world of time and space. Yet I believe that we may joyfully affirm the reality of inner experience, even if none of the terms presently available in the structure of language seems a suitable vehicle of that experience.

I do not reduce philosophy, and least of all metaphysics, to psychology. I refer rather to the existence of moral value. This returns us to the Greeks, with whom, as I have argued, a growing consciousness of moral dilemmas first led to an expression of belief in the primacy of mind.

Notes to Part III

Chapter 1

1. C. G. Jung, *The Zofingia Lectures. The Collected Works of C. G. Jung. Supplementary Volume A*, ed. William McGuire, trans. Jan van Heurck, with an Introduction by Marie-Louise von Franz, Bollingen Series XX (Princeton: Princeton University Press, 1983), para. 168.

2. Ibid., para. 179, 181.

3. Ibid., para. 183.

4. Ibid., para. 224, 225.

5. Ibid., para. 215, 216.

6. Ibid., para. 227.

7. See Paul Davies, *God and the New Physics* (New York: Simon and Schuster, Touchstone Books, 1984).

8. *The Zofingia Lectures*, para. 223.

9. C. G. Jung, *Psychology of the Unconscious: A Study of the Transformations and Symbolisms of the Libido, A Contribution to the History of the Evolution of Thought* (1912), trans. Beatrice M. Hinkle (New York: Dodd, Mead and Company, 1925) (hereafter cited as *Symbols of Transformation*, 1912), p. 493. Compare with the revised version, in *The Collected Works of C. G. Jung*, 20 vols., translated from the German by R. F. C. Hull, Bollingen Series XX (New York: Pantheon Books, 1953–79) (hereafter referred to as CW), vol. 5, para. 78.

10. "The Structure of the Unconscious," CW 7, para. 501.

11. "General Aspects of Dream Psychology," CW 8, para. 444, 462.

12. "On Psychic Energy," CW 8, para. 4 n.

13. "General Aspects of Dream Psychology," CW 8, para. 456. See also *Psychological Types*, CW 6, para. 701: "The product of the unconscious cannot be regarded as a finished thing, as a sort of end-product, for that would be to deny it any purposive significance. Freud himself allows the dream a

teleological role at least as the 'guardian of sleep', though for him its prospective function is essentially restricted to 'wishing'. The purposive character of unconscious tendencies cannot be contested *a priori* if we are to accept their analogy with other psychological or physiological functions."

14. "The Structure of the Unconscious," CW 7, para. 501 n. The practice of claiming an empirical attitude toward points of view that carried religious implications was much used by professors at the turn of the century who wanted to maintain a non-mechanistic view and still be respectable scientists. Wilhelm Wundt had a particularly ponderous way of doing it, while arguing for his psychophysics. For example: "Das Princip des psychophysischen Parallelismus in dem hier festgehaltenen Sinne ist hiernach ein heuristisches nicht nur, weil es sich ausschliesslich auf die Thatsachen beschränkt, für die es unmittelbar empirisch gefordert wird, sondern namentlich auch insofern, als es sich grundsätzlich auf die unmittelbare Wirklichkeit der Erscheinungen bezieht, nicht auf das metaphysische Wesen der Dinge. Denn es ist lediglich eine Betrachtungsweise, welche die beiden einander ergänzenden wissenschaftlichen Standpunkte, den rein objectiven der Naturwissenschaft und den subjectiven der Psychologie, widerspruchslos mit einander zu verbinden erlaubt...." *Grundzüge der Physiologische Psychologie*, 3 vols., 5th ed. (Leipzig: Verlag von Wilhelm Engelmann, 1903), part VI, p. 773.

What the man of religious temperament had been up against for the last fifty years may be seen in the forthright statement of Hermann von Helmhotz in his essay, "The Conservation of Force: A Physical Memoir," in *Selected Writings*, ed. with an Introduction by Russell Kahl (Middletown, Conn.: Wesleyan University Press, 1971), p. 49: "Cause, according to its original meaning, is the unchanging existent...which lies behind the changes of phenomena; the law of its effects is force. The impossibility...of conceiving of these in isolation from each other thus follows simply from the fact that the law of an effect presupposes certain conditions under which it is realized." "It is clear that science, the goal of which is the comprehension of nature, must begin with the presupposition of its comprehensibility and proceed in accordance with this assumption."

15. C. G. Jung, "Richard Wilhelm: In Memoriam" (1930), CW 15, para. 80.

16. C. G. Jung, "Commentary on 'The Secret of the Golden Flower',"
CW 13, para. 7.

17. Ibid., para. 51.

18. "Richard Wilhelm: In Memoriam," CW 15, para. 89 f.

19. Commentary of Wilhelm, in *The Secret of the Golden Flower: A Chinese Book of Life*, trans. and explained by Richard Wilhelm with a European Commentary by C. G. Jung (New York: Harcourt, Brace and Com-

pany, 1935), p. 17. Wilhelm gave different meanings to the terms *anima* and *animus* from those of Jung. As is apparent from the text, anima for Wilhelm is the dark yin-soul.

20. Ibid., p. 62. These phrases are from the text itself.

21. Ibid., p. 37.

22. Ibid., pp. 39, 62.

23. "Commentary on the Golden Flower," CW 13, para. 18.

24. Ibid., para. 24.

25. Ibid., para. 67. See also "The Relations between the Ego and the Unconscious," CW 7, para. 365.

26. "Commentary on the Golden Flower," CW 13, para. 71.

27. Ibid., para. 73.

28. Ibid., para. 82. See pp. 150 ff. above.

29. Two essays published in CW 9i illustrate the centering process: "A Study in the Process of Individuation" (first published in 1934) and "On Mandala Symbolism" (originally a seminar given in 1930). Each essay is accompanied by a series of illustrative plates.

30. See Part II, Chapter 4, above.

31. "The Soul and Death," CW 8, para. 798.

32. "Conscious, Unconscious, and Individuation," CW 9i, para. 498, 499.

33. *Aion: Researches into the Phenomenology of the Self,* CW 9ii.

34. Ibid., para. 48, 49.

35. Ibid., para. 52.

36. Ibid., para. 60.

37. Ibid., para. 64.

38. "The Relations between the Ego and the Unconscious," CW 7, para. 399.

Chapter 2

1. See Part I, Chapter 4, and Part II, Chapter 5, above.

2. Plato, *Timaeus and Critias*, trans. with an Introduction and an Appendix on *Atlantis* by Desmond Lee (Harmondsworth, England: Penguin Books, 1976), 29–30.

3. Ibid., 52–53.

4. Sir David Ross, *Aristotle* (1923) (London: Methuen & Co., 1974), p. 1. "It is reasonable to trace Aristotle's interest in physical science and above all in biology to his descent from a medical family. Galen tells us that Asclepiad families trained their sons in dissection, and it is possible that Aristotle had some such training; further, he may have helped his father in his surgery."

5. *Aristotle's Physics: Books I and II*, trans. with Introduction and Notes by W. Charlton (Oxford: Clarendon Press, 1970), 199a30–32.

6. *Aristotle's De Partibus Animalium I and De Generatione Animalium I* (with passages from II.1–3), trans. with Notes by D. M. Balme (Oxford: Clarendon Press, 1972), *De Partibus* 641b25–28.

7. Ibid., *De Partibus* 640b4–28.

8. *The Physics*, Charlton trans., 119a20–23.

9. *Aristotle's Metaphysics*, trans. with commentaries and Glossary by Hippocrates G. Apostle (Bloomington: Indiana University Press, 1975), 1072b2–4.

10. Aristotle, *On Generation and Corruption*, in *The Basic Works of Aristotle*, ed. and with an Introduction by Richard McKeon (New York: Random House, 1941), 337b10–338a16.

11. Marjorie Grene, *A Portrait of Aristotle* (Chicago: University of Chicago Press, 1963), p. 230; Mircea Eliade, *The Myth of the Eternal Return or Cosmos and History* (1949), trans. from the French by Willard R. Trask, Bollingen Series XLVI (Princeton: Princeton University Press, 1974), pp. 89 f. and n. "Just as the Greeks, in their myth of the eternal return, sought to satisfy their metaphysical thirst for the 'ontic' and the static (for, from the point of view of the infinite, the becoming of things that perpetually revert to the same state is, as a result, implicitly annulled and it can even be affirmed that 'the world stands still'), even so the primitive, by conferring a cyclic direction upon time, annuls its irreversibility. Everything begins over again at its commencement every instant. The past is but a prefiguration of the future. No event is irreversible and no transformation is final. In a certain sense, it is even possible to say that nothing new happens in the world, for everything is but the repetition of the same primordial archetypes; this repetition, by actualizing the mythical moment when the archetypal gesture was revealed, constantly maintains the world in the same auroral instant of the beginnings. Time but makes possible the appearance

Philosophical Issues in the Psychology of C. G. Jung

and existence of things. It has no final influence upon their existence, since it is itself constantly regenerated."

Chapter 3

1. Arthur O. Lovejoy has recounted the history of the idea up through the early 19th century in *The Great Chain of Being* (1936) (Cambridge: Harvard University Press, 1976).

2. See the epistemological discussion of Kant in Part I, Chapter 5, above.

3. Thomas S. Hall, *Ideas of Life and Matter: Studies in the History of General Physiology, 600 B.C.–1900 A.D.*, 2 vols. (Chicago: University of Chicago Press, 1969), 1:219.

4. This passage is cited in Lovejoy, *Chain of Being*, p. 241. A closely related passage from the *Prolegomena* is discussed in Part II, pp. 152 f., above.

5. "He rebelled against the fundamental principle of Rationalism, that reality has an inherent logical structure such that the laws of thought are also the laws of things." Maurice Mandelbaum, *History, Man and Reason: A Study in Nineteenth-Century Thought* (Baltimore and London: Johns Hopkins Press, 1971), p. 324.

6. See Part II above, pp. 162–66.

7. See Part I, Chapter 6, above.

8. "Some Thoughts on Psychology," in *The Zofingia Lectures*, para. 91.

9. *The World as Will and Representation*, 2 vols., translated from the German by E. F. S. Payne (New York: Dover Publications, 1969), p. 29.

10. C. G. Jung, *Analytical Psychology: Notes of the Seminar Given in 1925*, ed. William McGuire, Bollingen Series XCIX (Princeton: Princeton University Press, 1989), pp. 4, 12.

11. Arthur Schopenhauer, *On the Fourfold Root of the Principle of Sufficient Reason. On the Will in Nature*, trans. Mme. Karl Hillebrand (London: George Bell and Sons, 1907).

12. Ibid., p. 269.

13. Ibid., p. 255. Cf. also:

Ferocious animals, destined for combat and rapine, appear armed with formidable teeth and claws and strong muscles.... Timid animals, whose will it is to seek their safety in flight instead of contest, present themselves with light, nimble legs and sharp hearing in lieu of all weapons. (Ibid., p. 266)

According to M. Dutrochet, the direction in which plants grow, is determined by an inner principle.... Of all apparently voluntary movements of plants, the direction of their boughs and of the upper surface of their leaves towards the light and towards the moist heat, and the twining movements of creepers round their supports, are the most universal.... That which lives and moves in plant-nature and in the animal organism... presents itself in this newly rising consciousness as *will* and is here more immediately known than anywhere else. (Ibid., pp. 283, 286, 290 f.)

14. Ernst Cassirer, *The Problem of Knowledge: Philosophy, Science, and History since Hegel*, trans. William H. Woglom and Charles W. Hendel (New Haven: Yale University Press, 1950), p. 163; Mandelbaum, *History, Man and Reason*, p. 318.

15. *The Will in Nature*, p. 264.

16. Ibid.

17. Ibid.

18. Eduard von Hartmann, *Philosophy of the Unconscious: Speculative Results according to the Inductive Method of Physical Science* (1869), authorized translation by William Chatterton Coupland, new edition in one volume (New York: Harcourt, Brace and Company, 1931).

19. Bryan Magee, *The Philosophy of Schopenhauer* (Oxford: Clarendon Press, 1983), p. 282.

20. See for example Part I above, p. 65. Helmholtz insisted that metaphysicians might be listened to only when their results approached what "can be done by the inductive method." Von Hartmann thought that the inductive method could produce near proof of metaphysical hypotheses. So did Jung, at a very early stage of his career. See pp. 15–17, above.

21. *Philosophy of the Unconscious*, Part I, p. 30.

22. Ibid., p. 45.

23. Ibid., pp. 47–51.

24. *The Zofingia Lectures*, para. 175, 182.

25. Still another "empirical" demonstration of an invisible realm of spirit or psyche is found in Gustav Fechner's theory of psychophysics. See the Appendix, below.

Chapter 4

1. Stahl's pupil, Albert Lemoine, described Stahl's theory: "The principle of life is the soul, not a special soul, but the rational soul, that which alone constitutes man, and is manifestly united to his body. The soul is not the life of the body; it cannot even be said to be alive, but only to give life.... This life-giving act, the soul performs with complete intelligence in all details;... it is the soul that makes the lungs breathe, the heart beat, the blood circulate, the stomach digest, the liver secrete; it is the soul that, while preserving the body, also makes it live and that, in order to preserve it, maintains corruptible matter in its [condition of] essential corruptibility yet keeps it from the act of corruption; and it is the soul, finally, that ... nourishes [the body] and assimilates foreign substances to it, and makes repose follow movement and sleep follow waking." Cited in Hall, *Ideas of Life and Matter*, p. 363.

2. David L. Hull, *Philosophy of Biological Science* (Englewood Cliffs, N.J.: Prentice-Hall, 1974), pp. 145 ff.

3. Ibid., p. 147; Cassirer, *The Problem of Knowledge*, p. 188.

4. Helmholtz, "An Autobiographical Sketch" (1891), in *Selected Writings*, pp. 470 f.

5. Helmholtz, "The Aim and Progress of Physical Science" (1869), in *Selected Writings*, pp. 236 f., and "Thought in Medicine" (1877), ibid., pp. 348 f.; Hull, *Philosophy of Biological Science*, pp. 128 f.; Mandelbaum, *History, Man and Reason*, p. 291.

6. *Two Great Scientists of the Nineteenth Century: Correspondence of Emil Du Bois-Reymond and Carl Ludwig* (1927), collected by Estelle Du Bois-Reymond, Foreword, Notes and Indexes by Paul Diepgen, trans. Sabine Lichtner-Ayed, ed. with a Foreword by Paul F. Cranefield (Baltimore: Johns Hopkins Press, 1982), p. 13, Letter of April 22, 1848. The introductory passage to which Du Bois-Reymond refers is sharply satirical: "This force [the vitalists say] resides in the body as a whole, its essence, known yet unknown, holding forth on the mysterious metaphysical backstage of a theater on whose outermost forestage alone is enacted all that is accessible to sensation.... Before the vital force the physical and chemical forces must bow. It is granted it to bind and loose as it pleases.... After death, it withdraws modestly behind the wings without leaving a trace of itself. A helpmeet in all things ... it is the first cause of animal movement, and to the so-called soul it gives help at least to the extent of doing its thinking.... The trouble with such an agency is that it is both unnecessary and impossible. (Mit einen Wort, die sogennante Lebenskraft ist ein Unding.)... as something separate, something that can be hitched to matter, like a horse to a cart, and unhitched in the same manner, forces — especially vital forces — simply do not exist." Cited in Hall, *Ideas of Life and Matter*, 2:275 f.

7. Cited in William Coleman, *Biology in the Nineteenth Century: Problems of Form, and Transformation* (1971) (Cambridge: Cambridge University Press, 1977), p. 150.

8. *The Zofingia Lectures*, para. 85, 136.

9. Coleman, *Biology in the Nineteenth Century*, p. 12.

10. Claude Bernard, *An Introduction to the Study of Experimental Medicine* (1865), trans. Henry Copley Greene, with an Introduction by Lawrence J. Henderson (New York: Macmillan Company, 1927).

11. Ibid., p. 69.

12. Reino Vitranen, *Claude Bernard and His Place in the History of Ideas* (Lincoln: University of Nebraska Press, 1960), p. 46.

13. Bernard, *The Study of Experimental Medicine*, p. 66.

14. Ibid., p. 221.

15. Ibid., p. 24.

16. Ibid., p. 26.

17. Vitranen, *Claude Bernard*, p. 18. See also the general discussion by Coleman in his *Biology in the Nineteenth Century*, where Bernard may fairly be said to play the starring role.

18. Loren Eiseley, *Darwin's Century: Evolution and the Men Who Discovered It* (New York: Doubleday & Company, Anchor Books, 1961), p. 331.

19. Emil Du Bois-Reymond, "Ueber Neo-Vitalismus" (1894), in *Reden*, 2 vols. (Leipzip: Verlag von Veit & Company, 1912), 2:504. "So war der Vitalismus aus seiner mächtigsten Verschanzung getrieben und in die Flucht geschlagen. Wohl noch nie hat eine wissenschaftliche Schrift von rein theoretischem Interesse so schnell und in so weitem Umkreise die gesamte gebildete Welt ergriffen und entwurzelt. Besonders in England selber und in Deutschland feierte der Darwinismus seine Triumphe, bei den dort so mächtigen kirchlichen Einflüssen ein doppelt hoch anzuschlagender Erfolg. Sogar eine politische Partei sah sich bei uns bemüssigt von dem ihr gefährlich scheinenden Umschwung Notiz zu nehmen, und ein in diesem Salle gelesener Nachruf an Darwin wurde der Gegenstand gehässiger Beurteilung, welche bis auf die Rednerbühne des Abgeordnetenhauses ihren Weg fand." Helmholtz, on the other hand, whose writings reveal him as a man of generous spirit, beloved by fellow scientists throughout German-speaking countries, wrote consolingly: "That which arouses our moral feelings at the thought of a future, though possibly very remote, cessation of all living creation on earth is more particularly the question whether all this life is not an aimless sport, which will ultimately fall a prey to destruction by brute force.... [Yet] the individual, who works for the ideal

objects of humanity, even if in a modest position, and in a limited sphere of activity, may bear without fear the thought that the thread of his own consciousness will one day break." Herman Ludwig von Helmholtz, "The Mystery of Creation" (1871), in *The World's Best Orations*, vol. 7, ed. David J. Brewer (St. Louis, 1899), p. 2471.

20. See Part I, above, pp. 70 f., for Haeckel's epistemological confrontations.

21. Cassirer, *The Problem of Knowledge*, p. 162.

22. Heinrich Schmidt, *Der Kampf um die "Welträtsel." Ernst Haeckel, die "Welträtsel" und die Kritik* (Bonn: Verlag von Emil Strauss, 1900), p. 16. "Was Haeckel will, das ist eine Religion auf dem sicheren Boden der modernen Wissenschaft, eine Religion, die alle bisherigen Religionen überwindet, weil über sie hinausbauen will, — eine neue Religion dem neuen Menschen."

23. Ernst Haeckel, *Der Monistenbund: Thesen zur Organisation des Monismus* (Frankfurt a. M.: Neuer Frankfurter Verlag, 1905), p. 5. "Die Fortschritte der Entwickelungslehre haben uns überzeugt, dass die ganze Natur in kausalem Zusammenhang einem grossen einheitlichen Prozesse der Entwickelung unterliegt und dass diese Kosmogenesis aus einer ununterbrochenen Kette von Umbildungen besteht. Das gilt ebenso für die Entwickelung der anorganischen Natur (Kant, Laplace) wie für die Entwickelung der organischen Wesen (Lamarck, Darwin)....Dagegen muss die moderne Wissenschaft vollständig jede sogenannte 'Schöpfung' der Welt ablehnen, ebenso wie die mystische Annahme eines persönlichen Schöpfers, der die Welt aus 'Nichts' erschaffen und seine Schöpfungsgedanken in Form der Organismen verkörpert hat. Ein solcher anthropomorpher Schöpfer existiert ebensowenig, als eine von ihm geordnete 'sittliche Weltordnung' oder eine sogennante 'göttliche Vorstehung.'"

24. Ernst Haeckel, *The Riddle of the Universe at the Close of the Nineteenth Century*, trans. Joseph McCabe (New York: Harper & Brothers, 1900), p. 381.

25. Schmidt, *Kampf um die Welträtsel*, p. 25.

26. Ibid., p. 3.

27. William A. Cheney, *Can We Be Sure of Mortality?: A Lawyer's Brief* (New York: Roger Brothers, 1910), p. 2.

28. Ibid., pp. 199 f.

Chapter 5

1. The His-Weismann theory "regarded the individual cells of the embryo as being pre-ordained for a future function in building up the mature entity." Hans Driesch, *Man and the Universe*, trans. W. H. Johnson

from the German original (*Der Mensch und die Welt*) (London: George Allen & Unwin, 1929), p. 66. Life under this theory was a kind of plasmatic stream, and life forms were passed on from one generation to another, uninfluenced by environmental and somatic factors. The rediscovery of the Mendelian laws threw new light on the Weismann theory, but the phenomena observed by Driesch could not be thoroughly understood until the 1960s, with the discovery of the genetic code.

2. Cassirer, *The Problem of Knowledge*, p. 196; Hans Driesch, *The Science and Philosophy of the Organism*, 2 vols., The Gifford Lectures, 1908 (London: Adam and Charles Black, 1908), 2:168 f.: "Entelechy lacks all the characteristics of quantity: entelchy is order of relation and nothing else." "Entelechy is *not* a kind of energy, but in spite of that it does not disturb the validity of the first principle of energetics."

3. Ibid., p. 370. "This *primary* entelechy would not have created absolute reality, but would have *ordered* certain parts of it, and these parts therefore would show a sort of non-contingent constellation whilst all other constellations of the elementalities of the universe would be contingent." Driesch, *Man and the Universe*, p. 63: "There *are*, in fact, *two wholly different realms of reality* in so far as this manifests itself to us in the form of the material world. True, they both appear in a material form, but the laws which govern the happenings in them are wholly different."

4. W. K. C. Guthrie, *A History of Greek Philosophy*, vol. 6: *Aristotle: An Encounter* (Cambridge: Cambridge University Press, 1981), p. 124; F. E. Peters, *Greek Philosophical Terms: A Historical Lexicon* (New York: New York University Press, 1967), pp. 55–57.

5. Driesch, *Science and Philosophy of the Organism*, 2:338.

6. Driesch, *Science and Philosophy of the Organism*, 2:180 f., 329 ff.

7. Ibid., p. 82. This passage is quoted by Jung, "On the Nature of the Psyche," CW 8, para. 368. See Part III, Chapter 1, n. 14 above for another example of the empirical circumlocutions practiced by turn-of-the-century professors.

8. Cassirer, *Problem of Knowledge*, p. 205.

9. J. W. Jenkinson, "Vitalism," *The Hibbert Journal* 9 (1911): 545–59.

10. T. H. Morgan, "Review: *The Science and Philosophy of the Organism*," *The Journal of Philosophy*, vol. 6 (1909).

11. O. W. Griffith, "Review: *The Problem of Individuality* and *The History and Theory of Vitalism*," by Hans Driesch," *The Hibbert Journal* 13 (1915): 438–43.

12. Hilda D. Oakeley, "Review of Hans Driesch's *Wirklichkeitslehre: Ein Metaphysischen Versuch*," *Mind*, n.s. 30 (1921): 346–53.

13. Jung, *The Zofingia Lectures*, para. 56 f.

14. Ibid., para. 96.

15. "The mechanistic view is purely causal; it conceives an event as the effect of a cause.... The energic point of view on the other hand is in essence final; the event is traced back from effect to cause on the assumption that some kind of energy underlies the changes in phenomena." "On Psychic Energy," CW 8, para. 2–3.

16. See Part II, pp. 116 ff., above; also the Appendix on Fechner, below.

17. "On Psychic Energy," CW 8, para. 11.

18. Driesch, *Man and the Universe*, p. 70.

19. Driesch, *Science and Philosophy of the Organism*, 2:74. "Busse, in his book, *Geist und Körper, Seele und Leib*, brought forward an argument against so-called psycho-physical parallelism which is almost identical with my analysis down to the smallest details."

20. Ludwig Busse, "Die Wechselwirkung zwischen Leib und Seele und das Gesetz der Erhaltung der Energie," in *Philosophische Abhandlungen: Christoph Sigwart zu seinem siebzigsten Geburtstage* (Tübingen: J. C. B. Mohr, 1900), pp. 101 f.

21. Ibid., pp. 97, 115.

22. Ibid., p. 124.

23. Ibid., pp. 99 f. (Jung, "On Psychic Energy, CW 8, para. 9) "Man braucht bloss anzunehmen, dass eine Aequivalenz zwischen den geistigen und materiellen Processen besteht. Es würde dann das Energiequantum, das auf jener Seite verloren gehen müsste, damit ein entsprechendes Quantum geistiger Energie entstehen könnte, durch den abermaligen Umsatz der letzteren in eine neue materielle Energieform wieder eingebracht werden können. Es bliebe sich demnach ganz gleich, ob ein Quantum geistiger Energie sich in den Ablauf der materiellen Processe einschöbe oder nicht. Das Gesetz der Erhaltung der Energie in seiner bisherigen Auffassung würde nicht verletzt werden."

24. Wundt, *Grundzüge der physiologischen Psychologie*.

25. Ibid., pp. 736 f. I have made an informal translation of the passage preceding the sentences set in quotation marks.

26. Jung, *Psychological Types* (1921),CW 6, para. 748.

27. Jung, "General Aspects of Dream Psychology" (1916, revised in 1928 and 1948), CW 8, para. 529.

28. "On the Nature of the Psyche," CW 8, para. 367–70, 380. Jung refers to Driesch, *The Science and Philosophy of the Organism*, 2:82. I reproduced this passage on p. 249 above.

29. See the letter to Walter Schaffner, Feb. 16, 1961, in *C. G. Jung Letters*, 2 vols. translated from the German by R. F. C. Hull, selected and edited by Gerhard Adler in collaboration with Aniela Jaffé, Bollingen Series XCV (Princeton: Princeton University Press, 1973), hereafter cited as *Letters*.

30. Eugen Bleuler, *Die Psychoide als Prinzip der Organischen Entwicklung* (Berlin: Verlag von Julius Springer, 1925); Eugen Bleuler, *Mechanismus-Vitalismus-Mnemismus*, no. 6 of the series *Abhandlungen zur Theorie der Organischen Entwicklung*, published by H. Spemann, W. Vogt, and B. Romeis (Berlin: Verlag von Julius Springer, 1931).

31. Bleuler, *Mnemismus*, p. 144.

32. Ibid., pp. 51 f.

33. See Adolf Portmann, "Jung's Biology Professor: Some Recollections," *Spring* (1976), pp. 148–54, esp. p. 150. Jung's *Mysterium Coniunctionis*, CW 14, para. 768, 786 and 787, and his letter to Dr. H., Aug. 30, 1951, in *Letters*, 2, contain other references to a psychoid or "transcendental" factor in life. A comment in Jung's autobiography, *Memories, Dreams, Reflections*, recorded and edited by Aniela Jaffé, translated from the German by Richard and Clara Winston (New York: Pantheon, 1961), p. 338, reflects the more Schopenhauerian-von Hartmann cast of his thinking about final cause: "If the Creator were conscious of Himself, He would not need conscious creatures; nor is it probable that the extremely indirect methods of creation, which squander millions of years upon the development of countless species and creatures, are the outcome of purposeful intention. Natural history tells us of a haphazard and casual transformation of species over hundreds of millions of years of devouring and being devoured. The biological and political history of man is an elaborate repetition of the same thing. But the history of the mind offers a different picture. Here the miracle of reflecting consciousness intervenes—the second cosmogony. The importance of consciousness is so great that one cannot help suspecting the element of *meaning* to be concealed somewhere within all the monstrous, apparently senseless biological turmoil, and that the road to its manifestation was ultimately found on the level of warmblooded vertebrates possessed of a differentiated brain—found as if by chance, unintended and unforeseen, and yet somehow sensed, felt and groped for out of some dark urge."

34. Hans Driesch, *Die "Seele" als Elementarer Naturfaktor: Studien über die Bewegungen der Organismen* (Leipzig: Verlag von Wilhelm Engelmann, 1903), p. 80. "Das gewollte Ziel einer Handlung beruht, psychologisch gesprochen, teilweise auf blossen sogenannten 'Gefühl', indem ein Unlustgefühl hervorgerufen werden soll, teilweise beruht es auf Erfahrung. Ersteres tut es nur im Allgemeinsten, letzteres im Speziellen. Da nun jedes Handlungsziel irgendwie spezifiziert ist, so folgt, dass auch jedes gewollte Handlungsziel irgendwie durch Erfahrung bestimmt ist. Kein Wollen ohne Wissen."

35. "On the Nature of the Psyche," CW 8, para. 380.

36. "Synchronicity: An Acausal Connecting Principle," CW 8, para. 843, n. 38.

37. Ibid., para. 931.

Notes to Postscript

1. Arthur O. Lovejoy, "The Meanings of 'Emergence' and Its Modes," in *Proceedings of the Sixth International Congress of Philosophy* (New York: Longmans, Green and Co., 1927), pp. 24 f. See also Mario Bunge, *Causality and Modern Science* (1959), 3rd rev. ed. (New York: Dover Publications, 1979).

2. Charles Hartshorne, *Beyond Humanism: Essays in the New Philosophy of Nature* (Chicago: Willett, Clark & Company, 1937), pp. 194, 199.

3. W. H. Thorpe, *Purpose in a World of Chance* (Oxford: Oxford University Press, 1978).

4. Michael Polanyi, *Personal Knowledge: Towards a Post-Critical Philosophy* (Chicago: University of Chicago Press, 1958), pp. 358, 360.

5. Ibid., p. 389.

6. W. E. Agar, *A Contribution to the Theory of the Living Organism* (1943), 2nd ed. (Melbourne, Australia: Melbourne University Press, 1951).

7. Rainer Schubert-Soldern, *Mechanism and Vitalism: Philosophical Aspects of Biology*, trans. C. E. Robin (Notre Dame, Ind.: University of Notre Dame, 1962), pp. 223, 210.

8. Moritz Schlick, "Philosophy of Organic Life," in *Readings in the Philosophy of Science*, ed. Herbert Feigl and May Brodbeck (New York: Appleton-Century-Crofts, 1953), pp. 523–37.

9. Francisco J. Ayala, "Teleological Explanations in Evolutionary Biology," *Philosophy of Science* 37 (March 1970): 1–16, esp. p. 3.

10. Colin S. Pittendrigh, "Adaptation, Natural Selection and Behavior," in *Behavior and Evolution*, ed. Anne Roe and George Gaylord Simpson (New Haven: Yale University Press, 1958), p. 393.

11. Jacques Monod, *Chance and Necessity: An Essay on the Natural Philosophy of Modern Biology*, translated from the French by Austryn Wainhouse (New York: Alfred A. Knopf, 1971), p. 119. "The only acceptable mutations are those which, at the very least, do not lessen the coherence of the teleonomic apparatus, but rather, further strengthen it in its already assumed orientation or (probably more rarely) open the way to new possibilities."

12. Ibid., pp. 112 f. A restatement of these facts in the language of information systems was offered by Ernst Mayr in his essay, "Teleological and Teleonomic, a New Analysis," in *Methodological and Historical Essays in the Natural and Social Sciences*, ed. Robert S. Cohen and Marx W. Wartofsky, vol. 14 of *Boston Studies in the Philosophy of Science* (Dordrecht, Holland/Boston: D. Reidl Publishing Company, 1974). A DNA information program may be said to be teleologically decoded by the developing organism, but there is no way in which the process of genetic inheritance—the program itself—was produced by intention or design.

Appendix

Gustav Theodor Fechner

The life of Gustav Theodor Fechner (1801–87) spanned almost the entire nineteenth century. Fechner was a man of science and a man of deeply religious temperament; the struggle to be true to both these impulses of inner character was typical of many nineteenth-century intellectuals.

Though the expression of their characters was very different, Jung too embodied both scientific and religious inclinations. He was an astute and gifted psychiatrist who had almost immediately a large private practice. His earliest renown came on account of scientific experiments in disturbances of mental association patterns and led to applications which are still in use today, for example in polygraph tests. Both men shared at least one event of significance in their life histories. Mid-way in their careers, both Fechner and Jung suffered a mental/spiritual crisis, and emerged from it with a clearer orientation toward the primacy of inner, or religious truth. A sketch of Fechner's life may serve as a backdrop for understanding Jung more clearly.

Additionally, Fechner is of great academic interest in the history of psychological disciplines. He has long been regarded as the true founder of experimental and of physiological psychology. Freud drew from what he understood of Fechner's psychophysics in the establishment of a scientific base for his psychoanalysis. Jung rejected Fechner for what he thought was the materialist base of the psychophysics. Both men erred in their estimation of Fechner. Jung might have found in Fechner an earlier representative of some of his own views on the role of mind and of inner feeling in the discovery of truth. Jung would also have agreed with Fechner on the underlying unity of nature, and in the speculations of Jung's late years, on the universality of the life principle.

Fechner was born in a small Saxon village where his father and his grandfather had both been Lutheran pastors of the church. After the death of his father when Fechner was five years old, he grew up in the house of a maternal uncle, also a pastor, and came to the University of Leipzig at the age of sixteen as a student of medicine.

With a small scholarship, and what little help his mother could give him, Fechner still had not enough to live on, so he eked out a subsistence by translating scientific texts from French into German. Like Helmholtz, Fechner found he could not respect the medicine that was known and taught at that period. He determined to learn through books rather than attend lectures, and although he passed the medical exams he refused to take his doctoral degree. By this time his work in translation had already prepared him in another field, physics. He accepted a non-paid lectureship in physics and afterwards an appointment as extraordinary professor at the University, all the while continuing a heavy load of translations and literary activity and embarking on an assiduous program of physical experiments. He was elected as ordinary professor in 1834, but was able to exercise his professorial duties for only three years before a complete breakdown forced his retirement. The university granted him a life pension but he was not expected to live.

It was surely partly as a result of his experiments on afterimages on the retina, and of overwork in general, that Fechner's mental breakdown exhibited the kinds of symptoms that it did. He could neither eat nor drink for many months and afterwards only strange and highly spiced meats. He became completely blind and could not tolerate the least amount of light falling upon his eyes, suffered flight of thoughts, and inability to sleep.

Still, he himself never thought he would die from his illness. He was sustained, as he explained in a detailed memoir of his crisis, by the faithful care and devotion of his wife, and by religious thoughts which, he said, he did not consciously develop, but which seemed to develop themselves in his soul.

> [I experienced] a belief in a compensation in another life for all the pain endured here, and the conviction that all pain and evil is essentially only a means for producing a new good, whether in this or in another existence. . . . At times I actually thought of my present secluded situation as a kind of chrysalis from which I might emerge rejuvenated and with new strength, even in this life.[1]

For a brief period in his student days Fechner had become completely atheistic. But when he read Oken's *Philosophy of Nature* in the company of a theological student friend he discovered his own belief in a provident universe. Now, after three years of desperate illness,

Fechner recovered almost as suddenly as he had become ill, and lived for another forty-five years in stability of mind, pursuing the same quietly studious habits as before. When he died, all of Leipzig mourned him, for Fechner exemplified the ideals of the German scholar. He was, as William James noted, "as daringly original in his thought as he was homely in his life, a modest, genial, laborious slave to truth and learning."[2]

One important change marked Fechner's emergence from illness. He no longer cared, as such, for his original special field of physics. The religious vision which had supported him through the years of crisis became the only important truth of Fechner's life. He gave his remaining years, indeed, as it turned out, the larger portion of his life to the promulgation of his philosophical views. Though his pension left him free from teaching obligations, Fechner lectured once or twice a week to students on philosophical problems. The publication in 1848 of *Nanna oder das Seelenleben der Pflanzes* ("Nanna, or the Soul-Life of Plants") was followed in 1851 by his major work, the three-volume *Zend-Avesta oder über die Dinge des Himmels und das Jenseits* ("Zend-Avesta, or Concerning Matters of Heaven and the World to Come"), in 1860 by *Elemente der Psychophysik*, in 1863 by *Die Drei Motive und Grunde des Glaubens* ("The Three Motives and Grounds of Faith"), in 1876 by *Vorschule der Aesthetik* ("Propadeutic to Aesthetic") and in 1879 by *Die Tagesansicht gegenüber der Nachtansicht* ("The Daylight View as Opposed to the Night View"), to name only major works. A bibliography published in 1889 lists 175 of Fechner's writings.

The main item of Fechner's philosophical convictions was a belief in the unity of the entire universe—a unity based on shared life and ending in the living God who contains and *is* the universe. One may imagine a great circle and many small circles contained in the large one. Each small circle has a soul which it knows in and of itself. But each of the small circles is at the same time part of the large one, while separate from each of the other small ones. So we are all part of the larger whole, though we may not have direct knowledge of other individual circles. The great circle however knows all the small circles which comprise its own substance. We all are the small circles; the great circle is the earth and the greatest circle of all is God.[3]

Fechner read the philosophers of his time and was to some extent influenced by them. He reported having begun with the natural philosophy of Schelling's school, that he had then "plucked the best fruit from a branch of Hegel (a branch, to be sure, bent far from the tree), and that in the ashes of Herbart's fire he had found coals for his own hearth."[4] But Fechner completely circumvented the epistemological problems with which so much of post-Kantian philosophical thinking was concerned.[5] Why ever should we doubt the veracity of our perceptions of the visible world?, he asked. Why disbelieve in the material world? To do so is to disparage God himself, who is after all just as much a part of every rock and flower in the field as He is of the thoughts and feelings of we who meditate on Him. Body and soul are not two separate entities. They are two aspects of the same thing. We must only imagine God shifting position in order for us to see now matter, now spirit. Both are equally real, but the priority belongs to spirit, for all of nature is in some sense alive, being itself the body of God.[6] This is an identity theory, whose roots lie in Spinoza and in the Stoics. A passage from Fechner's *Soul Life of Plants* shows how his faith in an animate universe is supported by an analogical and poetic style:

> The question now is whether the *essential* signs of soul are lacking in the plant, or whether with respect to these it is perfectly analogous to us and to the animals....We must take to heart principally two things: first, that no conclusion whatever can be drawn from the fact that nothing whatever can be directly perceived of the soul of the plant, since the same thing can be said of the soul of my brother and of every other being; secondly that if plants look so unlike and are so different in their behavior from men and animals, men and animals too look so unlike and are so different in their behavior that one not only may but must ask whether this diversity can be carried further without prejudice to the possession of the soul....Can it perhaps be said that the manifestations of plant life exclude a psychic interpretation? But in addition to the souls which run about and cry and devour might there not be souls which bloom in stillness, which exhale their fragrance, which satisfy their thirst with the dew and their impulses by burgeoning? I cannot conceive how running and crying have a peculiar right, as against blooming and the emission of fragrance, to be regarded as indications of psychic activity.[7]

Fechner contrasted a Night View of reality with a Daylight View. A Night View sees the world as merely phenomenal, a subjective illusion, for it sees the true reality as something unknown and unknowable, as easily hell as heaven. If the material world is only phenomenal, it also means that the progress of science is illusory and that we can never understand reality or consciousness. From the standpoint of meaning, which is what interested Fechner, a phenomenalist view of reality is in no way different from a materialist view—both deny that there is any higher significance in our experience of life in the world we inhabit.

The Daylight View sees reality from the point of view of the inner eye. All things, if we see them from within, are besouled, and that includes atoms, crystals, heavenly bodies, and the earth.[8] If everything is alive—and this is I believe one of the main points, if not *the* main point, for Fechner—then it is not possible for there to be a passage from life to death, or from immaterial to material forms. Death does not exist. We may only pass from one form of life to another. It might appear that a child in the womb would die when it burst the bonds that contained it, but instead it passes into a new and freer empire, not detached from the former home, but contained in a more spacious room of that home. Our death may, again, seem to be the end of all, but if we proceed inductively, says Fechner, on the basis of what we already know of fetal life as the basis for independent existence, we may find that after death we emerge once more into a still freer domain.[9]

> When man dies...the soul will now return to nature with full freedom. He will no longer be conscious of the waves of light and sound only as they strike eye and ear, but, as the waves roll forth into the sea of ether and the sea of air, he will not merely feel the blowing of the wind and the wash of the waves against his body, but will himself murmur in the air and sea; no more wander outwardly through verdant woods and meadows, but himself consciously pervade both wood and meadow and those wandering there.[10]

William James, who in his 1890 *Principles of Psychology* had criticized Fechner's psychophysics as contributing nothing at all to the field of psychology, realized some ten or fifteen years later that Fechner's philosophical idealism was of exactly the right sort to help break up false intellectualist apriorism. In his 1908 Hibbert Lectures James used the example of Fechner's unexampled metaphoric "thickness," the richness of his love for the world of personal experience, in order to illustrate by contrast the "thinness" of current transcendentalisms. With their intellectual handling of concrete things they effect only a postmortem dissection of life. But reality, and the reality of experience, is far too rich to be encompassed by a single system. "If philosophy is more a matter of passionate vision than of logic—and I believe it is, logic only finding reasons for the vision afterwards—must not such thinness come either from the vision being defective in the disciples, or from their passion, matched with Fechner's or with Hegel's own passion, being as moonlight unto sunlight or as water unto wine?"[11]

The aspect of his theory for which Fechner has been remembered in the twentieth century is his psychophysics, which became the foundation stone of experimental psychology. It was devised, however, not for the sake of science but in order to demonstrate the reality of the relationship between mind and body by showing "the two modes of appearance of a single thing that is a unity."[12]

While Fechner was meditating on the need to provide a solid, scientific foundation for his philosophical views, it occurred to him one morning at mid-century, on October 22, 1850, still lying in bed, that an observation of his colleague, E. H. Weber, on the converse ratio between the intensity of a stimulus, for example a stimulus of touch, and the intensity by which it is perceived in the organism, might provide the necessary basis, if the relationship could be established mathematically. If an "arithmetic series of mental intensities might correspond to a geometric series of physical energies," then, "the relative increase of bodily energy" might serve as the measure "of the increase of the corresponding mental intensity."[13] Fechner undertook a complex program of logarithmic computations to demonstrate his theory. Ten years later his *Elements of Psychophysics* was published. It gained immediate recognition from scientists such as Helmholtz and Mach, and a considerable scientific discussion from such figures as Volkmann, Aubert, Delbouef, Vierordt, and Berstein. Fechner was the first scientist to make a careful study of the applicability of the thermodynamic laws to the problem of mental activity, and to attempt to answer the question whether the mind is also subject to physical laws. He thought that he had been able to demonstrate the connection between higher mental activities and physical processes. Surely it is no misfortune, he said, that the mind is subject to the same energic laws that govern the entire universe. Whether or not we must conclude that mental processes can exist only because of physical processes or whether, on the other hand, "the mind furnishes from its own sources the energy for the activities of the body" and might "be a creator of completely fresh energy in the body," thus negating the law of the conservation of energy, are questions which Fechner's experimentation sought to encompass.[14] It is true that there are occasions when the will alone, or voluntary effort, appears to create kinetic energy which would otherwise not have come into existence. We can see a person perform a tremendous physical or mental feat, when he/she was just before sitting indifferently and quietly in place. But this voluntary effort is nevertheless always at the cost of potential energy which could have been used for something else. Every activity exhausts us all the more, the more vigorously and the longer it is continued. Nothing happens contrary to the laws of energy. Both the idealist and the materialist may trace activity to, respectively, mental or material causes. Fechner, however, concluded from his experiments the case for simultaneity: "We take the facts as they appear directly on observation, where at one time the material side (or mode of appearance), at another the mental side provides the evidence for the change distribution."[15]

In spite of the apparent clarity of the above statement, Fechner's theory of psychophysics was fraught with conceptual difficulties, for he insisted on the *identity* of mind and body while at the same time believing that all of nature is in some degree alive and conscious. Those who did not share his metaphysical convictions would naturally interpret the results of his psychophysical data from a different perspective. Besides, in the psychophysical writings of his later years, Fechner tended toward silence concerning his metaphysical theses in order to make his scientific demonstrations more acceptable.[16]

An internal incoherence in the psychophysical method was pointed out by Wilhelm Wundt, who established the first experimental laboratory for psychology in 1879 in Leipzig, as the psychological heir of Fechner. Although Fechner proposed an identity between mind and body, his investigations of the relations between external stimulus and sensation actually presupposed a causal relation between two objectively different things.[17]

The difficulties of Fechner's concept, combined with the inherent interest in the body-mind problem and the novelty of applying the newly won scientific knowledge in thermodynamics to a philosophical problem released a spate of arguments. Heinrich Rickert analyzed the difficulties in comparing qualitative (psychic) with quantitative (mass) concepts. It is all very well to compare reality with the convex and concave sides of a hollow ball, he said. Here the parallel effect is exact, for every change in the concave side means also a change in the convex side. But this is a mathematical

image. In the real world we will scarcely find any points of comparison with any process which may conceivably be set in parallel
relationship.[18]

Biologists and psychologists of a materialist persuasion greeted
Fechner's work because it seemed that now for the first time matters
of psyche or soul, which had hitherto belonged to the exclusive
preserve of theologians and philosophers, might be transferred to the
sphere of science.[19] G. F. Lipps, whose book, *Grundriss der Psychophysik*,
is catalogued in Jung's personal library, was a pupil of Helmholtz.
The task of psychophysics, he wrote, consists in clarifying the
physical and especially the physiological bases of consciousness.[20]

The depth psychologies, in particular Freud and after him Jung,
profited from still another aspect of Fechner's psychophysical
parallelism, namely his theory that the laws of energy in the
physical world run parallel to but do not interact with the energic
processes operating within the psyche.[21] The important part of this
hypothesis for psychology lies in the idea that the psyche is a closed
system, never losing energic values. If nothing is passing in or out of
the system then we may propose a psyche with a relatively constant
amount of energic potential. Energy which once appeared in conscious life and has now disappeared may be presumed not to have
vanished but to have been converted; it will be found existing in
some other *psychic* form. Further, the flow of psychic energy within
the psychic system is regulated, according to Freud, by the pleasure-
unpleasure principle, an idea enunciated already by Fechner in his
1846 book, *Ueber das höchste Gut*. The clinical concepts of the unconscious, of psychic energy, and of defense mechanisms gained a
scientific basis in Freud's economic, dynamic, and topographical
concepts of the mind, but were based on ideas first made current by
Fechner's attempt to transfer thermodynamic laws to the arena of
mental functioning. Freud also took over from Fechner the constancy
principle, another derivative of the energy laws. It defines pleasure
as the stabilizing or equalizing of energic potentials and unpleasure
as the tension involved in higher levels of excitation. Freud's extension of the principle of constancy into his Nirvana principle, utilizing the sinister second law of thermodynamics, did *not* however
accord with Fechner's views, although it too is rooted in an application of general physical laws to mental life.[22]

Inasmuch as "depth psychology" as a field is partly defined in
terms of its concern for the interaction between the conscious and
the unconscious psyche, Jung naturally inherited from Freud some
of the views which Freud had first found in Fechner. The economic
view—that the psyche is a closed, or a relatively closed system of

energic potentials, and the dynamic view—that there is a dynamic and symptomatic interaction between conscious and unconscious realms, as well as the topographical view—which delineates a threshold of excitation marking a boundary between known (conscious) and unknown (unconscious) psychic areas, would in their most basic statements of definition (though not in their theoretical consequences) belong to the postulates shared by both men. Beyond this it is not entirely clear what Jung thought of Fechner. Jung's references to Fechner are mostly incidental. In the *Zofingia Lectures* Jung counts Fechner among the number of non-materialist scientists who could appreciate "the notion of man as a materialization of soul."[23] In later writings he noted favorably Fechner's plan to make psychology accessible to scientific method.[24] Elsewhere he finds that Fechner overdid it with the scientific approach, for at the most crucial point, "psychology stands outside natural science."[25] In his late essay, "On the Nature of the Psyche," Jung acknowledged Fechner's concept of the threshold, and of an unconscious psyche.[26]

Jung's references to psychophysics show that he believed it was "an epiphenomenalist point of view" and a "legacy from the old-fashioned scientific materialism" which reduced *psyche* to *physis*.[27] Besides, the prospect of two non-interacting parallel systems meant there could be no reciprocal action between psychic and physical energy systems. This seemed psychologically unreasonable and philosophically reprehensible. For the idealist, mind itself must be an effective cause.[28] Only in his very late essay on "Flying Saucers" did Jung, reflecting on para-psychological phenomena, propose that the experiments of Rhine "bring us a little nearer to understanding the mystery of psycho-physical parallelism, for we now know that a factor exists which mediates between the apparent incommensurability of body and psyche, giving matter a kind of 'psychic' faculty and the psyche a kind of 'materiality', by means of which the one can work on the other."[29] If we could overcome the prejudice, Jung goes on to say, that only body affects psyche, and could accept that the psychic "extends beyond the sphere of biochemical processes to matter in general...[then] in that case all reality would be grounded on an as yet unknown substrate possessing material and at the same time psychic qualities." Jung did not apparently realize that this had all along been Fechner's main point. Fechner shared with another physician turned philosopher, Paracelsus, the principal items of the ancient doctrine of sympathy.[30] If Jung had known this, the history of the psychologies of the unconscious may have been rather different. Freud borrowed from Fechner's *Psychophysics*. But the affinity of inner viewpoint lay rather between Fechner and Jung.

Notes to Appendix

1. Gustav Theodor Fechner, *Religion of a Scientist: Selections*, ed. and trans. Walter Lowrie (New York: Pantheon Books, 1946), pp. 40 f.

2. William James, *A Pluralistic Universe*, The Hibbert Lectures of 1908 (Cambridge: Harvard University Press, 1977), p. 70.

3. Oswald Külpe, *The Philosophy of the Present in Germany*, translated from the fifth German edition by Maud Lyall Patrick and G. T. W. Patrick (London: George Allen & Company, 1913).

4. Ibid., p. 149.

5. G. Stanley Hall, *Founders of Modern Psychology* (New York: Appleton, 1912), p. 139. "Kant was one pet abomination, whose invention of the *Ding-an-sich* he termed a fell plot to banish joy from the world. For Fechner epistemology did not exist.... To teach distrust of the senses or to call our experience with nature merely phenomenal is to make true knowledge impossible and to bring discontentment, unhappiness and disenchantment into the world."

6. Frederick Copleston, S. J., *A History of Philosophy* vol. 7: *Fichte to Nietzsche* (London: Burns and Oates, 1963), p. 375; Külpe, *The Philosophy of the Present in Germany*, p. 157; Kurd Lasswitz, *Gustav Theodor Fechner* (Stuttgart: Friedrich Fronmanns Verlag, 1896), p. 147. "Die Erdkrüste...[denkt Fechner] überhaupt niemals des Lebens bar gewesen ist."

7. Fechner, *Religion of a Scientist*, pp. 167, 169.

8. Hall, *Founders of Modern Psychology*, p. 138; Gustav Theodor Fechner, *Life after Death* (1836), trans. Mary C. Wadsworth, with an Introduction by William James, and several excerpts from philosophical works (New York: Pantheon Books, 1943). James writes: "Once grasp the idealistic notion that inner experience is the reality, and that matter is but a form in which inner experience may appear to one another when they affect each other from the outside; and it is easy to believe that consciousness or inner experience never originated, or developed, out of the unconscious, but that it and the physical universe are co-eternal aspects of the one self-same reality, much as concave and convex are aspects of one curve" (pp. 16 f.).

9. Fechner, *Life after Death*, pp. 123 f.

10. Ibid., p. 65.

11. James, *A Pluralistic Universe*, pp. 117, 81.

12. Gustav Fechner, *Elements of Psychophysics* (1860), vol. 1, trans. Helmut E. Adler, ed. Davis H. Howes and Edwin G. Boring (New York: Holt, Rinehart and Winston, 1966), p. 5.

13. Ibid., p. xiv.

14. Ibid., p. 31.

15. Ibid., p. 35; for a more poetic statement of this same conviction, see Fechner's *Life after Death*: "Man lives here at once an outer and an inner life, the first all visible and audible in look, word, writing, in outward affairs and works, the last perceptible to himself only through interior thoughts and feelings.... However small and fine the vibration or impulse may be by which a conscious emotion is carried to our minds, yet the whole play of conscious emotions is borne by an inward mental action, it cannot die out without producing effects of its kind in us and at last beyond us; only we cannot follow them into life outside. As little as the lute can keep its playing to itself, it is born out beyond it, so little can our minds; to the lute or the mind belongs only that which is closest to it" (pp. 58 f.). In a more sober moment Fechner later estimated the strength of his thesis: "The living strength of consciousness never really rises anew, is never lost, but, like that of the body upon which it rests, can only change its place, its form, its manner of dissemination in time and space.... [Note] Indisputably this law, analogous to the so-called law of the conservation of energy in the physical realm, is in some way connected with it through the fundamental relation of spirit to body, without the connection being clearly established, or shown to be derivable psychophysically from the physical law, since the essence of psychophysical energy itself is not clearly defined. The law must therefore be inferred from facts such as are above mentioned; and, without being exactly and fully proved, it acquires thereby a probability which qualifies it to serve as a basis for such views as are here in question" (p. 77).

16. Wilhelm Wundt, *Gustav Theodor Fechner: Rede zur Feier seines hundertjährigen Geburtstages* (Leipzig: Verlag von Wilhelm Engelmann, 1901), p. 43.

17. Ibid., p. 69.

18. Heinrich Rickert, "Psychophysische Causalität und psychophysischer Parallelismus," in *Philosophischer Abhandlungen: Christoph Sigwart zu seinem siebzigsten Geburtstage* (Tübingen: Freiburg in B. und Leipzig: Verlag von J. C. B. Mohr, 1900), p. 73.

19. Wilhelm Ostwald, *Monism as the Goal of Civilization*, ed. International Committee of Monism (Hamburg, 1913), pp. 20 f.; Ernst Haeckel, *The Riddle of the Universe at the Close of the Nineteenth Century*, trans. Joseph McCabe (New York: Harper & Brothers Publishers, 1900),·p. 98.

20. G. F. Lipps, *Grundriss der Psychophysik* (Leipzig: G. J. Göschen'sche Verlagshandlung, 1903), p. 12.

21. Hall, *Founders of Modern Psychology*, p. 153; Lasswitz, *Fechner*, pp. 153 f.

22. Henri F. Ellenberger, "Fechner and Freud," *Bulletin of the Menninger Clinic* 20 (1956): 201–14; Frank Sulloway, *Freud, Biologist of the Mind: Beyond the Psychoanalytic Legend* (New York: Basic Books, 1979), pp. 62 f., 339 f.; Ernest Jones, *The Life and Work of Sigmund Freud*, 3 vols. (New York: Basic Books, 1953–57), 3: 374 f.

23. C. G. Jung, *The Zofingia Lectures. The Collected Works of C. G. Jung. Supplementary Volume A*, ed. William McGuire, trans. Jan van Heurck, with an Introduction by Marie-Louise von Franz, Bollingen Series XX (Princeton: Princeton University Press, 1983), para. 108 f., 117.

24. C. G. Jung, *The Collected Works of C. G. Jung*, 20 vols., translated from the German by R. F. C. Hull, Bollingen Series XX (New York: Pantheon Books, 1953–79) (hereafter referred to as CW), vol. 7, para. 407; vol. 9i, para. 111.

25. Jung, CW 17, para. 162.

26. Jung, CW 8, para. 352, 364.

27. Jung, CW 8, para. 10, 33.

28. See Part III of this essay, p. 255 above.

29. Jung, "Flying Saucers: A Modern Myth of Things Seen in the Skies" (1958), CW 10, para. 780.

30. See Part I, Chapter 7b of this essay, pp. 79 ff. above.

Selected Bibliography

A. Works by C. G. Jung

This is a selected list of essays cited in the present book, or of special interest with regard to the problems discussed in it. Writings appearing in the *Collected Works* are cited by the letters CW. The year of first publication, in parentheses, is followed by the volume number of the CW. A general bibliography of Jung's writings published up to 1979 comprises Volume 19 of the *Collected Works*. Bibliographic essays on works *about* Jung are listed in Part B of this bibliography.

"Adaptation, Individuation, Collectivity" (1916). CW 18.

"The Aims of Psychotherapy" (1929). CW 16.

Aion: Researches into the Phenomenology of the Self (1951). CW 9ii.

Analytical Psychology: Notes of the Seminar Given in 1925. Edited by William McGuire. Bollingen Series XCIX. Princeton: Princeton University Press, 1989.

Answer to Job (1952). CW 11.

"Basic Postulates of Analytical Psychology" (1931). CW 8.

"Brother Klaus" (1933). CW 11.

The Collected Works of C. G. Jung. 20 vols. Edited by Herbert Read, Michael Fordham, and Gerhard Adler; executive editor (from 1967), William McGuire. Translated by R. F. C. Hull, except as otherwise noted. Bollingen Series XX. New York: Pantheon Books for Bollingen Foundation, 1953–60; Bollingen Foundation, 1961–67. Princeton, N.J.: Princeton University Press, 1967–79. London: Routledge & Kegan Paul, 1953–78.

With Emma Jung and Toni Wolff. *A Collection of Remembrances.* Edited by Ferne Jensen. San Francisco: Analytical Psychology Club, 1982.

"Commentary on 'The Secret of the Golden Flower'" (1929). CW 13.

"Concerning the Archetypes, with Special Reference to the Anima Concept" (1936/1954). CW 9i.

"Concerning Mandala Symbolism" (1950). CW 9i.

"Conscious, Unconscious, and Individuation" (1939). CW 9i.

"Freud and Jung: Contrasts" (1929). CW 4.

With Sigmund Freud. *The Freud-Jung Letters*. Edited by William McGuire. Translated by Ralph Manheim and R. F. C. Hull. Bollingen Series XCIV. Princeton: Princeton University Press, 1974.

"General Aspects of Dream Psychology" (1916/1948). CW 8.

"Instinct and the Unconscious" (1919). CW 8.

"Is Analytical Psychology a Religion?: Notes on a Talk Given by C. G. Jung" (1937). *Spring* (1972), pp. 144–48.

"Jung and Religious Belief: Extracts from H. L. Philp, *Jung and the Problem of Evil*, and the Correspondence between Jung and the Rev. David Cox" (1956–57). CW 18.

C. G. Jung Letters. 2 vols. Translated by R. F. C. Hull. Selected and edited by Gerhard Adler in collaboration with Aniela Jaffé. Vol. 1 of Bollingen Series XCV. Princeton: Princeton University Press, 1973.

C. G. Jung Speaking: Interviews and Encounters. Edited by William McGuire and R. F. C. Hull. Bollingen Series XCVII. Princeton: Princeton University Press, 1977.

Memories, Dreams, Reflections. Recorded and edited by Aniela Jaffé. Translated from the German by Richard and Clara Winston. New York: Pantheon, 1961.

"Modern Psychology: Notes on Lectures given at the Eidgenössische Technische Hochschule, 1933–35." Vols. 1 and 2. Zürich: Privately distributed.

Mysterium Coniunctionis (1955–56). CW 14.

"New Paths in Psychology" (1912). CW 7.

"On Psychic Energy" (1928). CW 8.

"On Psychological Understanding" (1914). CW 3.

"On the Nature of the Psyche" (1947/1954). CW 8.

"Paracelsus" (1929). CW 15.

"Paracelsus as a Spiritual Phenomenon" (1942). CW 13.

"Paracelsus the Physician" (1941). CW 15.

"The Phenomenology of the Spirit in Fairytales" (1945/1948). CW 9i.

Psychological Types (1921). CW 6.

Psychology and Alchemy (1944). CW 12.

"Psychology of the Transference" (1946). CW 16.

"The Psychology of the Unconscious" (1917/1926/1943). CW 7.

Psychology of the Unconscious: A Study of the Transformations and Symbolisms of the Libido. Translated by Beatrice M. Hinkle. New York: Dodd, Mead and Co., 1925. (This book is referred to by me in the text as *Symbols of Transformation*, 1912, and the 1952 revised edition is referenced by me as *Symbols of Transformation*, CW 5.)

"Psychotherapists or the Clergy" (1932). CW 11.

"Psychotherapy and a Philosophy of Life" (1943). CW 16.

Psychology and Alchemy (1944). CW 12.

"Psychotherapy Today" (1945). CW 16.

"The Relations between the Ego and the Unconscious" (1928). CW 7.

"Religion and Psychology: A Reply to Martin Buber" (1952). CW 18.

"Richard Wilhelm: In Memorium" (1930). CW 15.

"The Soul and Death" (1934). CW 8.

"The Spirit Mercurius" (1943/1948). CW 13.

"The Spiritual Problem of Modern Man" (1928/1931). CW 10.

"The Stages of Life" (1930–31). CW 8.

"The Structure of the Unconscious" (1916). CW 7.

"A Study in the Process of Individuation" (1934/1950). CW 9i.

Symbols of Transformation: An Analysis of the Prelude to a Case of Schizophrenia (1911–12/1952). CW 5.

"Synchronicity: An Acausal Connecting Principle" (1952). CW 8.

"The Transcendent Function" ([1916]/1957). CW 8.

The Zofingia Lectures. The Collected Works of C. G. Jung. Supplementary Volume A. Edited by William McGuire. Translated by Jan van Heurck, with an Introduction by Marie-Louise von Franz. Bollingen Series XX. Princeton: Princeton University Press, 1983.

B. *Other Works Cited*

Adickes, Erich. *Kant contra Haeckel: Erkenntnistheorie gegen naturwissenschaft-lichen Dogmatismus*. Berlin: Verlag fron Reuther & Reichard, 1901.

Adkins, A. W. H. *From the Many to the One*. London: Constable, 1970.

Agar, W. E. *A Contribution to the Theory of the Living Organism* (1943). 2nd ed. Melbourne, Australia: Melbourne University Press, 1951.

Allison, Henry E. *Kant's Transcendental Idealism: An Interpretation and Defense*. New Haven: Yale University Press, 1983.

Aristotle. *The Basic Works*. Edited and with an Introduction by Richard McKeon. New York: Random House, 1941.

_____. *De Partibus Animalium I and De Generatione Animalium I* (with passages from II.1–3). Translated with Notes by D. M. Balme. Oxford: Clarendon Press, 1972.

_____. *Metaphysics*. Translated with Commentaries and Glossary by Hippocrates G. Apostle. Bloomington: Indiana University Press, 1975.

_____, *Physics: Books I and II*. Translated with Introduction and Notes by W. Charlton. Oxford: Clarendon Press, 1970.

Ayala, Francisco J. "Teleological Explanations in Evolutionary Biology" *Philosophy of Science* 37 (March 1970): 1–16.

Beck, Lewis White. *A Commentary on Kant's Critique of Practical Reason*. Chicago: University of Chicago Press, 1960.

_____. "Neo-Kantianism." *Encyclopedia of Philosophy* 5:468–73. New York: Macmillan Publishing Co., 1967.

Beckner, Morton O. "Vitalism." *Encyclopedia of Philosophy* 8:253–56. New York: Macmillan Publishing Co., 1972.

Behavior and Evolution. Edited by Anne Roe and George Gaylord Simpson. New Haven: Yale University Press, 1958.

Berkeley, George. *A Treatise Concerning the Principles of Human Knowledge*. Edited with an Introduction by Colin M. Turbayne. The Library of Liberal Arts. New York: Bobbs-Merrill Company, 1957.

Bernard, Claude. *An Introduction to the Study of Experimental Medicine* (1865). Translated by Henry Copley Greene, with an Introduction by Lawrence J. Henderson. New York: Macmillan Company, 1927.

Bernfeld, Siegfried. "Freud's Earliest Theories and the School of Helmholtz." *The Psychoanalytic Quarterly* 13 (1944): 341–60.

Biology and the Exploration of Mars. Publication 1296. Edited by Colin S. Pittendrigh, Wolf Vishniac, and J. P. T. Pearman. Washington, D.C.: National Academy of Sciences, National Research Council, 1966.

Bleuler, Eugen. *Mechanismus-Vitalismus-Mnemismus.* Vol. 6 of *Abhandlungen zur Theorie der Organischen Entwicklung.* Published by H. Spemann, W. Vogt, and B. Romeis. Berlin: Verlag von Julius Springer, 1931.

————. *Die Psychoide als Prinzip der Organischen Entwicklung.* Berlin: Verlag von Julius Springer, 1925.

Burkert, Walter, *Greek Religion.* Translated by John Raffian. Cambridge: Harvard University Press, 1985.

Busse, Ludwig. "Die Wechselwirkung zwishen Leib und Seele und das Gesetz der Erhaltung der Energie." In *Philosophische Abhandlungen: Christoph Sigwart zu seinem siebzigsten Geburtstage,* pp. 89–126. Tübingen: J. C. B. Mohr, 1900.

Butts, Robert E. *Kant and the Double Government Methodology: Supersensibility and Method in Kant's Philosophy of Science.* Dordrecht: D. Reidel Publishing Company, 1984.

Cairns-Smith, A. G. "The First Organisms." *Scientific American* 252 (June 1985): 90–100.

Case, Thomas. "Metaphysics." *Encyclopedia Britannica,* 11th edition (1911), 18:225–53.

Cassirer, Ernst. *The Problem of Knowledge: Philosophy, Science, and History since Hegel.* Translated by William H. Woglom and Charles W. Hendel. New Haven: Yale University Press, 1950.

Cheney, William A. *Can We Be Sure of Mortality?: A Lawyer's Brief.* New York: Roger Brothers, 1910.

Coleman, William. *Biology in the Nineteenth Century: Problems of Form, and Transformation.* Cambridge: Cambridge University Press, 1977.

Conger, George Perigo. *Theories of Macrocosms and Microcosms in the History of Philosophy.* New York: Columbia University Press, 1922.

Copleston, Frederick, S.J. *A History of Philosophy.* Vol. 7; *Fichte to Nietzsche.* London: Burns and Oates Limited, 1963.

Cornford, F. M. *Greek Religious Thought from Homer to the Age of Alexander* (1923). New York: AMS Press, 1969.

————. *The Unwritten Philosophy and Other Essays.* Cambridge: Cambridge University Press, 1967.

Davies, Paul. *God and the New Physics*. New York: Simon & Schuster, Touch-stone Books, 1984.

Descartes, René. *The Meditations Concerning First Philosophy*. Translated by Laurence J. Lafleur. The Library of Liberal Arts. New York: Bobbs-Merrill Company, 1960.

Driesch, Hans. *The Crisis in Psychology*. Princeton: Princeton University Press, 1925.

_____. "Emergent Evolution." *Proceedings of the Sixth International Congress of Philosophy, 1926*. New York: Longmans Green and Co., 1927.

_____. *Man and the Universe*. Translated by W. H. Johnston from the German *Der Mensch und die Welt*. London: George Allen & Unwin, 1929.

_____. *The Science and Philosophy of the Organism*. 2 vols. The Gifford Lectures. London: Adam and Charles Black, 1908.

_____. *Die "Seele" als Elementarer Naturfaktor: Studien über die Bewegungen der Organismen*. Leipzig: Verlag von Wilhelm Engelmann, 1903.

_____. *Der Vitalismus als Geschichte und als Lehre*. Leipzig: Verlag von Johann Ambrosius Barth, 1905.

Du Bois-Reymond, Emil. "Ueber Neo-Vitalismus" (1894). In *Reden* 2:492–516. Leipzig: Verlag von Veit, 1912.

Du Bois-Reymond, Emil, and Ludwig, Carl. *Two Great Scientists of the Nine-teenth Century: Correspondence of Emil Du Bois-Reymond and Carl Ludwig* (1927). Collected by Estelle Du Bois-Reymond. Foreword, Notes, and Indexes by Paul Diepgen. Translated by Sabine Lichtner-Ayed. Edited, with a Foreword, by Paul F. Cranefield. Baltimore: Johns Hopkins Press, 1982.

Edwards, Paul. "Common Consent Arguments for the Existence of God." *Encyclopedia of Philosophy* 2: 147–55.

Eibl-Eibesfeldt, Irenaeus. *The Biology of Peace and War*. Translation of *Krieg und Frieden aus der Sicht der Verhaltensforschung*. New York: Viking Press, 1979.

Eiseley, Loren. *All the Strange Hours: The Excavation of a Life*. New York: Charles Scribner's Sons, 1975.

_____. *Darwin's Century: Evolution and the Men Who Discovered It*. New York: Doubleday & Company, Anchor Books, 1961.

Eliade, Mircea. *The Myth of the Eternal Return or Cosmos and History*. Translated from the French by Willard R. Trask. Bollingen Series XLVI. Princeton: Princeton University Press, 1974.

Elkana, Yehuda. "The Problem of Knowledge in Historical Perspective." *Proceedings of the 2nd International Humanistic Symposium, Athens, 1972.* Pp. 191–247.

Ellenberger, Henri F. *The Discovery of the Unconscious.* New York: Basic Books, 1970.

———. "Fechner and Freud." *Bulletin of the Menninger Clinic* 20 (1956): 201–14.

Epicurus: *Letters, Principal Doctrines and Vatican Sayings.* Library of Liberal Arts. New York: Bobbs-Merrill Company, 1964.

Fechner, Gustav Theodor. *Elements of Psychophysics* (1860). Vol. 1. Translated by Helmut E. Adler. Edited by Davis H. Howes and Edwin G. Boring. New York: Holt, Rinehart and Winston, 1966.

———. *Life after Death* (1836). Translated by Mary C. Wadsworth, with an Introduction by William James, and several excerpts from philosophical works. New York: Pantheon Books, 1943.

———. *Religion of a Scientist: Selections.* Edited and translated by Walter Lowrie. New York: Pantheon Books, 1946.

———. *Zend-Avesta oder Ueber die Dinge des Himmels und des Jenseits, vom Standpunkt der Naturbetrachtung.* 2 vols. Third edition supervised by Kurd Lasswitz. Hamburg and Leipzig: Verlag von Leopold Boss, 1906.

Feigl, Herbert. *The "Mental" and the "Physical": The Essay and a Postscript.* Minneapolis: University of Minnesota Press, 1967.

Feigl, Herbert, and Brodbeck, May, eds. *Readings in the Philosophy of Science.* New York: Appleton-Century-Crofts, 1953.

Flournoy, Th. *The Philosophy of William James.* Translated by Edwin B. Holt and William James, Jr. New York: Henry Holt and Company, 1917.

Freud, Sigmund. *The Origins of Psycho-Analysis: Letters to Wilhelm Fliess, Drafts and Notes, 1887–1902.* Edited by Marie Bonaparte, Anna Freud, and Ernst Kris. Authorized translation by Eric Mosbacher and James Strachey. Introduction by Ernst Kris. New York: Basic Books, 1954.

———. *The Standard Edition of the Complete Psychological Works.* 24 vols. Translated from the German under the general editorship of James Strachey, in collaboration with Anna Freud, assisted by Alix Strachey, and Alan Tyson. London: Hogarth Press and The Institute of Psycho-analysis, 1953–74.

Freud, Sigmund, and Jung, C. G. *The Freud-Jung Letters.* Edited by William McGuire. Translated by Ralph Manheim and R. F. C. Hull. Bollingen Series XCIV. Princeton: Princeton University Press, 1974.

Frey-Rohn, Liliane. *From Freud to Jung: A Comparative Study of the Psychology of the Unconscious.* Translated from the German by Fred E. Engreen and Evelyn K. Engreen. New York: G. P. Putnam's Sons, for the C. G. Jung Foundation for Analytical Psychology, 1974.

Furst, Charles. *Origins of the Mind: Mind-Brain Connections.* Englewood Cliffs, N.J.: Prentice-Hall, 1979.

Givens, David B. *Love Signals: How to Attract a Mate.* New York: Crown Publishers, 1983.

_____. "The Nonverbal Basis of Attraction: Flirtation, Courtship, and Seduction." *Psychiatry* 41 (November 1978): 346–59.

Gould, Stephen Jay. *Ontogeny and Phylogeny.* Cambridge: Belknap Press of Harvard University Press, 1977.

Grene, Marjorie. "Empiricism and the Philosophy of Science or *n* Dogmas of Empiricism." In *Epistemology, Methodology, and the Social Sciences.* Edited by Robert S. Cohen and Marx W. Wartofsky. Vol. 71 of *Boston Studies in the Philosophy of Science.* Dordrecht, Holland/Boston, U.S.A.: D. Reidel Publishing Company, 1983.

_____. *A Portrait of Aristotle.* Chicago: University of Chicago Press, 1963.

Griffith, O. W. "Review: *The Problem of Individuality* and *The History and Theory of Vitalism.*" *The Hibbert Journal* 13 (1915): 438–43.

Guthrie, W. K. C. *A History of Greek Philosophy.* 6 vols. Cambridge: Cambridge University Press, 1975.

_____. *Orpheus and Greek Religion: A Study of the Orphic Movement* (1934). New York: W. W. Norton & Company, 1966.

_____, trans. *Plato. Protagoras and Meno* (1956). Harmondsworth, Middlesex: Penguin Books, 1976.

Haeckel, Ernst. *Monism as Connecting Religion and Science: The Confession of Faith of a Man of Science.* Translated by J. Gilchrist. London: Adam and Charles Black, 1895.

_____. *Der Monistenbund: Thesen zur Organisation des Monismus.* Frankfurt a. M.: Neuer Frankfurter Verlag, 1905.

_____. *The Riddle of the Universe at the Close of the Nineteenth Century.* Translated by Joseph McCabe. New York: Harper & Brothers Publishers, 1900.

Hall, G. Stanley. *Founders of Modern Psychology.* New York: Appleton, 1912.

Hall, Thomas S. *Ideas of Life and Matter: Studies in the History of General Physiology, 600B.C.–1900 A.D.* 2 vols. Chicago: University of Chicago Press, 1969.

Hartmann, Eduard von. *Philosophy of the Unconscious: Speculative Results According to the Inductive Method of Physical Science* (1869). Authorized translation by William Chatterton Coupland. New edition in one volume. New York: Harcourt, Brace and Company, 1931.

———. *Die Weltanschauung der Modernen Physik.* Leipzig, 1902.

Hartshorne, Charles. *Beyond Humanism: Essays in the New Philosophy of Nature.* Chicago: Willett, Clark & Company, 1937.

———. *A Natural Theology for Our Time.* La Salle, Ill.: Open Court, 1967.

———. "The Necessarily Existent," from *Man's Vision of God* (1941). In *The Ontological Argument: From St. Anselm to Contemporary Philosophers.* Edited by Alvin Plantinga, with an Introduction by Richard Taylor. New York: Doubleday and Company, 1965.

Heisenberg, Werner. *The Physicist's Conception of Nature.* London: Hutchinson Scientific and Technical, 1958.

Heisig, James W. *Imago Dei: A Study of C. G. Jung's Psychology of Religion.* Lewisburg, Pa.: Bucknell University Press, 1979.

———. "Jung and Theology, a Bibliographical Essay." *Spring* (1973), pp. 204–55.

Helmholtz, Hermann von. "The Aim and Progress of Physical Science" (1869). In *Selected Writings.* Edited with an Introduction by Russell Kahl. Middletown, Conn.: Wesleyan University Press, 1971.

———. "An Autobiographical Sketch" (1891). In *Selected Writings.* Edited with an Introduction by Russell Kahl. Middletown, Conn.: Wesleyan University Press, 1971.

———. "The Conservation of Force: A Physical Memoir" (1847). In *Selected Writings.* Edited with an Introduction by Russell Kahl. Middletown, Conn.: Wesleyan University Press, 1971.

———. "The Facts in Perception" (1878). In *Epistemological Writings: The Paul Hertz/Moritz Schlick Centenary Edition of 1921 with Notes and Commentary by the Editors,* pp. 115–85. Edited, with an Introduction and Bibliography, by Robert S. Cohen and Yehuda Elkana. Dordrecht, Holland/Boston, U.S.A.: Reidel Publishing Company, 1977.

———. "The Mystery of Creation" (1871). In *The World's Best Orations,* vol. 7. Edited by David J. Brewer. St. Louis, 1899.

_____. "Recent Progress in the Theory of Vision" (1868). In *Selected Writings*. Edited with an Introduction by Russell Kahl. Middletown, Conn.: Wesleyan University Press, 1971.

_____. "Thought in Medicine" 1877. In *Selected Writings*. Edited with an Introduction by Russell Kahl. Middletown, Conn.: Wesleyan University Press, 1971.

Hesiod. *The Works and Days. Theogony. The Shield of Herakles*. Translated by Richmond Lattimore. Ann Arbor: University of Michigan Press, 1978.

Hull, David L. *Philosophy of Biological Science*. Englewood Cliffs, N.J.: Prentice-Hall, 1974.

Huyghe, Patrick. "Of Two Minds: Attempts to Build Intelligent Machines Have Caused a Revolution in Our Thinking about Thinking." *Psychology Today* 17 (December 1983): 26–35.

Iverach, James. "Epistemology." *Hastings Encyclopedia of Religion and Ethics* (Edinburgh, 1912), 5:337–56.

Jacobi, Jolande. *Complex, Archetype, Symbol in the Psychology of C. G. Jung*. Translated from the German by Ralph Manheim. Bollingen Series LVII. Princeton: Princeton University Press, 1959.

Jaffé, Aniela. "The Creative Phases in Jung's Life." *Spring* (1972), pp. 162–91.

Jaki, Stanley L. "The Last Century of Science: Progress, Problems and Prospects." *Proceedings of the 2nd International Humanistic Symposium, Athens, 1972*. Pp. 248–64.

James, William. *A Pluralistic Universe*. The Hibbert Lectures of 1908. Cambridge: Harvard University Press, 1977.

_____. *Pragmatism: A New Name for Some Old Ways of Thinking, together with Four Related Essays from The Meaning of Truth (1907)*. New York: Longmans, Green and Co., 1949.

_____. *The Principles of Psychology* (1890). New York: Dover Publications, 1950.

Jenkinson, J. W. "Vitalism." *The Hibbert Journal* 9 (1911): 545–59.

Jones, Ernest. *The Life and Work of Sigmund Freud*. 3 vols. New York: Basic Books, 1953–57.

C. G. Jung Bibliothek Katalog. Küsnacht-Zürich, 1967.

Kant, Immanuel. *Critique of Pure Reason*. Translated by Norman Kemp Smith. New York: Modern Library, 1958.

————. *Dreams of a Spirit Seer and Other Related Writings.* Translation and commentary by John Manolesco. New York: Vantage Press, 1969.

————. *Foundations of the Metaphysics of Morals.* Translated with an Introduction by Lewis White Beck. The Library of Liberal Arts. New York: Bobbs-Merrill Company, 1959.

————. *The Philosophy of Kant: Moral and Political Writings.* Edited with an introduction by Carl J. Friedrich. New York: Modern Library, 1977.

————. *Prolegomena to Any Future Metaphysics.* Introduction by Lewis White Beck. New York: Liberal Arts Press, 1950.

Körner, S. *Kant.* Harmondsworth, England: Penguin Books, 1955.

Külpe, Oswald. *The Philosophy of the Present in Germany.* Translated from the fifth German edition by Maud Lyall Patrick and G. T. W. Patrick. London: George Allen & Company, 1913.

Lange, Friedrich Albert. *The History of Materialism* (1865).Translated by E. C. Thomas. 3rd edition, 3 vols. in one. London: Kegan Paul, Trench, Trübner & Co., 1925.

Lasswitz, Kurd. *Gustav Theodor Fechner.* Stuttgart: Friedrich Frommanns Verlag, 1896.

Leibniz, Gottfried Wilhelm. *Monadology and Other Philosophical Essays.* Translated by Paul Schrecker and Anne Martin Schrecker. Library of Liberal Arts. Indianapolis: Bobbs-Merrill Educational Publishing, 1985.

Lipps, G. F. *Grundriss der Psychophysik.* Leipzig: G. J. Göschen'sche Verlagshandlung, 1903.

Lipps, Theodor. *Leitfaden der Psychologie.* 3rd ed. Leipzig: Verlag von Wilhelm Engelmann, 1909.

Lodge, Sir Oliver. *Life and Matter: A Criticism of Professor Haeckel's "Riddle of the Universe."* New York and London: G. P. Putnam's Sons, 1906.

Lorenz, Konrad. *Behind the Mirror: A Search for a Natural History of Human Knowledge.* Translated by Ronald Taylor. London: Methuen, 1977.

————. "Companions as Factors in the Bird's Environment: The Conspecific as the Eliciting Factor for Social Behaviour" (1935). In *Studies in Animal and Human Behaviour,* 1:101–258. Cambridge: Harvard University Press, 1970.

————. *King Solomon's Ring: New Light on Animal Ways.* Translated from the German by Marjorie Kerr Wilson. New York: New American Library, Signet Books, 1972.

Lovejoy, Arthur O. *The Great Chain of Being.* Cambridge: Harvard University Press, 1976.

_____. "The Meanings of 'Emergence' and Its Modes." *Proceedings of the Sixth International Congress of Philosophy, 1926.* New York: Longmans, Green and Co., 1927.

MacIntosh, Douglas Clyde. *The Problem of Religious Knowledge.* New York: Harper & Brothers, 1940.

Magee, Bryan. *The Philosophy of Schopenhauer.* Oxford: Clarendon Press, 1983.

Mandelbaum, Maurice. *History, Man and Reason: A Study in Nineteenth-Century Thought.* Baltimore and London: Johns Hopkins Press, 1971.

Mayr, Ernst. "Teleological and Teleonomic, a New Analysis." In *Methodological and Historical Essays in the Natural and Social Sciences.* Edited by Robert S. Cohen and Marx W. Wartofsky. Vol. 14 of *Boston Studies in the Philosophy of Science.* Dordrecht, Holland/Boston, U.S.A.: Reidl Publishing Company, 1974.

Mazia, Daniel. "What is Life?" In *Biology and the Exploration of Mars.* Publication 1296. Edited by Colin S. Pittendrigh, Wolf Vishniac and J. P. T. Pearman. Washington, D.C.: National Academy of Sciences, National Research Council, 1966.

Miller, S. L., and Horowitz, N. H. "The Origin of Life." In *Biology and the Exploration of Mars.* Publication 1296. Edited by Colin S. Pittendrigh, Wolf Vishniac and J. P. T. Pearman. Washington, D.C.: National Academy of Sciences, National Research Council, 1966.

Mind in Nature: Essays on the Interface of Science and Philosophy. Edited by John B. Cobb and David Ray Griffin. Washington, D.C.: University Press of America, 1978.

Mohilewer, Joseph. *Wundt's Stellung zum Psychophysischen Parallelismus.* Königsberg i. Pr., 1901.

Monod, Jacques. *Chance and Necessity: An Essay on the Natural Philosophy of Modern Biology.* New York: Alfred A. Knopf, 1971.

Morgan, T. H. "Review: *The Science and Philosophy of the Organism,* by Hans Driesch." *Journal of Philosophy,* vol. 6 (1909).

Nagel, Ernest. "Teleological Explanation and Teleological Systems." In *Readings in the Philosophy of Science,* pp. 537–58. Edited by Herbert Feigl and May Brodbeck. New York: Appleton-Century-Crofts, 1953.

_____. *Teleology Revisited and Other Essays in the Philosophy and History of Science.* New York: Columbia University Press, 1979.

Oakeley, Hilda D. "Review of Hans Driesch's *Wirklichkeitslehre: Ein Metaphysicher Versuch*." *Mind*, n.s. 30 (1921): 346–53.

Onians, Richard Broxton. *The Origins of European Thought about the Body, the Mind, the Soul, the World, Time and Fate*. Cambridge: Cambridge University Press, 1951.

Ostwald, Wilhelm. *Monism as the Goal of Civilization*. Edited by the International Committee of Monism. Hamburg, 1913.

Pagel, Walter. *Paracelsus: An Introduction to Philosophical Medicine in the Era of the Renaissance*. Basel, Switzerland: S. Karger, 1958.

Pap, Arthur. *Elements of Analytic Philosophy*. New York: Macmillan Company, 1949.

———. *An Introduction to the Philosophy of Science*. London: Eyre & Spottiswoode, 1963.

Peters, Eugene H. *Hartshorne and Neoclassical Metaphysics*. Lincoln: University of Nebraska Press, 1970.

Philosophy of Biology in the Philosophy Curriculum. San Francisco: Council for Philosophical Studies, San Francisco State University, 1982.

Pittendrigh, Colin S. "Adaptation, Natural Selection, and Behavior." In *Behavior and Evolution*, pp. 390–416. Edited by Anne Roe and George Gaylord Simpson. Hew Haven: Yale University Press, 1958.

Plato. *Euthyphro, Apology, Crito, and Phaedo*. In *The Last Days of Socrates*. Translated by Hugh Tredennick. Harmondsworth, Middlesex: Penguin Books, 1954.

———. *Phaedrus*. Translated by R. Hackworth. Cambridge: Cambridge University Press, 1952.

———. *Protagoras and Meno* (1956). Translated by W. K. C. Guthrie. Harmondsworth, Middlesex: Penguin Books, 1976.

———. *Timaeus and Critias*. Translated with an Introduction and an Appendix on *Atlantis* by Desmond Lee. Harmondsworth, Middlesex: Penguin Books, 1976.

Polanyi, Michael. *Personal Knowledge: Towards a Post-Critical Philosophy*. Chicago: University of Chicago Press, 1958.

Portmann, Adolf. "Die Bedeutung der Bilder in der lebendigen Energiewandlung." In *Eranos Jahrbuch, 1952*, vol. 21: *Mensch und Energie*, pp. 325–58. Zürich: Rhein Verlag, 1953.

———. "Die Biologie und das Phänomen des Geistigen." In *Eranos Jahrbuch, 1946*, vol. 14: *Geist und Natur*, pp. 521–67. Zürich: Rhein Verlag,

1947. Translated by Ralph Manheim as "Biology and the Phenomenon of the Spiritual." In *Spirit and Nature: Papers from the Eranos Yearbooks*. Edited by Joseph Campbell. Vol. I of Bollingen Series XXX. New York: Pantheon Books, 1954.

————. "Jung's Biology Professor: Some Recollections." *Spring* (1976), pp. 148–54.

————. "Das Problem der Urbilder in Biologischer Sicht." In *Eranos Jahrbuch, 1950*, vol. 18: *Aus der Welt der Urbilder: Sonderband für C. G. Jung zum Fünfundsiebsigsten Geburtstag*, pp. 413–32. Zürich: Rhein-Verlag, 1950.

————. "Das Ursprungsproblem." In *Eranos Jahrbuch, 1947*, vol. 15: *Der Mensch*, pp. 11–40. Zürich: Rhein Verlag, 1948.

Psychology and the Philosophy of Mind in the Philosophy Curriculum. San Francisco: Council for Philosophical Studies, San Francisco State University, 1983.

Rickert, Heinrich. "Psychophysische Causalität und psychophysischer Parallelismus." In *Philosophischer Abhandlungen: Christoph Sigwart zu seinem siebzigsten Geburtstage*, pp. 61–87. Tübingen, Freiburg in. B. und Leipzig: Verlag von J. C. B. Mohr, 1900.

Riehl, Alois. *Introduction to the Theory of Science and Metaphysics*. Translated by Arthur Fairbanks. London: Kegan Paul, Trench, Trübner, 1894.

Robinson, Daniel N. *Toward a Science of Human Nature: Essays on the Psychologies of Mill, Hegel, Wundt, and James*. New York: Columbia University Press, 1982.

Ross, Sir David. *Aristotle* (1923). London: Methuen & Co., 1974.

Sagan, Carl. "The Solar System as an Abode of Life." In *Biology and the Exploration of Mars*, pp. 73–113. Publication 1296. Edited by Colin S. Pittendrigh, Wolf Vishniac, and J. P. T. Pearman. Washington, D.C.: National Academy of Sciences, National Research Council, 1966.

Schiller, Francis. *A Möbius Strip: Fin-de-Siècle Neuropsychiatry and Paul Möbius*. Berkeley: University of California Press, 1982.

Schlick, Moritz. "Philosophy of Organic Life." In *Readings in the Philosophy of Science*, pp. 523–37. Edited by Herbert Feigl and May Brodbeck. New York: Appleton-Century-Crofts, 1953.

Schmidt, Heinrich. *Der Kampf um die "Welträtsel." Ernst Haeckel, die "Welträtsel" und die Kritik*. Bonn: Verlag von Emil Strauss, 1900.

Schopenhauer, Arthur. *On the Fourfold Root of the Principle of Sufficient Reason*.

On the Will in Nature. Translated by Mme. Karl Hillebrand. London: George Bell & Sons, 1907.

————. *The World as Will and Representation* (1818, 1958). 2 vols. Translated by E. F. J. Payne. New York: Dover Publications, 1969.

Schubert-Soldern, Rainer. *Mechanism and Vitalism: Philosophical Aspects of Biology.* Translated by C. E. Robin. Notre Dame, Ind.: University of Notre Dame Press, 1962.

Scruton, Roger. *From Descartes to Wittgenstein.* New York: Harper Colophon Books, 1981.

The Secret of the Golden Flower (1931). Translation and Commentary by Richard Wilhelm. Foreword and Commentary by C. G. Jung. Includes part of Chinese meditation text, *The Book of Consciousness and Life.* Translated from the German by Cary F. Baynes. Foreword by Salome Wilhelm. London: Routledge & Kegan Paul, 1962.

Slobodkin, Lawrence. "The Peculiar Evolutionary Strategy of Man." In *Epistemology, Methodology, and the Social Sciences.* Edited by Robert S. Cohen and Marx W. Wartofsky. Vol. 71 of *Boston Studies in the Philosophy of Science.* Dordrecht, Holland/Boston, U.S.A.: Reidl Publishing Company, 1983.

Smyth, Herbert Weir. "Greek Conceptions of Immortality from Homer to Plato." In *Harvard Essays on Classical Subjects.* Edited by Herbert Weir Smyth. Boston: Houghton Mifflin Company, 1912.

Spaulding, E. G. "Driesch's Theory of Vitalism." *Philosophical Review* 15 (1906): 518–27.

————. "Review: *The Science and Philosophy of the Organism,* by Hans Driesch, 1908." *Philosophical Review,* vol. 18 (1909).

Stevens, Anthony. *Archetypes: A Natural History of the Self.* New York: Quill, 1983.

Stewart, Walter A. *Psychoanalysis: The First Ten Years, 1888–1898.* New York: Macmillan Company, 1967.

Sulloway, Frank J. *Freud, Biologist of the Mind: Beyond the Psychoanalytic Legend.* New York: Basic Books, 1983.

Taylor, Eugene. "William James and C. G. Jung." *Spring* (1980), pp. 157–68.

Thorpe, W. H. *Purpose in a World of Chance: A Biologist's View.* Oxford: Oxford University Press, 1978.

Vincie, Joseph F., and Rathbauer-Vincie, Margreta. *C. G. Jung and Analytical*

Psychology: A Comprehensive Bibliography. New York: Garland Publishing Co., 1977.

Vitranen, Reino. *Claude Bernard and His Place in the History of Ideas.* Lincoln: University of Nebraska Press, 1960.

Wundt, Wilhelm. *Grundzüge der physiologischen Psychologie.* 5th ed. 3 vols. Leipzig: Verlag von Wilhelm Engelmann, 1903.

_____. *Gustav Theodor Fechner: Rede zur Feier seines hundert-jährigen Geburtstages.* Leipzig: Verlag von Wilhelm Engelmann, 1901.

_____. *Kleine Schriften.* 2 vols. Leipzig: Verlag von Wilhelm Engelmann, 1910.

_____. *Lectures on Human and Animal Psychology.* Translated from the 2nd German edition by J. E. Creighton and E. B. Titchener. London: Swann Sonnenschein & Co., 1907.

_____. *Outlines of Psychology.* Translated by Charles Hubbard Judd. Leipzig: Verlag von Wilhelm Engelmann, 1907.

_____. *Üeber den Einfluss der Philosophie auf die Erfahrungswissenschaften.* Akademische Antrittsrede Gehalten zu Leipzig, am 20. November 1875. Leipzig: Verlag von Wilhelm Engelmann, 1876.

Index

Adickes, Erich: as defender of Kantian "subjectivism," 71; and parallelism with Jung, 71–72

Agar, W. E., 261

Agrippa von Nettesheim, 82

Alchemy: and Jung's study of Paracelsus, 80, 83; and projective field, 83

Alexander, Samuel, 259

Allison, Henry: and epistemic condition described by Kant, 58

Anamnesis. *See* Recollection, theory of

Archetype: as alternative to primary process libido, 141; and American counter-culture, 107–8; definitions of, 143, 145; and emotion, 111; ethology equated with, 174; and fantasy image, 111, 137; "Instinct and the Unconscious," 141–44; and mind-body identity, 168; and moral basis for life, 158–61; as perceptive, 167; and phylogenetic origins, 135; and Plato's forms, 49, 157–61; and progression and regression of libido, 137–39; and prospective method, 139–41; as replacement for Kant's categorical imperative, 25; and Schopenhauer, 144, 162–65; as *spiritus rector* of instinct, 170; and symbolic approach, 138–39; and synchronicity, 185–86; and unconscious mind, typical components of, 140–41; and vitalist assumptions, 143, 255

Aristolelian Society, Mind Association and British Psychological Society, joint meetings, 3, 142

Aristotle: and actualized being in scholastic philosophy, 97n.15; and cyclic view of natural process, 225; and Jung's source in Schopenhauer, 234; *Metaphysics*, 225; *On Generation and Corruption*, 225–26; *Parts of Animals*, 224; *Physics*, 224–25; relationship to Plato's doctrine of forms, 157; and self, 219; and teleological view of nature, 223–25; and Unmoved Mover, 225

Autonomy of psyche, and Driesch's vitalism, 250

Berkeley, George, 51–52, 73

Bernard, Claude, 13, 240–42

Bernet, Pastor Walter, 12

Bernfield, Siegfried, 115–16

Berzelius, Jöns-Jakob, 238

Bleuler, Eugen, 126, 256

Body-mind unity, as solution to epistemological problem: in Berkeley, 51–52; in Fechner, 287–88; in Jung, 35; in Paracelsus, 81–82; in Schopenhauer, 72–73

Boehme, Jakob, 3

Boss, Medard, 199n.6

Breuer, Josef, 114–16

Broad, C. D., 259

Brücke, Ernst: *Lectures in Physiology*, 115; as mentor to Freud, 113–16; and the "School of Helmholtz,"

313